# Movies, Censorship, and the Law

# Movies, Censorship, and the Law

*Ira H. Carmen*

*Ann Arbor*
*The University of Michigan Press*

*To my wife, Sandra*

# Preface

The writer whose subject for analysis lies in the realm of current events faces many problems not shared by colleagues who confine their remarks to historical content. One thing that constantly nags at him, for example, is that he knows that before the year is out there may well be drastic changes in the body of knowledge he has endeavored to describe. In this volume, I have tried to bring the reader into the offices of motion picture censors throughout the United States so that he can see how these government officials go about their work. I have also attempted to spell out in some detail the legal guidelines which the Constitution imposes on their prerogatives. But movie censorship, as carried on through the medium of public enforcement, is a fluid field. New court decisions will undoubtedly be handed down. Laws will be amended, repealed, enacted. Censorship practices will change. In short, what is said here may, to some extent at least, have already undergone alteration.

In spite of the threat of built-in obsolescence, however, the author grits his teeth and publishes. In the present instance, I am fortified in my ambitions by the fact that not one in-depth analysis of motion picture censorship as practiced by state and local authorities has ever been presented to the public. It is time to suspend for a moment the flow of events; it is time to take a long, hard look at what these censorship norms are today so that we can better understand what they ought to be and what they will be in future years.

A few words are in order concerning the data that have been amassed in interviewing the various censors. Much of this information is of great interest but could not be embodied in the text because it was somewhat irrelevant to the dominant issues at hand. In order to place these materials at the disposal of those who might wish to explore the many facets of movie censorship in the future, I have included accounts of these interviews as appendixes. It is undoubtedly true that the inclusion of these data will also afford the reader the opportunity to cross-reference textual comments about particular responses with the context in which these answers were obtained.

As is the case with anyone who completes a study as large as this, I owe many thanks to many people. This investigation would not have been possible without the gracious courtesies shown to me by each of the movie censorship officials who took hours away from work to talk with me and who allowed me to draw freely in my remarks from these discussions. These include Mr. Louis Pesce in New York, Mr. Elwood L. Gebhart in Maryland, Mrs. Lollie Whitehead in Virginia, Mrs. Minter S. Hooker in Memphis, Mrs. Christine S. Gilliam in Atlanta, and Sergeant Robert Murphy in Chicago. It is to be hoped that these officials understand that the criticisms to be levied against the programs they help to supervise, and there are many, are in no sense personal, but stem from honest differences of opinion as to how motion picture fare ought to be regulated by public authority. Nothing in the succeeding pages should be taken to undercut what I believe to be their obvious dedication and integrity.

I also owe a debt of gratitude to Professor Joseph E. Kallenbach, who was helpful beyond measure in the preparation and redrafting of this manuscript. Nor can I forget Miss Barbara Scott of the Motion Picture Association of America, whose assistance and advice were invaluable aids in the preparation of the study, or my colleagues, Professors Morton M. Rosenberg and Herbert Hamilton, for their personal kindnesses.

# Contents

# Introduction

This study is, in an elemental sense, an examination of the American public's gradual acceptance of the most significant technical advancement in the development of the mass media in the past generation, the motion picture. Of course, the focus or emphasis of this book will be centered upon the film industry's constant clashes with prosecuting attorneys and policemen in the courtroom and, especially, with motion picture censors in behind-the-scenes skirmishes; but, in a large sense, these public officials, whether on the side of the movie maker or against him, represent in their thinking strongly held value sentiments that shape public opinion at the mass level. To this extent, the struggles of the motion picture producer, actor, and writer to win approval for the medium somewhere on the totem-pole of the arts in the United States can be traced by understanding what has happened to the movie industry in the arena of public law.

This book will deal not only with the Supreme Court's delineation of rights to be enjoyed by the moving picture medium in a free society, but also with the role of the local body politic, be it city or state, in conforming to or implementing judgments of the nation's highest court. This point needs further illumination. Much is written in case books and law review articles about what the Supreme Court has said in interpreting both the rights of states and the rights of individuals against the state under the Constitution. But the political scientist must dig deeper than the opinions of the justices. In order to understand the role of the judiciary in a federal system he must understand the real effect of important decisions upon relevant political activities through-

1

out the nation. As Peltason has maintained, the impact of court rulings can only be measured by noting the responses of given communities to such rulings. Suppose the Supreme Court hands down a decision on some critical issue and local authorities do nothing to make this decision applicable to the everyday affairs of government? Suppose, indeed, local officials do not even know about the Court's edict, and so continue to flout its will unintentionally? Clearly, the student of judicial behavior must be acquainted with the nature of this chain reaction of political decisions as it manifests itself in the enforcement of a variety of court judgments if he is really to comprehend the role that judges play in preserving the doctrine of national supremacy.[1]

This line of argument has more than mere theoretical importance. Several studies have been conducted in recent years which show clearly that the influence of Supreme Court pronouncements upon local law enforcement agencies can in no way be gauged by the apparent persuasiveness of the Court's rhetoric, or by the number of justices who concur in a decision. For example, in 1948 the Court announced in the well-known *McCollum* decision that it was unconstitutional for a public school board to adopt a released-time program that would allow religious teachers to hold classes in public schools and require students either to attend these classes or remain in a study hall.[2] What effect did this decision have on the thousands of school boards across the country? One political scientist after an exhaustive examination of the record reported that:

> . . . the central point which emerges from this study is that the *McCollum* decision was put into effect in diverse ways, and 'obeyed' to varying degrees; and that, in some states and communities, it was simply not put into effect at all.[3]

Though it was true that most of the programs which relied upon the simultaneous use of public property and regular school

---

[1] Jack W. Peltason, *Federal Courts in the Political Process* (Garden City, N. Y.: Doubleday and Co., Inc., 1955), pp. 56–59.

[2] *McCollum v. Board of Education*, 333 U.S. 203 (1948).

[3] Gordon Patric, "The Impact of a Court Decision: Aftermath of the *McCollum* Case," *Journal of Public Law*, VI (1957), 455.

hours were at least modified,[4] there were several exceptions even
to this especially, it seems, in Illinois.[5] And in Virginia, thanks to
a helping hand from the Attorney General of that state, it was
decided that such programs could be continued in classrooms
during public school hours so long as school authorities made no
attempt to administer the program.[6]

Two years later, another study appeared which attempted to
measure local adherence to *Zorach* v. *Clausen*,[7] a Supreme Court
decision that upheld a New York City released-time program
whose dominant features were religious education conducted off
school premises and the willingness of private organizations to
finance and, to some extent, administer the program.[8] After first
substantiating the essentials of Patric's analysis regarding the lack
of support given to *McCollum* at the local level,[9] Sorauf next
examined whether or not the terms of the *Zorach* judgment had
induced these communities to meet the Court half-way. He found
that "school systems in virtually every state violate in some way
the legal principles concerning religious instruction in the public
schools."[10] To his knowledge, most of the programs conducted
by the Virginia Council of Churches were, as late as 1959, still
being held in public school buildings as were programs run by
many communities in Texas. He also reported that in 1957 a
magazine called *Religious Education* had examined various released-time programs throughout the country and had discovered
that thirty-two percent were still holding classes in public school
facilities.[11]

These case studies provide needed guidance for analyzing
local film censorship statutes in the light of judicial pronouncements relating to the meaning of the First and Fourteenth Amendments as they protect the exhibition of motion pictures. Since

[4] *Ibid.*, p. 457.
[5] *Ibid.*, p. 459.
[6] *Ibid.*, p. 460.
[7] 343 U. S. 306 (1952).
[8] Frank J. Sorauf, "*Zorach* v. *Clausen*: The Impact of a Supreme Court
Decision," *American Science Review*, LIII (1959), 777-91.
[9] *Ibid.*, p. 782.
[10] *Ibid.*, p. 784.
[11] *Ibid.*, p. 785.

1952 the Supreme Court has handed down a series of decisions
which have severely narrowed the scope of censorship agencies
in their attempts to decide what films should be commercially
shown without legal molestation. Some of these decisions were
the result of appeals lodged by motion picture producers themselves, while others have arisen from protests brought by book
publishers and others who control various vehicles of the mass
media that have been afforded First Amendment shelter by the
courts. To what extent do the activities of these local film censorship agencies follow such Supreme Court mandates? What do
movie censors know about such holdings? These and other related
inquiries provide the prime touchstones for investigation in this
study.

One other question of immediate priority must now be considered. What is motion picture censorship? One assumption that
can readily be agreed upon for purposes of this examination is
that the movie censorship policies requiring investigation include
only regulatory policies which are utilized by some organ of
government. Of course, much has been written about the film
industry's own program of self-discipline as well as the goals and
operations of certain private groups such as the Legion of Decency;[12] but clearly these extralegal observers of the content of
motion pictures owe no obligation to the federal government in
terms of what is here being discussed. Nor does the regulation of
moving pictures by federal law enforcement agencies fall within
the purview of this analysis. While there is a wealth of evidence
indicating that the Bureau of Customs is involved in the censoring
of films as that term will presently be defined,[13] the impact of

[12] A very provocative and useful article which, in part, deals with the
work of the Production Code Administration and the Legion of Decency
in a context similar to this investigation is Thomas B. Leary and J. Roger
Noall, "Entertainment: Public Pressures and the Law," *Harvard Law Review*,
LXXI (1957), 354-62.

[13] The best study of these activities is James C. N. Paul and Murray L.
Schwartz, *Federal Censorship: Obscenity in the Mail* (New York: The Free
Press of Glencoe, Inc., 1961). Alleged censorship practices utilized by the
Post Office Department pose no threat for the movie industry because films
produced for commercial purposes are never transported through the mails.
Interviews with Barbara Scott, attorney for the Motion Picture Association

court decisions on these practices and the arguments pro and con regarding their justification do not bear directly on the major thrust of this investigation.

A more difficult problem is presented, however, by the typical obscenity statute that has been enacted, at last count, by as many as forty-seven states.[14] These laws usually proscribe the sale of obscene materials or their possession with intent to sell[15] and provide for subsequent criminal punishment when these offenses are proven. Clearly, enactments of this kind could be used to inhibit the distribution of motion pictures if police officials are led to believe that a given film is obscene. Nor can these possibilities be minimized because the overwhelming number of convictions obtained under such laws are against peddlers of so-called "stag" films.[16] The fact that Atlanta, Georgia has recently passed a law making the showing of "obscene" motion pictures a crime,[17] and that the State of Ohio was able to enforce successfully a similar statute against the distributors of the film *The Lovers* until overruled by the U. S. Supreme Court[18] is proof enough of the sting such laws can carry for the publicly exhibited movie.

It would appear feasible, however, to exclude a consideration

---

of America, and Sidney Lipston, staff member serving in the office of the General Counsel of the Post Office Department directly under the Assistant General Counsel, April 1963.

[14] Leary and Noall, *op. cit.*, p. 343.

[15] *Ibid.* For typical examples of such laws see *Connecticut Gen. Stat.*, Sect. 8567 (1949), or *New Jersey Rev. Stat.*, Sect. 2A: 115-2 (1951).

[16] *Ibid.*, p. 343. The regulation of such films, of course, falls beyond the purview of this investigation. Such materials are clearly pornographic (see *Roth* v. *U. S.*, 354 U. S. 467, 1957) and, unlike movies that are produced for consumption in the "open market place of ideas," are never shown publicly. Naturally, these films cannot be "censored" as that term will soon be defined.

[17] Section 1 of the ordinance reads, "It shall be unlawful for any person or corporation knowingly to show or cause to be shown in a motion picture theatre . . . in the city of Atlanta an obscene motion picture." This enactment was signed into law by the Mayor on June 20, 1962. No citation can be given because Atlanta's statute books have not been updated as of this writing to include laws passed since 1961.

[18] *Jacobellis* v. *Ohio*, 12 L. Ed. 2d 793 (1964).

of such enactments and cases that have arisen under them for more sophisticated reasons. Leary and Noall, for instance, differentiate between "censorship," under which material must be reviewed and approved before it can be disseminated to the public, and all forms of subsequent sanctions which regulate by punishing those who have already distributed proscribed matter.[19] This opinion is shared by most thoughtful scholars in the field including Chafee[20] and Pritchett.[21]

There is good reason for making a careful distinction between any kind of prior restraint and punishment after the fact. As Thomas I. Emerson puts it:

> . . . under a system of subsequent punishment the communication has already been made before the government takes action; it thus takes place, for whatever it may be worth, in the market place of ideas. Under a system of prior restraint, the communication, if banned, never reaches the market place at all.[22]

Pritchett further points out that there are other attributes of prior restraint which make it more dangerous than the typical penal statute. For one thing, "it is broader in its application to communication, for its machinery is geared to universal inspection, not to scrutiny in particular cases which are the subject of complaint."[23] A second, but certainly a more basic objection, is the fact that prior restraint decisions are usually made in private and are brought to the attention of the public only in the rare instances in which such matters reach the courts. Perhaps the censors are following statutory standards closely in deciding if a film should be granted a license. But perhaps they are not. They certainly do not have to be convinced beyond a reasonable doubt as does a jury in a criminal proceeding. Indeed, what sort of procedural due process of law will the censorship boards afford? Will they permit a motion picture producer or distributor to be represented

[19] Leary and Noall, *op. cit.*, p. 326.

[20] Zechariah Chafee, Jr., *Free Speech in the United States* (Cambridge, Mass.: Harvard University Press, 1941), p. 541.

[21] C. Herman Pritchett, *The American Constitution* (New York: McGraw-Hill, 1959), pp. 397-401.

[22] Thomas I. Emerson, "The Doctrine of Prior Restraint," *Law and Contemporary Problems*, XX (1955), 648-71.

[23] Pritchett, *op. cit.*, p. 397.

by counsel? Will they allow expert witnesses on aesthetics or on the nature of the arts to be heard? Perhaps they will. Yet, perhaps they will not. When Miss Barbara Scott, an attorney for the Motion Picture Association of America was asked, "Why does your organization object more strenuously to censorship than it does to subsequent punishment statutes?," she replied:

> For two reasons. First, you must submit all films for inspection under a prior restraint statute. It is a real financial burden because of the fees that are charged. Secondly, there are no safeguards. The burden of proof should be on them (state officials), not us. They should operate in accordance with due process in a subsequent punishment proceeding. Subsequent punishment is okay because we don't make obscene films.[24]

In view of the many apparent differences between the typical prior restraint enactment and subsequent punishment, none of which is trivial even when taken separately, it seems more than equitable for purposes of this examination to label the former as "motion picture censorship." However, the nature of the distinction between the two kinds of abridgment will vary in practice with a pragmatic assessment of the operation of a given statute in particular circumstances.[25] Yet, the fact that a court of law should not be satisfied with a priori distinctions between prior restraint and subsequent punishment in establishing the constitutionality of particular laws does not dismiss the assumption that there are important theoretical differences between the two. Only an empirical analysis of such factors as the nature of the conduct proscribed, the trier of the fact, and the clarity of the statute will disclose to what extent a prior restraint restriction can claim parity under the Constitution with the typical penal law.[26] Such a task will constitute one of the important objectives of this analysis when appropriate to a better understanding of the permissible scope of movie censorship.

[24] Interview with Barbara Scott, April 1963.

[25] Paul A. Freund, "The Supreme Court and Civil Liberties," *Vanderbilt Law Review,* IV ( 1951 ), 539. Professor Freund's comments along this line are most enlightening.

[26] *Ibid.* There are some forms of prior restraint that have more in common with the criminal law than with the workings of movie censorship bureaus extant. See comments relative to footnote 237, *infra,* and especially *Kingsley Books, Inc.* v. *Brown,* 354 U. S. 436 ( 1957 ).

There is another breed of state legislation which, though far less frequent than criminal laws against the obscene, constitutes an even graver threat, if adequately implemented, to the motion picture industry's freedom to circulate film. The typical statute of this kind looks innocent enough. Under its authority to protect the health, safety, and good order of the community a state parcels out to each city certain lesser responsibilities for the purpose of adjusting the peculiarities of smaller localities to the demands of the body politic. For instance, a state might delegate to each city and town the power to regulate, license, or prohibit public dance halls, billiard parlors, circuses, theaters, and theatrical exhibitions.[27] It is evident that when theaters and, with the aid of a not unreasonable interpretation of the statute, movie houses are placed in the same general category as circuses and pool halls for purposes of regulation there is potential trouble for the motion picture maker.

If such legislation is implemented by just one of the many towns in a particular state so that all movie houses in that small area are closed down, has not an act of prior restraint or censorship been committed? The answer would seem to be that such restraint will make it impossible for a motion picture to reach the "market place of ideas." Under this kind of law movie houses may be closed or refused a required license by a community for many diverse reasons. For example, the town council may have evidence that gatherings at such theaters have a history of provoking trouble, or the council may feel that movies in general are too "dirty." Regardless of how rational or irrational the reason for rejection, in such cases it is clear that no board has been entrusted with the responsibility of accepting some films and rejecting others. If a city did set up a licensing system of this kind and rely upon such a state law for support, then the primary condition for analysis within the scope of this examination would have been met. This, indeed, is precisely what the city of Chicago has done.

The major guidelines for the main body of this investigation

[27] See, for example, *Iowa Code Ann.*, Vol. 18, Sect. 368.8 (1949) and *Code of Alabama*, Title 37, Sects. 751-52.

are now clearly in view. First, a careful examination will be made of the several Supreme Court holdings that are relevant to an understanding of what film censorship may constitutionally accomplish or which will give insight into the rights of the motion picture industry as opposed to those of the other media of speech and press under the First Amendment. The moving picture is a relatively new mode of communicating ideas and artistic values and any discrepancy between the rights accorded it and those granted to other channels of expression by the judiciary is obviously of the most essential import. Secondly, a detailed examination will be presented of the motion picture censorship programs of four large cities (Detroit, Chicago, Atlanta, and Memphis) and of the four state-wide agencies which, as of March 1965, were involved in prior restraint abridgment (in New York, Virginia, Kansas, and Maryland). Though stress will be placed on how adequately these governmental units abide by Supreme Court edicts as they go about their work, much attention will also be devoted to the relative statutory schemes under which the personnel involved in each program contribute to the overall tasks of a particular board, the differing idiosyncrasies of each agency in terms of how each performs similar duties, and the opinions of key members of each unit on a variety of provocative issues of relevance. Finally, a concluding chapter will evaluate how successful the American political system has been in transmitting the Court's views on free expression in this area into legislative and administrative policy-making at the local level. Of equal importance, a normative analysis will be made of what kind of film censorship is desirable, if any, in a free society.

# Chapter I

# The Supreme Court and the Right of Free Speech for Motion Pictures under the Constitution: The "Early Period," 1915-52

The Supreme Court has heard only a scant number of controversies dealing with motion picture censorship and most of these have been of modern vintage. However, the paucity of decisions does not reflect the complexity of the issues these cases have managed to raise. Surprisingly, many of these rulings were per curiam and, hence, evidently disposed of with ease. As will become apparent, however, the complexities have become even more formidable when considered in the light of decisions dealing with other media of speech bearing directly on the nature of permissible governmental censorship of the movies.

It is important to an understanding of these controversies that certain "facts of life" about the production and dissemination of movies be set out. The business of making motion pictures for a profit was, and is, divided into three basic branches; that is to say, it is conducted by manufacturers, distributors, and exhibitors. Manufacturers, or producers, do not sell their film directly to exhibitors, but sell instead to distributors who, in turn, rent to movie house owners. The tasks of a distribution agency may be likened to those of a clearing house or a circulating library and the growth of such companies is attributable to the great popularity of movies and the great expense the purchase of films would be to exhibitors.

### The Supreme Court's Initial Encounter with the Issue
The Supreme Court first gave an indication of its views on the matter of film exhibitions and freedom of speech in the case of *Mutual Film Corporation* v. *Industrial Commission of Ohio.*[28]

[28] 236 U. S. 230 (1915).

Ohio had passed, in 1913, one of the first state film censorship statutes.[29] It provided for the creation of a motion picture censorship board whose duty it was to examine all film that was to be shown publicly for profit in any part of the state. Section 4 of the act stated that "only such films as are in the judgment and discretion of the board of censors of a moral, educational or amusing and harmless character shall be passed and approved...." Section 3 made mandatory the payment of an inspection fee by those submitting movies to the censorship agency.

Appellant, the Mutual Film Corporation, was engaged in the business of purchasing films and leasing them to movie house owners in Ohio. Its distribution agency was located in Detroit and it was the company's usual practice to consign shipments of film to Ohio exhibitors for their use. Because these exhibitors would not rent uncensored films for fear of prosecution, the complainant would have been forced to bear all expenses for having the movies inspected by the state. Consequently, the corporation sought out an injunction to restrain the enforcement of the applicable law, and, meeting with failure, it appealed to the Supreme Court.

As the Court pointed out in its preliminary analysis of the case,[30] the complaint lodged against the statute was voluminous. First of all, it attempted to show that the law violated several sections of Article I of the Ohio Constitution because it deprived appellant of due process of law by placing, in the hands of a censorship bureau, the power to determine what films could legally be shown in that state. In short, the use of such a prior restraint mechanism constituted a deprivation of a judicial determination. Secondly, it maintained that the law violated the First and Fourteenth Amendments of the Constitution of the United States as well as Article I of the Ohio Constitution in that it restrained appellant from freely publicizing ideas and sentiments contained in these movies.[31] And, finally, it contended that the standards set forth in the statute were far too vague to be responsibly in-

[29] 103 *Ohio Laws* 399.

[30] 236 U. S. 230 at p. 231.

[31] The written brief filed on behalf of appellant laid heavy stress on the free speech aspects of the case. *Ibid.*, pp. 236-37.

terpreted and thus were an unconstitutional delegation of legislative power.[32]

In deciding against these claims a unanimous court, which numbered among its members Mr. Justice Holmes, specifically dismissed two of these charges as unsound. Speaking through Mr. Justice McKenna, the Court, after first putting to one side the notion that the statute might constitute an unreasonable burden upon interstate commerce,[33] refused to construe the Constitution of Ohio so as to include the motion picture medium.[34] To be sure, he clearly noted, the film industry did not claim that movies cannot be made to conform to standards which the state had set up under its police powers, but only that prior censorship was foreign to due process of law as provided for in the Ohio Constitution. Nonetheless, the exercise of similar powers had been wielded by many states in the years prior to passage of the Ohio law and, after citing several precedents to establish the veracity of this contention, he went on to state with impeccable clarity a principle that was to relegate motion pictures for decades to come to the status of the side show as a medium for artistic expression and the dissemination of ideas:

> It seems not have occurred to anyone in the cited cases that freedom of opinion was repressed in the exertion of the power which was illustrated. . . . It cannot be put out of view that the exhibition of moving pictures is a business pure and simple, originated and conducted for profit, like other spectacles, not to be regarded, nor intended to be regarded by the Ohio Constitution, we think, as part of the press of the country or as organs of public opinion. They are mere representations of events. . . .[35]

It is most important to note that at no time did the Court allude to the claim posed by the Mutual Film Corporation that

[32] No particular passage of the Ohio Constitution was mentioned by the Court in its discussion of this point.

[33] 236 U. S. 230 at p. 241.

[34] Section 11 of Article 1 of the Ohio Constitution stipulates that: "Every citizen may freely speak, write, and publish his sentiments on all subjects, being responsible for the abuse of the right; and no law shall be passed to restrain or abridge the liberty of speech, or of the press."

[35] *Ibid.*, p. 244.

a censorship law of this sort violated the First Amendment of
the Federal Constitution. To be sure, another ten years were
to pass before it would rule that liberties protected by this
Amendment applied substantively to state actions as well as to
those of the national government through the due process provision of the Fourteenth Amendment.[36] Nonetheless, Justice
McKenna made no attempt to anticipate this position by suggest-
ing that such an allegation might have merit if motion pictures
were protectable as speech, nor did he even bother to suggest
that an application of the First Amendment to state activities was
an entirely dubious contention. Whether the Court really believed
that the Bill of Rights could not be properly interpreted as a
limitation on states' powers, or whether the consensus among the
Justices was that a construction of the free speech clause of the
Ohio Constitution that excluded motion pictures from protection
certainly would also apply by analogy to the commands of the
First Amendment and that such a step in logic was too apparent
for exposition is certainly a moot point.

The rest of the opinion was anticlimactic. It was only necessary to show that the passage of the Ohio ordinance did not constitute a delegation of legislative power which, in effect, would
allow the censorship bureau to roam at will with no precise
standards as to what was educational, moral, or harmless. Such
an attack was brushed aside with the argument that the statute
guarded against this danger in that its terms obtained precision
"from the sense and experience of men" and that all administrative bodies must, of necessity, ascertain facts and conditions to
which policies are applicable.[37]

Few decisions which the Supreme Court has handed down
in the area of civil liberties have been treated to more adverse
criticism in recent years than this case. Perhaps the most search-
ing analysis of the underlying motifs of the Court's position
appeared several years ago in an article in the *Yale Law Journal*.[38]
The authors of this study tried to pinpoint the basic premises

[36] *Gitlow* v. *New York*, 268 U. S. 652 (1925).

[37] 236 U. S. 230 at p. 246.

[38] Note, "Motion Pictures and the First Amendment," *Yale Law Journal*,
LX (1951), 696-719.

that they believed were most influential in the minds of the Justices as they rendered their judgment, and concluded that the decision was predicated upon three fundamental suppositions, each of which was highly dubious.[39]

Two of these assumptions clearly emerge from a careful examination of Justice McKenna's argument, quoted earlier, which deprived motion pictures of free speech protection under the Ohio Constitution. The first is that movie making is "a business pure and simple" conducted solely for the purpose of monetary reward. As the article pointed out in regard to this observation, the question of whether speech is uttered freely or at a price has never been a conclusive factor in determining if it is censorable.[40] And, as Professor Kauper has characterized this situation:

> It may be said of all book publishers and most newspaper publishers that they are engaged in the business for profit, but this does not in any way impair the fact that they are engaged in the business that involves the freedom of the press.[41]

The second of these premises centers around the claim that moving pictures were mere spectacles such as circuses or other novelty acts and that, as such, they were not meant to be protected by free speech clauses in state constitutions. Challenging this assumption, critics have noted that this value judgment reflects "traditional judicial suspicion of the arts in general, expressed in terms of a dichotomy between entertainment and ideas." Indeed, the legitimate theater can point to a long history of arbitrary censorship restraint that was buttressed by judicial approval.[42] The authors of the study in the *Yale Law Journal*

[39] *Ibid.*, pp. 702-5.

[40] The point was stated without qualification in *Schneider* v. *State*, 308 U. S. 147 (1939).

[41] Paul G. Kauper, *Civil Liberties and the Constitution* (Ann Arbor: The University of Michigan Press, 1962), pp. 75-76.

[42] See Note, "Motion Pictures and the First Amendment," *op. cit.*, p. 703, and especially footnote 19 for a brief résumé of the trials and tribulations of stage productions and censorship in Great Britain and the United States. For a more detailed analysis see Chafee, *op. cit.*, pp. 529-40 as well as the cases reported in Annotation, "What Amounts to an Obscene Play or Book Within Prohibition Statute," *American Law Reports*, LXXXI (1932), 801-8.

spent much time trying to show that modern communication research has largely disproved the existence of such a distinction.[43] It hardly seems necessary to muster empirical evidence to verify this criticism since special ideas of importance have been contained in countless fictionalized accounts other than the dramatic ranging from the plays of Shakespeare to the movies of Charlie Chaplin and the comic-strips of Al Capp. Nor can the classification of films as spectacles be excused because of the fact that talking pictures were not produced until 1926, since many books whether worthwhile or of little interest are entirely devoted to entertainment while always having received constitutional protection.[44] It should also be noted that while sound has been the dominant factor in leading to the production of "quality" films, the fact remains that by 1915 such intellectually significant silent movies as *The Birth of a Nation, Hamlet, The Life of Abraham Lincoln,* and *Quo Vadis* had already been released.[45]

A third value judgment which was advanced by the authors of this commentary in the *Yale Law Journal* as being a basic supposition for the Court's ruling is more difficult to substantiate. They maintained that much of the hostility in Mr. Justice McKenna's opinion towards movies was predicated on the belief that this new medium, if misused, possessed a great capacity for evil which a community could legitimately shield itself against. It is true that the Court did allude on several occasions to this inherent frailty of the motion picture when, for example, it mentioned films could be more "insidious in corruption" when shown, as they usually were, to mixed audiences of male and female adults and children.[46] Nonetheless, a finding that motion pictures did possess a greater capacity for evil than other forms of mass communication by the very nature of the utilized techniques was unnecessary to establish the fact that the medium itself was not protected by the free speech clause in the Ohio Constitution. The authors were perfectly correct, however, in pointing out that a threat of

[43] *Ibid.,* pp. 704-5.

[44] Kauper, *op. cit.,* p. 76.

[45] Edward Lasker, "Censorship of Motion Pictures Pursuant to Recent Supreme Court Decisions," *U.C.L.A. Law Review,* I (1954), 583.

[46] 236 U. S. 230 at p. 242.

evil consequences arising out of uses of speech and press "has never meant that all expression within a medium will be restricted at the outset," but only that the nature of the evil will help determine how the community's need for protection will be balanced against free speech privileges.[47]

Over and above the normative aspects of the decision its effect upon the film industry was profound. Many state and lower federal courts construed its meaning in such a way that it might just as well have stated in so many words that motion picture censorship was permissible under the national Constitution.[48] And, as might have been anticipated, many state courts upheld similar censorship laws directed against movies by interpreting free speech guarantees contained in their respective state constitutions as the Supreme Court had construed the fundamental law of Ohio.[49]

## Free Speech Protections of the United States Constitution Extended to the States

It was not until 1925 that the Supreme Court again dealt, even tangentially, with problems of concern to the motion picture industry. No doubt the fact that *Gitlow* v. *New York*[50] was to prove to be the seed from which almost all of the constitutional rights that movies now enjoy would sprout escaped the vision of even

---

[47] Note, "Motion Pictures and the First Amendment," *op. cit.*, p. 703. The nature of the type of "balancing test" now adhered to by the courts is best exemplified in Judge Learned Hand's opinion in *Dennis* v. *U. S.*, 183 F. 2d 201 at p. 215 (1950). For an analysis of the *Mutual Film Corp.* case that concludes that the Court's decision was essentially consistent with Judge Hand's "test," see P. D. McAnany, "Motion Picture Censorship and Constitutional Freedom," *Kentucky Law Journal*, L (1962), 431.

[48] Albert W. Harris, Jr., "Movie Censorship and the Supreme Court: What Next?" *California Law Review*, XLII (1954), 122. See also *Buffalo Branch, Mutual Film Corporation* v. *Breitinger*, 250 Pa. 225 (1915) and the very important *RD-DR* v. *Smith*, 183 F. 2d 562, *cert. den.* 340 U. S. 853 (1950).

[49] Many of these cases are discussed in Annotation, "Constitutionality, Construction, and Effect of Censorship Laws," *American Law Reports*, LXIV (1929), 505-13.

[50] 268 U. S. 652 (1925).

the most optimistic of film producers. Though the facts of the matter in no way involved members of the industry and though censorship of speech and press, as defined, was also not at issue, nonetheless this case merits careful attention as a step toward the position ultimately to be approved by the Court on the issue of movie censorship.

Gitlow was an active member of the Left Wing Section of the Socialist Party. Indeed, for all practical purposes he could easily have been designated a Communist. As the business manager of a pamphlet called *The Revolutionary Age* he arranged for its printing and, in part, its distribution. Contained in one of the editions of this paper was a Manifesto setting forth the tenets of this segment of the Party. Among other things, it condemned "moderate Socialism" for its recognition of the necessity of the democratic parliamentary state; repudiated its policy of introducing Socialism by legislative measures; and advocated, in plain and unequivocal language the necessity of accomplishing the "Communist Revolution" by a militant and "revolutionary Socialism."[51]

He was indicted and convicted of violating a New York State law which had made it a felony to print, publish, edit, or knowingly circulate or distribute any written matter "containing or advocating, advising or teaching the doctrine that organized government should be overthrown by force, violence, or any unlawful means."[52] Defendant's counsel pointed out that as a matter of law the Manifesto was not in contravention of the statute and that, even if it were, the statute itself ran contrary to the due process clause of the Fourteenth Amendment. Clearly, however, these arguments would fall on deaf ears just as did the pleas of the Mutual Film Corporation unless the Court was willing to grant the premise that the free speech and free press guarantees of the First Amendment bound the states as well as the federal

[51] Much of this "Manifesto" was appended to the Court's opinion. See 268 U. S. 652 at pp. 656-60.

[52] *New York Penal Laws,* Sect. 161, Part 2. See also *New York State Laws,* Ch. 88 (1909). While appellant was also indicted and convicted of Sect. 161, Part I, most of the Court's opinion seems to be directed towards his guilt under the quoted portion of the statute.

government because they were a part of the "liberty" of the Fourteenth Amendment which the states could not abridge. Indeed, just three years earlier the Court had found that "the Constitution of the United States imposes upon the States no obligation to confer upon those within their jurisdiction . . . the right of free speech."[53] Such is the fate of judicial precedents, however, that this principle was discarded in two sentences. "For present purposes," the majority announced, "we may and do assume that freedom of speech and of the press . . . are among the fundamental personal rights and 'liberties' protected by the due process clause of the Fourteenth Amendment. . . ." The point of view expressed in the *Prudential Insurance* decision was relegated to the role of an "incidental statement" not to be regarded as "determinative of this question."[54]

Having once established this position, the Court, through Mr. Justice Sanford, went on to uphold the constitutionality of the law. That a state could pass laws protecting the public peace and welfare could not be questioned. The State of New York had determined that utterances advocating the violent overthrow of the government were so dangerous to the general welfare that they might reasonably be proscribed. Such statements, prima facie, threatened breaches of the peace and other criminal acts. The fact that immediate strife might not be accurately foreseen from such comments was no bar because "the State cannot reasonably be required to measure the danger from every such statement in the nice balance of a jeweler's scale."[55]

Once the law had been found constitutional, Judge Sanford had no trouble concluding that all remarks and writings of such character were brought within the confines of its scope. In reply to

[53] *Prudential Insurance Co.* v. *Cheek,* 259 U. S. 530 (1922) at p. 543.

[54] 268 U. S. 652 at p. 666. Undoubtedly the fact that property rights were receiving so much protection from state regulation under the due process clause at this time helped to give the Court an added incentive to place other personal liberties in this sheltered category. Prior to *Gitlow* two other important cases had been recently decided which placed personal freedoms before state regulatory policies and both contained elements of private property deprivation for appellant. See *Meyer* v. *Nebraska,* 262 U. S. 390 (1923) and *Pierce* v. *Society of Sisters,* 268 U. S. 510 (1925).

[55] *Ibid.,* p. 669.

plaintiff's contention that his beliefs did not constitute a clear and present danger to the community the Court distinguished the facts of the present case from those presented in the famous _Schenk_ v. _U. S._[56] That case had revolved around the federal Espionage Act of 1917 which by its terms had prohibited certain acts promotive of substantive evils which Congress could prevent and the Court had then found it necessary to decide how closely speech might serve as a provocation to such deeds without coming within the confines of the law. In _Gitlow_ it was the speech itself that had clearly, and for just cause, been outlawed.[57]

Mr. Justice Holmes, with Mr. Justice Brandeis concurring, dissented from the Court's judgment in the _Gitlow_ case and, consequently, voted to reverse his conviction. They felt that appellant's "redundant discourse" posed no threat to the community's tranquility and that as a matter of law the "clear and present danger" test should be used to define the applicability of the law to oratory and pamphleteering.

It is of interest to note that while dissenting from the Court's judgment both Holmes and Brandeis agreed that free speech was indeed constitutionally protected against state acts. It cannot be safely stated that Holmes had at this time changed his mind in regard to the principles enunciated in _Mutual Film Corporation_ v. _Industrial Commission of Ohio_ for he might have still believed the production of motion pictures to be merely a business, or that movies were still more like circuses than literature. In any event, the fact that in a ten-year interim he had decided to challenge one of the root assumptions of an opinion he had supported in 1915 was a small but significant illustration of a trend in the Court's thinking that was to revolutionize the role of the First and Fourteenth Amendments in American life.[58]

_Gitlow_ v. _New York_ had established the principle that the states must be mindful of the guarantees of free speech and press as set forth in the Constitution of the United States. However, it

[56] 249 U. S. 47 (1919).

[57] 268 U. S. 652 at pp. 670-71.

[58] Justices Van Devanter, McReynolds and, curiously, McKenna were other members of the Court who had participated in _Mutual Film Corp._ but who concurred in Judge Sanford's opinion in _Gitlow_ v. _New York_.

offered only a small hint as to how far a state might go to protect its citizens from kinds of speech it felt ought to be proscribed. Of immeasurably greater concern to the aims of this examination, it left wide open the issue of when a state could properly censor speech.

### Constitutional Limitations on Prior Restraints on Speech

The Court came to grips with this second inquiry six years later.[59] Near and his associates were publishers of a newspaper known as *The Saturday Press*. For a period of more than a week this daily ran a series of articles viciously attacking the city government of Minneapolis, Minnesota. The publishers charged that a "Jewish gangster" was in control of gambling, bootlegging, and racketeering in the city while the chief of police, district attorney, and mayor were not only inefficient and incompetent but were engaged in illicit relations with this gangster and his organization.

At that time, Minnesota had on its statute books a law that stipulated that anyone who published or distributed (a) any obscene or lewd newspaper, or (b) any "malicious, scandalous and defamatory newspaper, magazine or other periodical" was guilty of a nuisance and, further, that such newspaper could be perpetually abated in an injunctive proceeding brought to court by either a government attorney or a private citizen. In actions brought under this law there was to be available as a defense the fact that "the truth was published with good motives and for justifiable ends."[60] Near and several of his business partners were brought to court under a charge of having violated this statute. After a speedy hearing *The Saturday Press* was branded as a public nuisance and was thereupon abated. The judgment perpetually enjoined the defendants from further operating this newspaper. The Supreme Court of Minnesota upheld the convictions but added that it saw no reason for appellants to construe the verdict as restraining them from expressing their views in

[59] *Near* v. *Minnesota*, 230 U. S. 697 (1931).
[60] *Mason's Minn. Stats.*, Sects. 10123-1 to 10123-3 (1927).

print so long as they observed decencies consistent with the public welfare.[61]

It was a closely divided Supreme Court that carefully weighed the appeal lodged by Near. Speaking for a majority of five, Chief Justice Hughes examined in great detail the provisions of the statute to see if they in any way deprived plaintiff of his freedom of the press. Several facts weighed heavily on the Chief Justice's mind. First, the statute was not aimed at a redress of individual wrongs. Remedies for libel remained available. The purpose of the enactment was to ban written materials "detrimental to public morals." Secondly, in order to obtain an injunction it was not necessary to prove the falsity of the charges set forth. What was necessary was that the defendant in such a proceeding must establish not only the truth of his assertions, but also that the truth was published with good motives and for justifiable ends. Thirdly, the object of the law was not merely to punish criminal offenses against the law, but to suppress speech. In the present case, appellant had defamed the city officials of Minneapolis and so had helped to create a public scandal. Such diatribes were unlawful under the statute and could be permanently enjoined.

Having satisfied himself that he had accurately described the functioning of this "unusual, if not unique" law, the Chief Justice then went on to characterize those aspects of free speech and press which were protected under the First and Fourteenth Amendments. He found that it had been a generally accepted maxim of constitutional law that the major purpose of these guarantees was to prevent previous restraints upon publication. This liberty, he said, had been described by Blackstone in these terms:

> The liberty of the press is indeed essential to the nature of a free press; but this consists in laying no previous restraints upon publications, and not in freedom from censure from criminal matter when published. Every freeman has an undoubted right to lay what sentiments he pleases before the public . . . but if he publishes

[61] 230 U. S. 697 at p. 706.

what is . . . illegal, he must take the consequences of his own temerity.[62]

This was not to be taken to mean that prior restraint was forbidden at all times, however. There were exceptional cases when censorship could be justified constitutionally and Hughes had no compunctions about setting forth when such conditions might arise. If, for example, the success of the nation's armed forces was at stake in time of war, or if the security of the community needed to be protected against impending acts of violence, then censorship might be justified. Perhaps, indeed, such laws might be necessary to protect private rights according to principles that were at the disposal of equity courts. And, lastly, "the primary requirements of decency may be enforced against obscene publications."[63] How ironic it is that this last dictum so cavalierly assumed to be sound law should capture the essence of a continuing struggle between censors and movie makers so that the issue it poses is still very much alive and smoldering.

Such threats to public peace and order or private rights, the opinion of the Court went on to say, were nowhere to be found in the facts of this case. Nor was the Chief Justice impressed by the contentions that the statute did not constitute a prior restraint because court verdicts were to be issued against crimes already committed, or because the forum of judgment was a courtroom where due process of law was available. If such a law were found permissible then it would be equally sound for a legislature to provide that a publisher could be brought into court at any time and be required to produce proof of the truth of his publication, or of what he intended to publish, and of his motives. And if these things could be done, then the legislature could provide machinery for determining what were the justifiable ends that a defendant must be prepared to demonstrate he is supporting. In short, though the enactment possessed many of the forms of subsequent punishment it was "of the essence of censorship."[64]

---

[62] *Ibid.*, pp. 713-14. This contention as well as Blackstone's beliefs further cement the validity of the claim that censorship and subsequent punishment do not share a common theoretical or practical justification.

[63] *Ibid.*, p. 716.

[64] *Ibid.*, p. 713.

Mr. Justice Butler, supported by Justices Van Devanter, McReynolds, and Sutherland, dissented from these conclusions. The first section of his opinion stressed the fact that a state might constitutionally protect its citizens from defamatory and scandalous pamphlets under its police power. He pointed out with great care that the articles that had been published in *The Saturday Press* might reasonably be expected to disturb the peace of the community, and to support this position he appended several portions of these articles to his dissent. To capture the real flavor of what was at stake in the Court's ruling it might be worthwhile to quote some of the remarks that appeared in defendant's newspaper:

> . . . It is Jewish men and women—pliant tools of the Jew gangster, Mose Barnett, who stand charged with having falsified the election records. . . .
>
> Practically every vendor of vile hooch, every owner of a moonshine still, every snakefaced gangster and embryonic yegg in the Twin Cities is a Jew. . . .
>
> It was a Jew who employed Jews to shoot down Mr. Guilford. It was a Jew who employed a Jew to intimidate Mr. Shapiro and a Jew who employed Jews to assault that gentleman when he refused to yield to their threats. . . .
>
> It is Jew, Jew, Jew, as long as one cares to comb over the records.[65]

What Justice Butler was implying, of course, was that the so-called "reasonable man" test should be applied to cases of this kind. In other words, no state law should be declared unconstitutional unless reasonable people were unable to justify it as a proper exercise of the police power.[66] The majority had argued, contrarywise, that the First Amendment precluded this approach to the problem since its major purpose was to protect the people against the typical prior restraint. In order to meet this contention, the minority attempted to demonstrate that the statute in question was not censorship at all. The law, said Butler, did not authorize

[65] *Ibid.*, pp. 725-26.
[66] For an incisive statement of the "reasonable man" theory see *Lochner v. New York*, 198 U. S. 45 (1905), dissenting opinion of Holmes, J.

administrative control in advance but prescribed a remedy to be enforced at equity. As such, procedural due process of law governed the tribunal's decisions. And, to press his point to the hilt, he aimed a verbal dagger at what was seemingly a weak point in the majority's conclusions:

> The opinion seems to concede that under clause (a) of the Minnesota law the business of regularly publishing and circulating an obscene periodical may be enjoined. . . . It is difficult to perceive any distinction, having any relation to constitutionality, between clause (a) and clause (b) under which this action was brought. Both nuisances are offensive to morals, order and good government.[67]

The *Near* case is one of the most important ever handed down by the Supreme Court in the area of First Amendment rights. It set forth the binding principle that censorship of the press by states was to be considered unconstitutional unless proof could be clearly established that such legislation was needed to protect fundamental public and/or private rights. The Court had been unanimous on this point. And, of equal import, a majority of the Justices had refused to be limited by definitions of censorship that had been formulated in prior years. If new laws were passed that possessed in substance the "evils" of censorship these enactments would be cited as repugnant to the Constitution regardless of the fact that they might contain refined techniques for wielding power not utilized in Blackstone's time.

It was only a short jump from the Court's findings in this case to its holding unconstitutional a local ordinance that required the written permission of the city manager of Griffin, Georgia before literature of any kind could be distributed within the limits of the community.[68] Speaking for a unanimous court, Chief Justice Hughes began by asserting that it was settled law that municipal statutes adopted under state aegis constituted state action and so fell under the jurisdiction of the Fourteenth Amendment. He then noted the sweeping terms of the ordinance.

---

[67] 230 U. S. 697 at p. 737.

[68] *Lovell* v. *Griffin*, 303 U. S. 444 (1938). The city statute is incorporated in the Court's opinion at pp. 447-48.

It did not confine itself to literature that was obscene or contrary to the public morals. The law was applicable to every conceivable sort of writing. Nor was the statute limited in its authority to certain modes of distribution such as, for instance, activities which might be thought of as inconsistent with the maintenance of public order. It covered every means of circulation "either by hand or otherwise."

In the particular controversy at hand, Alma Lovell, a member of Jehovah's Witnesses, had distributed some of the organization's literature in the form of handbills and circulars on the streets of Griffin without the mandatory permit. In response to her appeal to the Supreme Court following arrest and conviction, the attorneys for the city claimed that she was not a member of the press and so not entitled to invoke the constitutional privileges that protected newspaper and book publishers. The Court squarely rejected this notion by declaring the ordinance "invalid on its face" because it subjected to a program of prior restraint all who wished to disseminate written matter. The liberty of the press could not be limited to newspapers, periodicals, or other forms of written communication that one might usually encounter. It necessarily included leaflets and pamphlets. As the work of Thomas Paine well illustrated, the spread of ideas through the publication of such documents could be of vital importance in the fight for just causes. It must be remembered, concluded the Chief Justice, that the press in its historic connotation embraced every sort of written publication and that the freedom to distribute such materials was as necessary to the maintenance of a free press as was the freedom to write down one's thoughts.[69]

Lovell v. Griffin is an important link in the chain of decisions dealing with censorship that the Court has evolved over the years because it brings all media of written communication under the purview of the First and Fourteenth Amendments. At the same time, Chief Justice Hughes's opinion did not anticipate the dual questions of whether more limited state or local censorship statutes aimed at outlawing specific kinds of matter or certain means of distributing such material that might be detrimental to

[69] Ibid., pp. 451-52.

the public health and safety would be consistent with the Constituton. In this regard, his opinion was clearly in accord with his generally cautious attitude expressed in *Near*.[70]

In contrasting the rights of individuals to write and to read what is presented on the printed page with similar rights to speak and to hear what is orally stated it is essential to keep in mind that there are inherent differences between communicating by voice and communicating by the medium of the press. Reading is a "solitary process." It is most fruitful when a single person is left alone and permitted to concentrate and absorb. The essence of speech, however, consists in an audience-speaker relationship where one person tries to reach at least one other person. By its nature, the freedom to speak is best utilized by those with a cause to champion when it attracts the attention of a crowd of people whether the utterances are to be delivered on private property or on public grounds. It is evident then, that freedom of speech presents far more problems for the preservation of public order than does a free press, for a magazine or book can always be read at home whereas speech, especially when presented in a public park or on public streets, is a more social activity which may, and often does, reach the ears of listeners easily offended by the orator's remarks.[71]

In an early decision regarding free speech problems, the Supreme Court had upheld a Boston ordinance that had required any person who wished to make a public address, discharge any firearm, or who wished to peddle goods on Boston Common to first receive a permit from the mayor.[72] The law, said Chief Justice White, was not directed against free speech generally but only speech to be voiced on the Common which was city property. If the Boston City Council could curtail the public's right to enter

---

[70] In *Schneider* v. *State*, 308 U. S. 147 (1939), the Court, per Justice Roberts, struck down several other local censorship ordinances aimed at the dissemination of handbills. To the argument that these laws were justified to prevent littering of the streets, the Court said that some other means would have to be found to deal with this problem for, by itself, it was not a sufficient reason to justify censorship of the press.

[71] Pritchett, *op. cit.*, pp. 413-14.

[72] *Davis* v. *Massachusetts*, 167 U. S. 43 (1897).

upon this stretch of land then certainly it could take the lesser step of excluding certain activities from its premises. This ruling, as will be seen, was rarely supported in later rulings by the Court and may now be said to be obsolete. As it was adjudicated twenty-eight years before *Gitlow* v. *New York*, it is not difficult to see why the Court at that time did not even remotely consider the constitutional nuances of local prior restraint laws raised by the facts of this case.

The first controversy of modern vintage to be decided dealing with the censorship of speech was *Hague* v. *CIO*, a 1939 decision.[73] Jersey City, New Jersey, then under the vice-like control of Mayor Frank Hague, had passed an ordinance prohibiting all public assemblies "in or upon the public streets, highways, public parks, or public buildings" of the city unless a permit could be obtained from the local Director of Public Safety who was authorized to grant such requests unless he deemed it necessary to do otherwise for the purpose of "preventing riots, disturbances or disorderly assemblage."[74]

The CIO repeatedly tried to obtain a permit under this law to hold a series of public meetings in furtherance of its attempt to unionize workers in the area, but was refused each time on the ground that it was a Communist organization. By a vote of 5-2, with Justices Frankfurter and Douglas excusing themselves, the Court found the statute invalid, but so diverse were the reasons by which the majority arrived at its verdict that three separate opinions were filed in support of this conclusion. In a remarkably unscholarly analysis Mr. Justice Roberts, with Justice Black concurring, felt that the ordinance was a clear violation of the privileges and immunities guaranteed to citizens of the United States by the Fourteenth Amendment. The record clearly demonstrated, in his view, that the CIO had no other purpose in mind than to inform citizens of Jersey City by oral persuasion that trade unionism was a movement in support of their best interests. The opinion went on to declare that the rights to peaceably as-

---

[73] 307 U. S. 496.

[74] For a statement of the ordinance in its entirety see the opinion of Roberts, J. at p. 502.

semble and debate public issues were attributes of national citizenship which could not be abridged.

In response to petitioner's claim that the city statute was nothing more than the rightful exercise of a community's police power as sanctioned by *Davis* v. *Massachusetts*, Roberts replied that the Boston ordinance upheld in that case was of a different species from the one at issue in this dispute for that law was a device not aimed solely at a curtailment of the civil rights of citizens but was merely a general enactment drafted to promote an aspect of public order and so also directed toward a regulation of other activities which were well within the competence of the city to control. Then, as if to apologize for the weakness of this rebuttal, the learned Justice as much as overruled the *Davis* precedent by stating that regardless of whether that verdict had been rightly or wrongly decided it could not govern the facts of the present dispute because no matter who possessed a title to public facilities it had always been assumed that they could be used for free discussion and assembly.[75] This being the case, Roberts concluded that the Jersey City ordinance was void on its face because it gave an almost complete discretion to a public servant to decide who could exercise these rights. Only more precise standards drafted by the city for the general comfort and convenience of all and administered impartially by the officers in charge could be given approval, in his estimation.[76]

Mr. Justice Stone, with Mr. Justice Reed in agreement, filed an opinion that disagreed with virtually everything Justice Roberts had presented except his conclusion. It had been clearly established, he said, that freedom of speech and of assembly for any lawful purpose were secured to every person by the due process clause of the Fourteenth Amendment. It had never been seriously argued that these rights were privileges and immunities of citizens of the United States. Indeed, this contention had been rejected by the Court in the *Slaughter-House Cases*.[77] Why, in the

---

[75] *Ibid.*, pp. 514-15.
[76] *Ibid.*, p. 516.
[77] 16 Wall. 36 (1873).

light of the *Gitlow, Near,* and *Lovell* decisions was it necessary to revive a dead horse?

This argument gained some support from Chief Justice Hughes who, in another concurring opinion, seemed to be trying to mediate this dispute. He felt that the union's right to discuss the particular kinds of issues it claimed it wanted to talk about was indeed a privilege inherent in United States citizenship, but that the record did not establish beyond doubt that it wished to confine itself within these bounds so that the decision properly should have been argued in terms of the meaning of the due process clause.

In dissent, Justices McReynolds and Butler generally hewed to the line expressed in *Davis* v. *Massachusetts,* claiming there was no appreciable difference between it and the instant case.[78]

A ruling of unusual significance because of the broad play it gave to freedom of speech rights and because the state statute under scrutiny contained concomitants of both censorship and subsequent punishment legislation was *Thornhill* v. *Alabama*[79] which came before the Court in 1940. The State of Alabama had enacted a law the substance of which was to ban picketing throughout the state and Thornhill was found guilty of so demonstrating.[80] With only Justice McReynolds disagreeing, the Court again invoked the "void on its face" doctrine and swept the statute aside as it had the prior restraint enactments of Jersey City and Griffin even though, historically, courts were not usually disposed to grant relief to those convicted on a charge of picket-

[78] In *Thomas* v. *Collins,* 323 U. S. 516 (1945), the Court voided a Texas law requiring all labor union organizers to obtain a permit before soliciting members for their organizations. Though public officials were given no power to reject an application form properly filled out, a majority of five judges found that only unusual circumstances could justify such a burden on free speech. Ordinarily, however, licensing provisions that do not place discretionary powers in the hands of public authorities as to the use of public parks and streets for meetings and the dissemination of literature are constitutional. See, for instance, *Poulos* v. *New Hampshire,* 345 U. S. 395 (1953).

[79] 310 U. S. 88.

[80] *Ibid.,* p. 91.

ing. The reason for this general rule was that such conduct had been traditionally held to be tortious; indeed, the concept of peaceful picketing had usually been thought of as a contradiction in terms.

Speaking for the majority, Mr. Justice Murphy made note of the fact that the law was not aimed at specific evils that might be threatened by speech in a given context, but included a ban on all picketing. The statute, indeed, had been construed by the courts of Alabama to prohibit an individual from walking back and forth on a sidewalk, outside a place of business, carrying a placard that informed the public that that particular establishment did not employ men affiliated with the American Federation of Labor. "In the circumstances of our times," said Murphy in appraising the situation, "the dissemination of information concerning the facts of a labor dispute must be regarded as within that area of free discussion that is guaranteed by the Constitution."[81] Nor could the state justify a statute of this kind on the grounds that it was protecting the community from the possible evil consequences of picketing, namely, violence, disorder, and unruly conduct. Going much further than either Chief Justice Hughes had in the *Near* and *Lovell* decisions or Justice Roberts in *Hague*, Murphy asserted that "abridgment of the liberty of such discussion can be justified only where the clear danger of substantive evils arises under circumstances affording no opportunity to test the merits of ideas by competition for acceptance in the market of public opinion."[82] This dictum seemed to place the Court much closer to Justice Holmes's position in *Gitlow* than it had ever been before. The general principle enunciated, if applied stringently in other actions brought against state and local censorship statutes that limited aspects of speech or press, would certainly push most of them outside the ambit of constitutional protection.

One aspect of this decision should be noted carefully. Unlike other ordinances discussed thus far, the Alabama enactment voided in *Thornhill* did not place discretionary power in a public official to determine who might speak or publish and on what

[81] *Ibid.*, p. 102.
[82] *Ibid.*, p. 105.

occasions. It was one of the few laws ever challenged before the Supreme Court that simply proscribed a medium of communication which is, in and of itself, the essence of speech.[83] Of course, this unique situation is readily explainable given the unusual nature of picketing; that is, that it inherently contains an element of speech as well as an element of economic coercion. The point is, however, that in a sense the law in question was simply a typical penal restraint; i.e. a certain mode of behavior involving an expression of views was declared to be contrary to the public welfare and was found to be punishable in a criminal proceeding. Yet, the enactment, without doubt, smacked of censorship because it banned a type of communication that had historically come to be the chief means of disseminating information to the public about a special kind of economic controversy. And that communication had been specifically found by the Court to be, absent extenuating circumstances, one of the many forms that free speech might take. This case, then, is of great importance because it is sui generis; it is illustrative of the fact that the Court may rule that under some conditions, at least, a state cannot proscribe outright a means of communicating ideas.[84]

Thus far, no controversy had come before the Court which tested the right of a community to subject religious liberties to previous restraint. Such was the issue at stake in *Cantwell* v. *Connecticut*.[85] A state law made it a crime for a person to solicit money for any "alleged religious . . . cause . . . unless such cause shall have been approved by the secretary of the public welfare council." When anyone wished to solicit funds on behalf of some religious sect he was to file a request with the secretary who would then make a judgment as to whether the organization to be aided

[83] Somewhat similar is *Kovacs* v. *Cooper*, 336 U. S. 77 (1949), to be discussed in this section, where the applicable statute was aimed at another particular technique for transmitting speech, the sound truck.

[84] See footnote 27, *supra*, and the commentary relevant thereto. Local ordinances banning the exhibition of movies within town or city limits would seem to be invalid for much the same reasons. It is worth noting that Pritchett's discussion of the *Thornhill* decision, at *op. cit.*, p. 424, is included in his chapter on "Censorship of Speech."

[85] 310 U. S. 296 (1940).

was "a bona fide object of charity or philanthropy and conforms to reasonable standards of efficiency and integrity. . . ."[86]

A unanimous court with Mr. Justice Roberts formulating its argument began by adducing that the religious liberties enshrined in the First Amendment—that Congress could make no law respecting an establishment of religion or prohibiting the free exercise thereof—were as binding upon the states as the dual freedoms of press and speech. In temperate language Justice Roberts explained that the free exercise of one's religious convictions, clearly at issue in this dispute, was not undilutable; for such freedom might, if carried too far, impinge on the rights of others. It was evident, for example, that a state might regulate the times, the places, and the manner in which all forms of solicitation were to be conducted in the streets and parks of the city. No one would contest, however, the proposition that a community could not, under the Constitution, censor the right to preach or to distribute religious literature. In Justice Roberts' opinion, the law at issue was an impermissible regulation of solicitation because it involved a religious test. The secretary was impowered to determine if a religious sect or organization met prescribed standards. Such an enactment constituted "a censorship of religion as the means of determining its right to survive" and so was clearly void. In reply to the state's argument that appellant retained the right of appeal to the courts following a refusal to issue a permit, Justice Roberts, with a nod towards *Near* v. *Minnesota*, responded by asserting that unconstitutional prior restraints were null whether enforced by administrative tribunals or judicial officers.[87]

---

[86] *Ibid.*, pp. 301-2.

[87] *Ibid.*, pp. 305-6. In *Kunz* v. *New York*, 340 U. S. 290 (1951), a New York City ordinance making it unlawful to hold meetings for religious worship on the streets without first obtaining a permit from the police commissioner was struck down because it gave "an administrative official discretionary power to control in advance the right of citizens to speak on religious matters on the streets of New York" with "no appropriate standards to guide his action." The twin cases of *Jones* v. *Opelika*, 316 U. S. 584 (1942), and *Murdock* v. *Pennsylvania*, 319 U. S. 105 (1943), though involving taxes to be paid by vendors of religious tracts prior to their being given a license to sell, were not truly germane to the subject here being dealt with because the fees exacted were nondiscriminatory in nature,

Judging from the cases presented thus far, it would not be hasty to conclude that local censorship statutes aimed at rights granted under the First Amendment are rarely able to surmount the rigid standards that have traditionally guided the Supreme Court in this area of litigation. It might profitably be pondered at this point if any prior restraint statutes that delegate some flexibility to the censor in the decisions he is to make are constitutional. For example, what of the right of the community to limit parades and processions in the streets? As the tactics of Martin Luther King, Jr. and other integration leaders illustrate, the parade can be a useful means of marshaling the sympathies of onlookers to support an ideological commitment. A parade dramatizes the marchers' point of view and gives to a movement a certain cohesion and militancy—not afforded by the mere distribution of literature or by speeches in the public park—in its determination to enlist the aid of others. At the same time, a parade can tie up motor vehicle traffic in a large city for miles in all directions and the aid of an entire police force of a smaller town might be required to keep such proceedings orderly and make it possible for a procession to run its course. Requiring a permit for a parade thus raises the question whether this form of prior restraint, in view of the attendant circumstances, might be constitutionally justifiable even though the communication of ideas is the primary object of the demonstration.

In *Cox v. New Hampshire*,[88] the Court was asked to decide whether a state could demand that those who wished to organize a parade that would pass upon any public way first procure a license from the locality where the procession was to be held. The statute went on to require that each license that was issued should specify the day and particular time of day when the parade

being required of all door-to-door peddlers and other transient merchants. If the taxes had been designed to curtail the selling of these pamphlets (which was not their intent) the situation would have been analogous to the plight of motion picture companies if a community chose to close down all movie houses in the area as an exercise of its police power. See the discussion in the Introduction, *supra*. Of course, a discriminatory tax aimed at driving certain newspapers out of business is unconstitutional. *Grosjean v. American Press Company*, 297 U. S. 233 (1936).

[88] 312 U. S. 569 (1941).

was to be held and, also, that each licensee was to pay in advance of receiving a permit a sum not to exceed $300.00 for the use of public facilities.[89]

Speaking for a unanimous court, Chief Justice Hughes upheld the constitutionality of this law as applied to a parade staged without a license by the Jehovah's Witnesses in Manchester, New Hampshire. The control of travel on the streets is the most fundamental kind of protection a community can afford to all its citizens, he pointed out, and when a state sought to regulate the times, places, and manner of activities that could, if left uncontrolled, result in total confusion, such laws should be presumed to be valid. It was important to note, moreover, he maintained, that the applicable statute in no way infringed on the countless other ways by which a segment of society might wish to make known its views on various questions of interest. Of equal importance was the fact that there was no evidence to support an allegation that the law was being used to prevent appellant from utilizing a medium of speech. Indeed, the organizers of the parade had made no attempt to obtain a license because they believed such a law to be void on its face. In the light of the obvious consequences unrestricted parades and demonstrations in the streets could have on the tranquility and order of a neighborhood the Court could not support such a finding.[90]

There remained the question of the license fee demanded of each group wishing to stage such a procession. Here, the Chief Justice upheld the state court's conclusion that a town might reasonably assess a "tax" of this sort to pay for the expenses of policing such demonstrations and that a flexible schedule of fees could be invoked so as to charge organizations in accordance with the size of their respective parades, given the fact that the adopted schedule had never been used to curtail the rights of anyone wishing to stage such a march.[91]

The Court had shown, then, that some form of prior restraint on street parades was constitutionally acceptable. In try-

[89] The terms of the statute in their entirety are set forth at *ibid.*, pp. 571-72.
[90] *Ibid.*, pp. 574-76.
[91] *Ibid.*, p. 577.

ing to decide whether this holding represents a departure from previous doctrine in the area of censorship, one should note that the New Hampshire law did not summarily proscribe a form of idea communication as had the Alabama enactment at issue in the *Thornhill* case. A statute making it illegal to stage parades in all likelihood would be regarded by the Court as unconstitutional as one banning picketing.[92]

The applicable New Hampshire law, it can be seen, delegated some discretionary powers to a licensing agent. He could decide what day and at what hour a procession might be held. But he had no authority to decide if a parade could be held at all. The statute on its face was therefore not nearly as constricting as the one presented in *Hague*. Yet, did it differ markedly from the ordinance at stake in the *Lovell* decision? There, a statute that made mandatory the permission of a public official to distribute literature on the streets was found to be void on its face. Nor should it be forgotten that in *Thomas* v. *Collins* the Court, four years later, was to strike down an enactment requiring trade union organizers to register before carrying on their work. In neither case was it shown that the applicable law was a guise for discrimination against certain segments of the community wishing to circulate ideas through speech or press.

Clearly the difference between these decisions rests on the respective cause and effect relationships each of the claimed rights desired by appellants entails when exercised in society. What great threat is posed which would justify a community's making each and every distributor of literature seek a license from a city official? And what emergency, short of the threat of labor sit-downs or widespread use of the secondary boycott, would justify making every person who wanted to encourage workers, in their presence, to join a union register with the state? But a parade is of a different genre. It traditionally involves large masses of people walking for miles at a time, making a great deal of noise, and creating traffic stalemates that could make it impossible for others to get from place to place in times of great importance. In short, the social context in which freedom to express ideas is exercised must inevitably be evaluated against

[92] Compare *Kovacs* v. *Cooper*, 336 U. S. 77 (1949).

community rights and the rights of other individuals. In *Cox* v.
*New Hampshire*, therefore, it is not surprising that the law at
issue could not be found void on its face, nor in the absence of
any discrimination against appellant could it be voided at all
in so far as it demanded that a license be sought out by those
wishing to stage such marches.

The question of a license tax to be paid by prospective
paraders must be treated separately. There was nothing in the
record of the case to indicate that this section of the enactment
had been used to forbid any particular kinds of parades. But if
the discriminatory evils of *Grosjean* were not present how does
one distinguish the fee declared constitutional in *Cox* with the
nondiscriminatory tax declared null in *Murdock* v. *Pennsylvania*
as applied to peddlers of religious tracts? In that case the merchants were involved in the commercial activity of selling books
for a profit. In *Cox* there was no commercial activity at all. The
problem is basic to an understanding of what constitutes a justifiable previous restraint under the Constitution; but because both
taxes were nondiscriminatory and because no discretion was
placed in the hands of public officials as to whom should or should
not be taxed under either system it is only tangentially relevant
to the basic questions of concern here.

The Court had spelled out in relatively clear terms that a
community possesses some inherent power of censorship over
activities that, though protected by the First Amendment, were
by their very nature a serious intrusion into the peace and order
of a locality. But what of the rights of those whose exercise of
free speech was such that it, in some measure, interfered with
the privacy of other citizens? A person need not, unless he wishes,
take a handbill that is offered him on the streets. He may remove
himself from a public park if he disapproves of a speech being
delivered there. But what of loudspeakers and other devices
that amplify sound so that it reaches hundreds of yards into
private houses, libraries, and so forth? What may a city do to
protect its citizens from such disturbing noises?

The Court first grappled with this problem in *Saia* v. *New
York*.[93] Lockport, New York had passed an ordinance forbidding

[93] 334 U. S. 558 (1948).

the use of any loudspeaker on public or private property unless for the purpose of disseminating "public information" such as "items of news and matters of public concern" and then only after permission had been granted by the Chief of Police.[94] Plaintiff was a member of Jehovah's Witnesses whose license to use a sound truck in a park provided by the city for recreational and other purposes was not renewed by the police department on the ground that "complaints had been made." He filed suit in federal court claiming that the law prevented him from expressing his religious views in a manner guaranteed under the Constitution.

In a short opinion a five-man majority, per Justice Douglas, held the ordinance void on its face. This law demanded the prior approval of a public official before sound equipment could be used to propagate information of "public concern." Yet, this duly constituted authority was not vested with precise standards to guide him in accepting or rejecting applications for permits. If the statute had been narrowly drawn so as to cope with what reasonable men would term a substantive evil (the unrestricted use of sound paraphernalia) the question presented to the Court, he felt, might have been different. In this era of a highly refined technology, however, the sound truck had become recognized as an important means for reaching large numbers of people. Consequently, he believed that the facts as presented were in line with those at issue in *Hague* v. *CIO, Lovell* v. *Griffin,* and *Cantwell* v. *Connecticut* where the Court had come to the aid of citizens whose rights to engage in propagandizing activities under the First Amendment were at the mercy of the prior approval of local public officials. As for the New Hampshire parade case, "courts must balance the various community interests in passing on the constitutionality of local regulations" of this character and therefore *Cox* v. *New Hampshire* did not depart from that basic assumption.[95]

Four judges, however, filed dissents in opposition to the majority's assertions. Mr. Justice Frankfurter, for himself and Justices Reed and Burton, seriously questioned some of the root suppositions latent in Douglas' analysis. To be sure, the Court

[94] *Ibid.,* pp. 558-59.
[95] *Ibid.,* pp. 561-62.

had decided such cases as *Cantwell* and *Lovell* correctly. But the facts of this dispute were far different. The rights of speech and press when exercised in accordance with a technology of 1787 could interfere little with the rights of others to carry on their daily activities in relative peace and quiet. But a state might reasonably find, as New Hampshire had with processions in the streets, that loud, ear-piercing noises constituted a threat to the comfort and convenience of others. Hence, a finding that the law was void on its face was unacceptable. Of course, even the power to issue permits for sound amplifying devices could not be wielded with bias, but no one had claimed that the police officials had acted arbitrarily. A license had been denied to appellant only because complaints had been registered by people who felt the din of his sound truck in operation was disconcerting. It was not unreasonable, Frankfurter believed, for the Chief of Police to decide that these protests were good grounds for protecting the rights of others picnicking and playing in the park.

Mr. Justice Jackson filed a dissent of his own in which he heatedly attacked the Court's reasoning. In his view, the majority had wrested away from the states and their subdivisions all control of their property so that they could not regulate the use thereon of something as dangerous to the average citizen (if handled carelessly) as a public address system. What could be a more legitimate exercise of local police power than an ordinance giving the police authority to decide where and when such equipment with its electrical wiring strung across sidewalks and pathways would be utilized, he asked. The Court's verdict had treated this case as a free speech controversy; yet, this was exactly what it was not. The city had not interfered, even in its parks, with all the "facilities of speech with which nature had endowed the appellant." To the contention that the Chief of Police had not been given sufficient guidance to determine who should be awarded permits, he asserted that it was not the work of the Supreme Court to act as a council of revision and that without a showing of discrimination against appellant his claim should be disregarded in the light of *Cox* v. *New Hampshire*.

The divergent opinions expressed in the *Saia* case were only a prelude to the dispute that followed a short time later in *Kovacs*

v. *Cooper*.[96] This decision is probably the most confusing of all those discussed thus far in view of the fact that the Trenton, New Jersey ordinance which had been enforced against appellant was not very precise in its language. A statement of this law serves to highlight this point. It read as follows:

> 4. That it shall be unlawful for any person . . . to play, use or operate for advertising purposes, or for any other purpose whatsoever, on or upon the public streets, alleys or thoroughfares in the City of Trenton, any device known as a sound truck, loud speaker or sound amplifier . . . or any other instrument of any kind or character which emits therefrom loud and raucous noises and is attached to and upon any vehicle operated or standing upon said streets or public places aforementioned.[97]

It appeared that plaintiff was using a sound truck in the streets of Trenton to comment on a labor dispute then in progress. He was arrested and charged with violating the aforementioned enactment. He was subsequently convicted and the verdict against him was upheld by the appeals courts of the state.

The Supreme Court was so split in its position that five opinions were filed. Upon announcing the judgment of the Court as contrary to appellant's claim, Mr. Justice Reed, with Chief Justice Vinson and Justice Burton supporting his view, delivered what has been called a "cloudy opinion."[98] After first stating that the words "loud and raucous" had, through everyday usage, acquired a meaning sufficiently clear to stand against a claim of "void for vagueness," Reed went on to say that a state or city might reasonably find that an unlimited use of devices restricted in the instant statute "would be intolerable." He then argued that "absolute prohibition within municipal limits of all sound amplification, even though reasonably regulated in place, time and volume, is undesirable and probably unconstitutional."[99] What he seemed to be saying was that the law only forbade, as applicable to this case, sound trucks that were loud and raucous, not sound trucks per se.

[96] 336 U. S. 77 (1949).
[97] *Ibid.*, p. 78.
[98] Pritchett, *op. cit.*, p. 419.
[99] 336 U. S. 77 at pp. 81-82.

He then attempted to distinguish the issue at hand with the one presented in *Saia*. There, the Chief of Police had been given powers that were tantamount to making him a censor in the use of sound equipment within that community. But the Trenton ordinance was something else again. It was merely the "run of the mine" criminal statute drafted for the purpose of preventing disturbing noises in the streets. Users of sound truck equipment could proceed at their own risk. Sound trucks, even of a loud and raucous kind, might still be used in public parks and on private property, he concluded, without violating the provision in question.

Mr. Justice Frankfurter, in a concurring opinion, devoted most of his salvos to a ringing denial of the "preferred position" doctrine which he believed bottomed the thinking of both the Court's position and that of the dissenters. He felt that the conclusion arrived at in *Kovacs* clearly overruled the *Saia* decision and that oversimplified formulas should not be used to lump all aspects of communication into one category for purposes of sheltering them all under First Amendment aegis. Each form of idea distribution should be treated in accordance with its effect upon the social community in which it operates. In short, a "balancing of conflicting interests" must be made. Thus, he pointed out in an extremely enlightenting statement, "movies have created problems not presented by the circulation of books, pamphlets, or newspapers, and so the movies have been constitutionally regulated."[100] Here was a ringing endorsement of the *Mutual Film Corporation* case and its treatment of motion pictures as a "mere spectacle" thirty-four years after that decision had been handed down.

In another concurring opinion Mr. Justice Jackson reiterated for the most part Justice Frankfurter's views. Each medium of idea transmission should be treated separately when pertinent local regulations came before the Court, he contested, and he could see no difference between the principle set forth in the *Saia* case and the one in *Kovacs*. He parted company with all other members of the majority group, however, when he criti-

[100] *Ibid.*, p. 96.

cized Justice Reed's construction of the Trenton ordinance. To him, this law banned all sound trucks from the streets regardless of the noises they made, but was still a legitimate exercise of the police power nonetheless.

In a powerful dissent Mr. Justice Black, with Justices Douglas and Rutledge in agreement, hit hard at Justice Reed's findings. Appellant had been neither charged nor convicted, he contended, because he had operated a sound truck that emitted loud and raucous noises. The complaint lodged against him was only that he had used a sound truck. The minority demanded to know what evidence there was in the record to substantiate the claim that the noises heard by the policeman were loud or raucous. They felt that the statute "in simple, unambiguous language" prohibited "the use upon the public streets of any device known as a sound truck" and that the sounds it transmitted were of no consequence.[101]

Having questioned the way in which the majority had interpreted the ordinance, Black and his associates then branded the law as far more dangerous than the Lockport statute involved in the *Saia* case because it barred the use of all loudspeakers mounted upon any vehicle in the city's streets. The basic assumption of the First Amendment, they said, is that all forms of speech are protected by its terms. There are many people who do not have the money to buy newspaper space or time over the airways to communicate ideas. The sound truck is for these people an inexpensive means for disseminating opinion. Black then made a most startling statement:

> Ideas and beliefs are today chiefly disseminated to the masses of people through the press, radio, *moving pictures,* and public address systems. . . . The result of today's opinion in upholding this statutory prohibition of amplifiers would surely not be reached by this Court if such channels of communication as the press, radio, or *moving pictures* were similarly attacked.[102] (Emphasis added.)

For anyone interested in the welfare and growth of the motion picture medium this rejoinder must have been received as the

[101] *Ibid.,* p. 98.
[102] *Ibid.,* p. 102.

happiest of news.[103] By asserting that movies were a chief carrier of ideas and beliefs three judges on the Court had knocked the strongest pillar out from under the *Mutual Film Corporation* case. Of almost equal importance, they had said in so many words that the Court would hold unconstitutional any law, such as the one at issue in the *Thornhill* verdict or similar to the one being contested in *Kovacs*, which sought to ban the showing of motion picture film to the public in a given community or which so attempted to limit where film houses could be opened that the restriction might be termed, at the very least, arbitrary or capricious.[104] Justice Black concluded his remarks by saying that narrowly drawn ordinances could be enacted to protect a city from the blare of sound trucks but that it was unconstitutional to ban all such trucks from the streets.

In a short dissenting opinion, Justice Rutledge found it necessary only to state that appellant stood convicted but of what crime no one could determine because a majority of the judges were in agreement that the statute had been misconstrued by Justice Reed. Any law that could so thoroughly confuse the Supreme Court as to its meaning should be held violative of due process for reasons of vagueness.

Taken together, these two cases leave much that is unanswered about the role of sound trucks as disseminators of speech under the First Amendment. A majority of the Justices had initially found that censorship authority could not be vested in a public official which gave him the blanket right to determine if and when sound trucks and other amplifying instruments could be used. In the *Kovacs* case, however, a different majority (the dissenters along with Jackson and Frankfurter) concluded that the doctrine expressed in *Saia* had been overruled. Yet, two of the

[103] But, because it had been upstaged by the *Paramount Pictures* decision decided a few months earlier (see *infra,* this section), it was not regarded of itself as an entering wedge for broader constitutional sanctions for the film industry.

[104] Of course this opinion, which today would be sound law, would not threaten legitimate zoning laws that restricted movie houses to certain parts of a locality.

Justices (Reed and Burton) who voted to uphold the Trenton ordinance attempted to distinguish it from the Lockport law as if to imply that they were willing to concede that *Saia* was settled law. If this was so, then both cases must now be assumed to be "the law of the land," for surely the views of Black, Douglas, Rutledge, and Murphy (who had dissented without comment in *Kovacs*) had not changed with regard to the merits of the *Saia* judgment.

Given the fact then, that Mr. Justice Reed held, in his opinion in *Saia*, that each decision could stand on its own premises and logic without violating the commands of the other, what primary deductions can be formulated about the importance of the principles set forth therein? In *Saia v. New York* the Court had refused to sanction a form of censorship which imparted unchecked discretionary powers to a police official. To be sure, a community could restrict the times and places during and at which sound equipment could be used and subsequently punish anyone who transgressed such regulations. Whether or not a locality could constitutionally impose an ordinance on the use of sound trucks of the kind that was upheld in the *Cox* street parade case, where public officials were vested with narrowly defined discretionary powers, remained an open question. It would depend upon whether the Court felt that instrumentalities that amplified speech were as much an impingement on the rights of others as parades are on the tranquility and needs of society and, also, upon whether such a statute was administered without prejudice.

As to *Kovacs v. Cooper* the Court had there determined that a locality might mark off certain areas of public property and exclude "obnoxious" sound amplifying paraphernalia therefrom. This was not a censorship statute at all, it had held, because no public authority was given any power to decide when or where such equipment could be used. Unlike the situation in the *Thornhill* case, owners of sound trucks were not prohibited entirely from utilizing such media. Indeed, a law that demanded compliance to such a rigid rule would be null. These trucks could be used in other public areas and make as much noise as they wished and, if kept from being "loud and raucous," could even be used in the streets.[105]

The basic point in the minority's arsenal of arguments (over and above the question of statutory interpretation which may be put aside) was that this law was even more invidious than the Lockport ordinance because it banned sound trucks that were capable of emitting enough noise to attract an audience from the streets at all times. This was a form of censorship because it grievously hindered access to "the market place of ideas" in Trenton by proscribing at the outset any speech, regardless of its content, transmitted by amplifying devices. At the heart of this debate, in short, were questions of the deepest significance: What is censorship? What is a subsequent restraint? In the light of the analysis of these problems made earlier in the Introduction to this investigation it would appear that the scales of justice are tilted slightly in behalf of public authority. That a city might reasonably find amplified sound equipment to be a burden on the community, and at the same time preserve some substantive rights for those who wished to disseminate ideas in this way, would appear a constitutional balancing of the right to speak with the right of states and local communities to exercise their police powers. The right of free speech in dispute was not subject to the unrestricted whim of the censor. Nor was the right to use a sound truck proscribed ab initio. As far as scholarly examination has thus far been able to distinguish a form of prior restriction from the usual kind of subsequent punishment penal law, it would seem proper to place the Trenton ordinance case in the latter category.[106]

Of course, the opinion of Justice Black relative to the scope to be allotted to motion pictures under the terms of the First

[105] Though Justice Reed never did explain if it was possible for such devices to be anything but "loud and raucous."

[106] Professor Freund might contend that this kind of deduction is a form of theorizing which amounts to "label thinking." See his remarks, *op. cit.* Nonetheless, Chief Justice Hughes's comments in the *Near* decision *re* the especially odious character of censorship statutes in the light of the demands of the First Amendment and the Court's insistence, as described *supra,* that this precedent be vigorously implemented would appear to be determinative of the value of such assessments.

Amendment was most revealing. Much of the shock was removed from its impact, however, because a few months earlier a dictum touching upon the same point, but of far more grandiose proportions, was enunciated by the Court itself, with Mr. Justice Douglas as its spokesman, in *U. S. v. Paramount Pictures*.[107] This was a case involving the highly intricate matter of whether the leading motion picture companies were, in some of their dealings with exhibitors, in violation of the Sherman Act. Though freedoms guaranteed under the Bill of Rights had no bearing on the facts of the controversy, as Douglas freely admitted, he felt it necessary to assert that if such were the case then the Court's focus upon the issues would be regulated by the basic principle that "we have no doubt that moving pictures, like newspapers and radio, are included in the press whose freedom is guaranteed by the First Amendment."[108] It is an ironic twist indeed that the movie industry should come of age before the "bar of justice" in a manner so anticlimactic. Though Justice Douglas' statement was only a dictum of the most obvious sort, it was apparent that the death knell had been sounded for the *Mutual Film Corporation* precedent. Justice Black's announcement in *Kovacs* v. *Cooper*, then, was really only an afterthought; the ceiling had already caved in.

Curiously, Justice Frankfurter, who dissented in part in this antitrust proceeding, made no attempt to counter Douglas' premature finding. Yet, in the *Kovacs* decision he seemed to imply that the Court's treatment of motion pictures in 1915 was defensible. As time was to demonstrate, however, what Frankfurter was really saying was that movies were a part of speech and press but that they raised special problems for a community which might reasonably be remedied by legislation not constitutionally applicable to other media of expression such as books, newspapers, or word of mouth.

### Motion Pictures Accorded Status of Free Speech

Apparently, it would be only a matter of time before a case which demanded a modern scholarly appraisal of rights held by movie

[107] 334 U. S. 131 (1948).
[108] *Ibid.,* p. 166.

companies under the First Amendment would reach the Supreme
Court. In the light of Justice Douglas' declaration in the *Paramount* decision, and of Justice Black's observations in *Kovacs* v.
*Cooper,* it was somewhat of a shock that, when such a controversy
was presented for certiorari two years later, only one judge
(Douglas) felt that the petition deserved to be granted.[109] In that
dispute Miss Christine Smith, the chief motion picture censor in
Atlanta, Georgia, had ruled that the film *Lost Boundaries,* which
dealt with a Negro doctor and his family who were able to pass as
white for years without notice, was "likely to have an adverse
effect upon the peace, morals, and good order of the city" and
so could not be shown. This ruling had been upheld first by a
lower federal District Court[110] and, later, by a Court of Appeals.[111]

Speaking for a unanimous three-judge District Court, Chief
Judge M. Neil Andrews reluctantly decided in the censor's behalf. Despite Douglas' statement in *Paramount,* he felt that he
could not properly anticipate that the Court was ready to discard
the *Mutual Film* precedent. Nonetheless, he could not hold himself back from stating that ordinances of the type in question
should be put away "in the attic which contains the ghosts of
those who arrayed in the robe of Bigotry, armed with the spear
of Intolerance, and mounted on the steed of Hatred, have through
all the ages sought to patrol the highways of the mind." He made
it perfectly clear that so far as he could ascertain that part of the
Atlanta ordinance under scrutiny was indefensible because it
"empowers the censor to determine what is good and what is bad

[109] *RD-DR* v. *Smith,* 340 U. S. 853 (1950). In *United Artists Corp.* v.
*Board of Censors,* 339 U. S. 952 (1950), the Board of Censors of Memphis,
Tennessee had refused to allow the movie *Curley* to be shown. Appellant
asked the Court to declare the entire censorship ordinance unconstitutional
but, without dissent, certiorari was denied. An analysis of a decision rendered
by the Tennessee Supreme Court, 189 Tenn. 397 (1949), prior to this
appeal, lends appreciable weight to the belief that appellant's lack of success
before the Supreme Court was attributable to procedural factors rather
than a rejection of his constitutional grounds for initiating the suit. See
further discussion of this matter in Chapter IV.
[110] 89 F. Supp. 596 (1950).
[111] 183 F. 2d 562 (1950).

for the community and that without any standard other than the censor's personal opinion."[112]

Judge Andrews' uncertainties were not shared by his superiors on the Fifth United States Circuit Court of Appeals. They were positive that states and localities still had an untrammeled power to censor motion pictures, and they could not imagine that the Supreme Court would overrule or in any other way subvert a decision that had been on the books for years, had been followed with the greatest consistency by the states, and had almost never been criticized. Further, it was their belief that moving pictures had not in any sense "emerged from the business of amusement into instruments for the propagation of ideas and, therefore, like newspapers, freedom of assembly, freedom of speech, must be regarded as within the protection of the Fourteenth Amendment."[113] In any event, they believed it out of their range of responsibilities to attempt to outguess the Supreme Court; individual judges may have stated that the *Mutual Film Corporation* decision was shopworn but far more evidence was needed to convince them that they should act on the assumption that this judgment had been overturned.

It is difficult to explain why the Court declined certiorari at that point, given the fact that two years later the *Mutual Film Corporation* case, as had been presaged, was to be thrust aside. It is even less apparent why Justice Black, who had dissented so vigorously in *Kovacs* and who had talked with so much conviction about the rights of motion pictures being coequal with those of other media of expression, did not join Douglas in a desire to hear oral argument on the merits of enforcing a statute at least as amenable to arbitrary manipulation as those declared void in such cases as *Saia* v. *New York* and *Lovell* v. *Griffin.*[114]

If the Court had, for some unexplainable reason, wavered in

[112] 89 F. Supp. 596 at p. 598.

[113] 183 F. 2d 562 at p. 565 (1950).

[114] The Atlanta statute, at that time, demanded a pre-screening for each full-length movie to see if it met with prescribed standards which included, among others, whether a film was "likely to have an adverse effect upon the peace, morals, and good order" of the city.

the *Lost Boundaries* case, it was decisive indeed in *Burstyn* v. *Wilson*.[115] Appellant was a distributor which owned exclusive rights to lease to American exhibitors an Italian film entitled *The Miracle*. After examining the movie the motion picture division of the New York Education Department, which under state law was vested with the power to preview all films before they were given a permit allowing them to be shown,[116] issued a license authorizing the film to be exhibited as one part of a trilogy entitled *Ways of Love*. Thereafter, for a period of approximately two months this movie was presented daily in a New York theater. During this time the New York State Board of Regents, which by law governed the work of the movie censorship board,[117] received hundreds of letters and telegrams demanding that the movie not be shown. Meanwhile, Edward T. McCaffrey, Commissioner of Licenses for New York City, declared the film "officially and personally blasphemous" and ordered it withdrawn at the risk of suspension of the license to operate the Paris Theater where the movie was playing. This action was short-lived, however, when the New York Supreme Court ruled that the City License Commissioner had exceeded his authority in that he was without powers of movie censorship. This responsibility had been placed by the state in other hands.[118] Resolving himself to investigate the nature of the turmoil surrounding *The Miracle,* the Chancellor of the Board of Regents requested three members of the Board to view the picture and to make a report to the entire membership. After viewing the film this committee reported to the parent body that in its opinion there were just grounds for finding that the picture was "sacrilegious" and thus should not, under the state law, be exhibited.[119] After another hearing, the Commissioner of Education rescinded appellant's license to show the film.

---

[115] 343 U. S. 495 (1952).

[116] *McKinney's N. Y. Laws*, Education Law, Book 16, Sect. 122.

[117] *Ibid.*, Sect. 132.

[118] *Burstyn* v. *McCaffrey*, 101 N.Y.S. 2d 892 (1951).

[119] The law stated that a film shall be given a license unless deemed to be "obscene, indecent, immoral, inhuman, sacrilegious, or is of such a character that its exhibition would tend to corrupt morals or incite to crime. . . ." See *op. cit.*, Sect. 122. Mr. Justice Clark, in his opinion for the full court, seemed to assume that the Board had implicit power to

Among the claims advanced by petitioner in the brief it presented before the New York Court of Appeals were (1) that the statute violated the First and Fourteenth Amendments because it was a prior restraint upon the rights of freedom of speech and press; (2) that it impinged upon the right of a free exercise of religion guaranteed against state action by the same Amendments; and (3) that the term "sacrilegious" violated due process because it was an indefinable standard whose vagueness provided no guidelines for the scope of administrative authority. In each instance, the New York court found in favor of the Regents' ruling.[120]

In his examination of these assertions, Mr. Justice Clark in speaking for a unanimous Supreme Court found that it was only necessary to consider the contention that the New York law was an unconstitutional abridgment of free speech and a free press. Agreeing wholeheartedly with Douglas' dictum in the *Paramount* case, he found that movies were, without question, a significant medium for the dissemination of ideas. He clearly refuted the conclusions to the contrary Justice McKenna had reached thirty-seven years earlier by stating that it was of no consequence either that many motion pictures were designed merely to entertain, or that the film industry was a large-scale business conducted for private profit. To the former charge, he merely observed that the line between what informs and what entertains was too elusive to determine what aspects of speech were constitutionally sheltered, and that one man's amusement was another man's dogma. To the latter contention, he asserted that if books and newspapers could be sold for profit and yet be protected as privileged communication then so could motion pictures.[121]

In order to soften the blow of what seemed would inevitably be a reversal of the *Mutual Film Corporation* decision, Clark tried to distinguish that case on two grounds, neither of them especially persuasive. First, he demonstrated that the 1915 decision was decided solely upon an interpretation of the Constitution of Ohio and that consequently Justice McKenna's opinion had not dealt

---

rescind a license for a movie even though it had been passed by the film censorship bureau.

[120] 303 N. Y. 242 (1951).

[121] 343 U. S. 495 at p. 501.

with appellant's rights under the federal Constitution. Though on the surface this was a correct statement of the Court's train of thought, the point was purely academic because plaintiff had at that time asked, in part, for relief based upon an interpretation of the Fourteenth Amendment and, by not granting such aid, the Court had clearly denied its validity sub silentio. Secondly, Clark advanced the notion that much significance should be placed on the fact that the film industry did not ripen into maturity until 1926 with the advent of the talking movie. As mentioned earlier, this supposition is highly fallacious.[122] At the same time, however, he was eminently clear in his belief that wherever the 1915 judgment was out of harmony with the Court's new position, "we no longer adhere to it."

Phase one of the new status of motion pictures had been set forth. No longer could movies, it seemed, be treated as second-class citizens of the mass media. They had been granted tangible rights under the Constitution as a protectable expression of beliefs and artistic values. As Justice Clark was quick to point out, however, the fact that movies were now to be regarded as sheltered speech did not mean that the Constitution required that the showing of all films at all times and at all places be placed beyond legal regulation. This was not a startling statement in the light of the several exceptions to the doctrine of "uninhibited speech" that the Court has always insisted upon.[123] "Nor does it follow," he went on, "that motion pictures are necessarily subject to the precise rules governing any other particular method of expression."[124] This was a sentiment reminiscent of Justice Frankfurter's embittered dissent in *Saia* v. *New York*. If it possessed any practical meaning at all, it might prove to be a source of disappointment and disillusionment for motion picture producers.

The nature of the facts of this particular case were such, however, that *Burstyn* v. *Wilson* would for years be remembered only

[122] See Lasker, *op. cit.*, and the discussion centering around footnote 45, *supra*.

[123] The threat of inciting to riot, for example, has generally been held to be a valid reason for the police to keep a close watch on public utterances of speakers. *Feiner* v. *New York*, 340 U. S. 315 (1951).

[124] 343 U. S. 495 at p. 503.

as a kind of Emancipation Proclamation for movie exhibitors. Justice Clark went on to point out that as a general rule prior restraint legislation, from the days of the *Near* decision, had almost never received the blessings of the Court. New York's highest court had said that the term "sacrilegious" was readily understandable: "It simply means this: that no religion, as that word is understood by the ordinary, reasonable person, shall be treated with contempt, mockery, scorn and ridicule. . . ."[125] To Clark and his brethren this was far from the closely circumscribed exception that Chief Justice Hughes had indicated in the *Lovell* and *Near* cases might serve as the justifiable basis for a censorship law in the face of the general presumption that such statutes were unconstitutional. "In seeking to apply the broad and all-inclusive definition of 'sacrilegious' given by the New York courts," Justice Clark forcefully pointed out, "the censor is set adrift upon a boundless sea amid a myriad of conflicting currents of religious views, with no charts but those provided by the most vocal and powerful orthodoxies."[126] In conclusion, Clark found it again necessary to issue a word of warning. The Court was not deciding, he said, such questions as whether or not a city or state might censor movies under a "clearly drawn statute designed and applied to prevent the showing of obscene films." It was only concluding that the term "sacrilegious" was an unconstitutional guideline upon which censors might decide if a movie was proscribable.

Two concurring opinions were filed as well. In a two-sentence statement, Mr. Justice Reed expressed the view that if a state could license movies for given reasons, a question still left open by the Court's ruling, then it was the function of the judiciary in each case to look into the question of whether the principles of the First Amendment had been honored. To him, *The Miracle* did not appear to be the kind of movie which could be permissibly banned consistent with the guarantees of free speech and press.

In a highly scholarly but long-winded concurring opinion, Mr. Justice Frankfurter, with the approval of Justice Burton, centered

125 *Ibid.,* p. 504.
126 *Ibid.,* pp. 504-5.

his attack upon the vagueness of the word "sacrilegious." After examining countless dictionaries and religious tracts he was unable to find a suitable definition for the term. Indeed, it appeared to him that the New York Court in framing its definition had added attributes of similar, but clearly different, concepts such as apostasy, heresy, and blasphemy. Nor did the use of the standard by the state itself shed light on how it had been operationally defined. Of the many appeals lodged with the Board of Regents from denials of licenses by the motion picture board,[127] only three had involved the meaning of "sacrilegious."[128] In these cases, the records of the Board showed only if the films were found to be sacrilegious. No description of what part or parts of each film that were deemed sacrilegious was presented, nor was a definition of the term ever once posited. In his view, history did not encourage the use of such vast, unchecked, and unchartered powers by censors when the creative processes of literature and art were at stake.

Initial reaction to the Court's pronouncement was generally favorable. In only one contemporaneous article published in a well-known legal periodical was there a definite negative response.[129] Even though most students of constitutional law were apparently happy to see motion pictures attain the lofty elevation of First Amendment coverage, many of them appeared to be uneasy about what they saw as a key ambiguity in the Court's opinion. A typical appraisal of this kind was voiced by Professor C. H. Pritchett in one of his more influential works.[130] He had no trouble with the first segment of Justice Clark's analysis which had resulted in the overturning of the *Mutual Film Corporation* decision; but to him the rest of the opinion seemed to be "a little

[127] Rights of appeal from adverse decisions rendered by the New York film censorship board are to be taken first to the Board of Regents. See *op. cit.*, Sect. 124.

[128] These movies were *The Puritan* (1939), *Polygamy* (1939), and *Monja y Casada—Virgen y Martir* (1935).

[129] See Howard N. Morse, "A Critical Analysis and Appraisal of *Burstyn v. Wilson*," *North Dakota Law Review*, XXIX (1953), 38-41.

[130] C. Herman Pritchett, *Civil Liberties and the Vinson Court* (Chicago: The University of Chicago Press, 1954), p. 41.

puzzling." Had the Court decided that *The Miracle* could not be banned because motion pictures were to be treated as free speech, or "on the rather narrow ground that 'sacrilege' is too loose and meaningless?"[131]

In my opinion, it is hard to see the dilemma Mr. Pritchett poses. The Court had, on several occasions prior to this, struck down previous restraint enactments limiting the dissemination of ideas as unconstitutional impediments on speech; but this had been done usually, as in this case, with a warning that the door was not being closed on "tightly drawn statutes aimed at specific evils." Here, Justice Clark had simply placed movies in the same general category as "speech and press" and then said the same thing. To be sure, he had referred to the term "sacrilegious" as "all-inclusive," but he had also been pointed in his view that "the state has no legitimate interest in protecting any or all religions from views distasteful to them which is sufficient to justify prior restraints. . . ."[132] Furthermore, if he believed that "sacrilegious" was solely an unconstitutionally vague standard, then he could have merely invoked due process as guaranteed by the Fourteenth Amendment without even commenting on whether or not motion pictures should receive First Amendment privileges. This he had chosen not to do. His disagreement with the principle enunciated in the *Mutual Film* case was stated forthrightly; and his willingness to regard the exhibition of films as a form of speech protected by the First and Fourteenth Amendments was clear.

[131] *Ibid.*
[132] 343 U. S. 495 at p. 505.

# Chapter II

# Motion Pictures and the Right of Free Expression under the Constitution: The "Modern Period," 1953-65

### The Extension of *Burstyn* v. *Wilson* and the Split on the Supreme Court

During the next several years, the Supreme Court was afforded numerous opportunities to expand upon its statement in the *Burstyn* case as motion picture distributors, encouraged by this new turn of events, began to protest more vigorously against local censorship enactments. In each of these disputes, however, a majority of the Justices managed to dispose of the questions at issue without shedding much light on the basic problem that vexed students of First Amendment interpretation in this area of litigation: Was motion picture censorship, in and of itself, in conflict with the constitutional protection accorded to free speech and a free press?

The first of these cases was adjudicated just one week after the issues presented in *Burstyn* had been settled. The town of Marshall, Texas had on its books an ordinance setting up a film censorship agency which was empowered to preview all movies before they were shown publicly and to refuse to license any picture if it was "of such character as to be prejudicial to the best interests of the people of said city." Ignoring a finding that a permit should not be granted, appellant had shown the movie *Pinky*, a Stanley Kramer production dealing with a Negress who attempts to pass for white in a Southern town. The exhibitor was subsequently convicted of a misdemeanor as specified by the statute.

This decision was upheld by the Court of Criminal Appeals of

Texas in a unanimous opinion.[133] The only claim advanced by petitioner was that the law was invalid on its face as a violation of the Fourteenth Amendment. Speaking for his colleagues, Mr. Justice Beauchamp readily dispensed with this argument by paraphrasing at length from Chief Justice Hutcheson's decision in *RD-DR* v. *Smith.* If the Supreme Court wished to reverse its holding in the *Mutual Film Corporation* decision, it was free to do so. This, however, was not the task of state courts. Though he might have mentioned that the Court had denied certiorari following Hutcheson's ruling in the *RD-DR* controversy, he neglected to do so.

In a one-sentence per curiam holding the Supreme Court reversed,[134] citing its decisions in *Burstyn* and *Winters* v. *New York.*[135] In the latter case, a New York statute prohibiting the dissemination of printed matter "devoted to the publication . . . of criminal news" or stories of deeds of bloodshed, lust, or crime had been struck down as unconstitutionally vague. It was apparent, then, that the Court felt that the Marshall ordinance as applied against *Pinky* was of the same genre as the "sacrilegious" standard invoked by New York State against *The Miracle* and that, furthermore, it was too nebulous a guideline to be constitutionally acceptable. Justice Frankfurter, as he had done in *Burstyn* v. *Wilson,* appended a short concurring opinion to the per curiam statement in which he specifically pinpointed "indefiniteness" as the fatal weakness of the statute.

In another concurring opinion, however, Mr. Justice Douglas ignored the question of vagueness, concluding rather that the law was invalid because it was a "flagrant form" of prior restraint which had been condemned in *Near* v. *Minnesota* and *Burstyn.* He felt that the "great purpose of the First Amendment" was undermined whenever a censorship agency was able to tell Americans what it was in their best interests to see.

In analyzing this opinion, one critic finds it difficult to understand how Douglas could have construed *The Miracle* decision, as he believed he evidently had, to mean that the Court was declaring

[133] *Gelling* v. *State,* 247 S. W. 2d 95 (1952).
[134] *Gelling* v. *Texas,* 343 U. S. 960 (1952).
[135] 333 U. S. 507 (1948).

all motion picture censorship to be violative of the fundamental law.[136] And yet Douglas' obvious uneasiness over Frankfurter's approach to the problem, a mode of analysis which stressed statutory precision as a relevant tool of constitutional adjudication, laid bare a thorny question in logic for the Court: If the states were to be equated with Congress so far as their authority to impinge on speech and press was concerned (sanctioned in *Gitlow* v. *New York*) and movies were protected speech, then what sense did it make even to imply that some elements of censorship for movies were constitutionally permissible?

Two years later, the Court again was given an opportunity to deal with a similar situation when motion picture distributors in New York and Ohio appealed state supreme court decisions in these states that had sustained findings by censorship boards that movies which they owned might properly be proscribed. In the New York controversy,[137] the state film censorship bureau had refused to license the movie *La Ronde* on the grounds that it was "immoral" and "would tend to corrupt morals."[138] This determination was upheld by the Board of Regents.[139]

Speaking for a majority of his colleagues on the New York Court of Appeals, Mr. Justice Froessel felt that there were three basic issues at stake before the tribunal. First, did *Burstyn* v. *Wilson* exempt motion pictures from all manner of censorship?[140] Secondly, if not, were the words "immoral" and "tend to corrupt morals" adequate standards to satisfy the requirements of due process? Thirdly, if so, had such guidelines been properly applied to the movie in question?

In answer to this first inquiry, he had no difficulty in deciding that the *Burstyn* judgment did not close the door to all manner of

[136] McAnany, *op. cit.*, p. 436.

[137] *Commercial Pictures Corp.* v. *Regents*, 305 N. Y. 336 (1953).

[138] *McKinney's N. Y. Laws*, Education Law, Book 16, Sect. 122.

[139] The appeal system as spelled out in the New York statute is discussed in connection with *Burstyn* v. *Wilson* earlier in this chapter. See also Chapter III for a detailed examination of the New York law.

[140] The State of Texas, it must be remembered, had dealt with the *Gelling* case prior to the Supreme Court's ruling in *Burstyn* so that Judge Froessel's opinion was really the first opportunity a state supreme court had had to construe this decision.

prior restraint against motion pictures. The U. S. Supreme Court, he noted, had on numerous occasions upheld state laws governing speech and press if a "clear and present danger" to the community could be demonstrated. In so far as the New York law afforded protection against such acts, it was clearly constitutional.

Passing on to his second query Froessel next sought to explain what the New York legislature had meant when it used the term "immoral." Many state and federal laws, he found, used similar language in their commands; for instance, the phrases "moral turpitude" and "good moral character" were terms which could be found in the civil service laws of New York and the immigration laws of the nation to determine conduct which could result in the loss of a job or disqualify one from entering the country. The word "immoral," he believed, was no more difficult to define than these two terms. Of course, words of that kind gathered meaning from their context. The fair sense of the particular law under discussion, he felt, was that "immoral" referred to sexual immorality because it seemed to be coupled with such other words as "obscene" and "indecent."[141] As such, it was not vague or indefinite because when viewed in this perspective it was a word commonly used and readily understood by any person of normal intelligence.

As to the application of this law to *La Ronde,* Justice Froessel stated that the movie itself dealt from beginning to end "with promiscuity, adultery, fornication and seduction." The board of censors, then, had not made an unreasonable determination in classifying such a film as immoral.

> That a motion picture which panders to base human emotions is a breeding ground for sensuality, depravity, licentiousness and sexual immorality can hardly be doubted. That these vices represent a 'clear and present danger' to the body social seems manifestly clear. . . . Now we have a commercially feasible three dimensional projection, some forms of which are said to bring the audience 'right into the picture.' There can be no doubt that attempts will be made to bring the audience right into the bedchamber if it be held that the State is impotent to apply preventive measures.[142]

[141] See footnote 119 for the wording of the statute.
[142] 305 N. Y. 336 at p. 342.

To the suggestion that the Court itself form an independent judgment as to the legitimacy of the censors' ruling, the majority stated that this would be a judicial usurpation of power granted by the legislature to an administrative agency. It was not the constitutional duty of courts, the opinion concluded, to review such fact-finding proceedings de novo.

In a concurring analysis, Mr. Justice Desmond added one more point of note to the majority's argument when he asserted that most valid laws limiting speech and press involved subsequent punishment rather than prior censorship, but that the system of distribution and exhibition of movies made it "feasible, if not necessary, to examine and license or refuse to license them before exhibition to audiences." Only in this way would the community be effectively shielded from "evil" movies.[143]

In a long and exhaustive dissent, Mr. Justice Dye disagreed with almost every contention the Court had attempted to formulate. To be sure, Justice Clark had been able to clear *The Miracle* from prior restraint inhibition by finding that the statutory use of the term "sacrilegious" afforded an adequate basis for reversal in and of itself and so found it unnecessary to deal with the overriding problem of the constitutionality of movie censorship per se. Nonetheless, the Supreme Court had long ago found previous restraints an especially abhorrent infringement on freedom of expression.

> Since the courts no longer see any distinction separating motion picture film from the protection afforded other media of communication, it follows as a matter of reason and logic that prior censorship of motion pictures is as to them as it is in other fields of expression, a denial of due process.[144]

This was the same kind of argument Mr. Justice Douglas had maintained should have been adopted by the Court in the *Gelling* decision. Of course, Judge Dye said, the "clear and present danger" test could be constitutionally adopted by political agencies to limit First Amendment freedoms, but *La Ronde* had been shown without incident or complaint in sixteen states and the District

143 *Ibid.*, p. 351.
144 *Ibid.*, p. 357.

of Columbia. This was a "convincing testimonial" that it was not inimical to the welfare and good order of society.

Even if one accepted the premise that the censorship of motion pictures was, in some measure, constitutional the New York law as applied could not be upheld because of the indefiniteness of the word "immoral." The law itself supplied no definition for the term, nor did juxtaposing it with the word "obscene" help establish its meaning so far as this case was concerned because *La Ronde* was never thought to be obscene. Of course, the theme of illicit love was usually looked upon as immoral but so were murder and countless other sins. The records of the Regents themselves clearly substantiated the point, he believed, that the theme itself did not furnish a valid ground for previous restraint. Otherwise the infamous *The Outlaw* and many others could not have received permits. As to its presentation corrupting the morals of the public, this issue was highly debatable. The record certainly indicated that the film received high praise by reviewers in a number of states. Since reasonable men might differ on the impact of *La Ronde*, it followed that a "clear and present danger" was not sufficiently imminent to override the terms of the First Amendment. In any event, it was the duty of the judges themselves to determine if this movie violated given statutory commands, because such a decision involved a matter of law, namely, appellant's right of free speech.

An Ohio decision,[145] rendered shortly after the *Commercial Pictures* case was adjudicated in the New York courts, presented strikingly similar questions of law to those which Justices Froessel and Dye had disagreed so completely upon. There, plaintiff had submitted the movie *M* to the Division of Film Censorship of the State Department of Education, as required by state statute, for censorship and approval. The film was rejected by the Bureau "on account of being harmful."[146] By a vote of 5-2 the Ohio Supreme

[145] *Superior Films, Inc.* v. *Dept. of Education of Ohio,* 159 Ohio St. 315 (1953).

[146] This was the same statute declared constitutional by the Supreme Court in *Mutual Film Corporation* v. *Ind. Comm. of Ohio,* 236 U. S. 230 (1915). Under the terms of this law "only such films . . . of a moral, educational or amusing and harmless character shall be passed and approved

Court affirmed this conclusion. There was nothing startling about the first segment of Justice Hart's majority opinion. With the recent decision of the New York Appeals Court before him he followed with precision the arguments that Justices Froessel and Desmond had propounded. There was no inherent right to publicity, he felt, for motion pictures which tended to "destroy the very social fabric of the community." In such instances the mantle of the First Amendment did not shield the offender. To be sure, the Supreme Court in *Burstyn* had declared that the use of the word "sacrilegious" as a test to determine if speech could be suppressed was violative of the First and Fourteenth Amendments; but surely this did not inhibit a state from invoking its police power to protect citizens from "baneful and harmful matter." Further:

> In these times of alarming rise in juvenile delinquency . . . attributed by social agencies, at least in part, to the character of the exhibitions put on in the show houses of the country, criminal prosecution after the fact is a weak and ineffective remedy to meet the problem at hand.[147]

He then went on to point out that the state censorship agency had found that *M* would have an adverse effect on unstable persons of any age because it could lead to the commission of immoral and criminal acts by such people. Also, the presentation of actions and emotions of a pathological child killer throughout the movie emphasized the complete perversion of the man "without serving any valid educational purpose" and "creates sympathy rather than a constructive plan for dealing with perversion."[148] Though the Court had not viewed the movie, it was willing to accept the petitioner's claims that the film was a serious attempt to probe the social ramifications of the perverted acts depicted. Nevertheless, Justice Hart came to the amazing conclusion that such a motion picture would have appeal for this reason only to a small number of viewers whereas "the great

---

by such board." For a short history of the evolution of the dictates of the statute as revised by the Ohio legislature over the years, see 159 Ohio St. 315 at p. 320.

[147] 159 Ohio St. 315 at p. 328.

[148] *Ibid.*

majority of a promiscuous audience, including children" might very well find the film interesting only because of its "portrayal of evil conduct."[149] Such a movie could reasonably be suppressed.

In defending the guidelines for licensing in the Ohio statute as lucid, Justice Hart approvingly noted the Supreme Court's judgment in the 1915 decision which had upheld the standards set forth in the law as acquiring precision from "the sense and experience of men." The court in *Burstyn* had not rebuked this assertion and so the law must still be held constitutional against a charge of being void on account of vagueness.

In a short dissenting opinion, Justices Taft and Stewart (now Supreme Court Justice Stewart) contended that the scope of the Court's rulings in *Burstyn* and *Gelling* required the Ohio courts to rule that the state film censorship law was void. Unfortunately, however, they did not indicate whether they believed these precedents made this conclusion obligatory because of the terms of the First Amendment as reflected through the Fourteenth or because of the dictates of due process.

The assumptions and reasoning put forward by these state appellate court judges were of unusual importance because they represented the highest level of judicial determination where any attempt was made to explain in detail how these disputes should be resolved. This state of affairs resulted once again from the fact that the Supreme Court, as it had in *Gelling* v. *Texas,* dispensed with appellants' appeals per curiam by simply combining both of these disputes into one suit[150] and reversing them summarily on the authority of *Burstyn* v. *Wilson.*

Once again, however, Mr. Justice Douglas, this time with Justice Black siding with him, refused to abdicate his right to speak for himself on the issue of film censorship. No law could be found constitutional, he explained, which demanded that a newspaper submit its news dispatches to a board of approval. Nor could a community require book publishers to submit novels, poems, or essays to a censorship agency. So much was clear, he assumed, from the Court's findings in *Near* v. *Minnesota* and

---

[149] *Ibid.,* p. 329.
[150] *Superior Films, Inc.* v. *Dept. of Education of Ohio,* 346 U. S. 587 (1954).

assorted other cases. To be sure, motion pictures were a different medium of expression from the radio, the stage, or the novel; but "the First Amendment draws no distinction between the various methods of communicating ideas." Here again was the argument Douglas had presented in *Gelling*, an appraisal evidently not shared by his colleagues, yet a point of view which as yet had not been rebutted in any real sense.

It is hardly surprising that the Court would find a statute unconstitutional that delegated to a censorship agency the power to ban a film if it was deemed "harmful" to a community. Such a criterion was clearly as arbitrary as the "best interests of the community" guideline set aside in *Gelling* and, perhaps, an even more stifling inhibition of free expression than the "sacrilegious" standard invoked by New York State. One might have reasonably imagined, however, that a majority of the Justices would have thought it necessary to write a full-length opinion on the matter, in view of the fact that the Ohio statute involved was the same one that had been found to be constitutional in the earlier *Mutual Film Corporation* decision.

As to the *Commercial Pictures* holding, a good case could undoubtedly be made which would be highly critical of the Court's per curiam format. Of course, scholars of constitutional law certainly could defend with great plausibility the notion that a state may not censor an "immoral" film any more than it could censor a "harmful" movie. Nonetheless, this is a word commonly used to denote sexual promiscuity and the Court might have exerted itself to demonstrate that the term, as defined by the New York Appeals Court, did not constitute a type of speech which was so harmful to the mores that its proscription via prior restraint would lie beyond the "outer limits" of the First Amendment. If, as the Court had hinted in *Burstyn*, a censorship edict aimed at banning obscene films might be allowable then why not movies whose only theme was sexual promiscuity? Indeed, could not motion pictures such as this one, assuming it was everything the New York board said it was, be labeled obscene? Such questions certainly were deserving of most careful judicial scrutiny.

An even plainer example of the Court's woeful lack of forthrightness at this point in the evolution of judicial pronouncement in the area of local motion picture censorship rights occurred a year later.[151] The Kansas State Board of Review, the motion picture censorship organ in that state, had refused to issue a permit to *The Moon is Blue* for the reasons that, "Sex theme throughout, too frank bedroom dialogue: many sexy words; both dialogue and action have sex as their theme." Under authority granted by the state law the movie was reexamined and found to be "obscene, indecent and immoral, and such as tends to debase or corrupt morals,"—all statutory reasons for refusing to issue a permit.[152] At this point an appeal was lodged with the district court of Wyandotte County, Kansas which ruled that the guidelines contained in the enactment were invalid because the State Board of Review had construed them in such a way that they conveyed "a meaning so broad and vague" as to rob them of any precision.[153]

The Supreme Court of Kansas, however, reversed unanimously.[154] After belaboring the point that no court had the power to substitute its opinion for that of the censorship board's unless the initial judgment by the Bureau was totally unreasonable,[155] Justice Robb passed on to the problem of whether the applicable standards of the statute were void on account of indefiniteness. Though he felt that each of these guidelines had a precise meaning, he concentrated his defense on the term "obscene" which, he said, had been well defined in several legal dictionaries and lower federal court decisions.[156]

He then went on to quote approvingly from the majority view in *Near* v. *Minnesota* which, he maintained, conceded the constitutionality of local prior restraints against obscene publications, and from Justice Clark's oft-quoted reservation in *Burstyn* to buttress his belief that a state might censor films falling into this category.[157] Since the Kansas State Board of Review had found the film, among other things, "obscene" and since no evi-

---

[151] *Holmby Productions* v. *Vaughn*, 350 U. S. 870 (1955).

[152] *G. S. 1949*, Sect. 51-103.

[153] 177 Kansas 728 at p. 730.

[154] *Holmby Productions* v. *Vaughn*, 177 Kansas 728 (1955).

[155] See his comments, *ibid.*, pp. 731 and 733.

[156] *Ibid.*, p. 732.

[157] *Ibid.*, p. 734.

dence had been presented which challenged that finding, the Court had no power to review this judgment. Naturally, this train of thought negated the necessity of deciding if the Board of Review had overstepped its authority in its application of the other terms of the law it had invoked—words which, in part, the Supreme Court had already found to be in violation of free speech and press when used to perpetuate prior restraint.

The Supreme Court once again, however, had no trouble placing the facts of this case in line with those of *The Miracle* holding. In another per curiam statement, it reversed the Kansas ruling, citing the recent *Superior Films* decision along with *Burstyn* as precedents. Here, now, was an anomalous situation, indeed. Chief Justice Hughes in *Near* had been very frank in stating his convictions regarding censorship laws aimed at obscenity. Mr. Justice Clark in *Burstyn* had suggested that a statute designed to accomplish such a task would be examined with great care by the Court. Yet, in a one-sentence appraisal a unanimous decision of the Justices had seemingly swept the concept of "obscenity" under the table along with the several other guidelines that had gone by the boards. It was possible, however, that the Court was really saying nothing more than what the Wyandotte tribunal had stipulated; viz., that the Kansas State Board of Review had indiscriminately applied several statutory commands to curtail a showing of *The Moon is Blue* and that this utilization of these terms, taken together, had rendered all the guidelines invalid. In other words, the word "obscene" was not being judged in and of itself but only as used in conjunction with other legislative standards, some of which had already been found constitutionally unacceptable. It had also been meaninglessly defined by the Board when it made the pronouncement "sex theme throughout, too frank bedroom dialogue" etc., as the record had stipulated.

Yet, in the light of the Court's judgment, how could one presume to say that obscenity still constituted a legitimate basis for prior restraint? After all, the Kansas Supreme Court had clearly grounded its decision on the assumption that a community could censor the obscene; and the Supreme Court had reversed on the grounds set forth in *Burstyn* without saying a word about "void for vagueness," which had appeared to backbone the position taken by the Wyandotte court. Once again, the Court had missed a chance to set up some clear-cut limits as to what scope film censorship authorities were to have, assuming they possessed any valid authority to censor at all. It is rather evident that the refusal of the Court in *Burstyn* to thrust all motion picture censorship laws into the discard was the main factor responsible for state appellate courts in Kansas, New York, and Ohio upholding the constitutionality of licensing criteria contained in their respective prior restraint enactments. These tribunals were unsure of the limits the Supreme Court had established for censorship bureaus in that case; consequently they had simply resolved all matters of doubt in favor of state and local police power.

It is much more difficult, however, to understand why the Court found it necessary to "blur" the constitutional issues at stake in these cases by constantly resorting to the per curiam format. In choosing this technique as an avenue for disposing of these disputes, the Justices succeeded only in confusing many of those most interested in the Court's investigation of such problems.[158] Clearly, the fact that they were widely split on the means to be utilized in dealing with the constitutional question inherent in movie censorship constituted the primary reason for invoking this procedure. What better way to shield a breakdown in consensus from public scrutiny than to join hands in drafting one-sentence opinions for the Court!

In spite of such camouflage certain obvious differences of opinion among the Justices were readily discernible. Black and Douglas, for instance, as their concurring statements indicated, were quite willing to eliminate all vestiges of prior restraint, including those inhibiting movies. Justice Clark's position was more moderate, judging from his views as set forward in *Burstyn*. He was willing to set aside most film censorship enactments as viola-

[158] A most notable instance of this dilemma is seen in McAnany, *op. cit.*, p. 436. He found that the Court in each of these per curiam decisions had voided the state statutory commands at issue on account of vagueness. Of course, this conclusion is predicated on the patently false assumption that "sacrilegious" had been struck down in *The Miracle* decision because it had contravened only due process considerations. See *ibid.*

tive of the First Amendment, but apparently he also felt that it was necessary to take a long, hard look at prior restraints clearly aimed at meeting precise dangers to the good order of community life. Justice Reed, if one may judge from his concurring opinion in *The Miracle* controversy, also seemed amenable to accepting some aspects of censorship as constitutional; but it was his view that the Court should stress the nature of the movie itself in reviewing such controversies so as to be certain no motion picture was banned that met the minimal requirements (as yet undefined) of free speech protection. Frankfurter, if his views in *Burstyn* and *Gelling* v. *Texas* were a correct reflection of his overall position, was first and foremost disposed to examine such statutes in terms of how narrowly they defined the essence of the objectionable in films which communities wished to inhibit, rather than to subject them to First Amendment examination. Given this factionalism on the Court it was not surprising, perhaps, that its members chose the per curiam opinion as a means of support for its rulings so as to postpone until another day the time when the really basic constitutional issues inherent in the scope of motion picture censorship would have to be met.

### The Supreme Court Defines Obscenity

It will be recalled that one of the chief reasons that motion picture censorship had been treated with great delicacy by many courts in the course of years was the fear that movies would have a deleterious effect on the thoughts and behavior of children. This supposition certainly constituted one of the root beliefs expressed by Mr. Justice McKenna in his early vindication of prior restraints when used to inhibit the commercial presentation of films. Moreover, Justice Hart had alluded to the sharp rise in juvenile crimes as being partially a product of risqué movies in his *Commercial Pictures* opinion.

In 1957 the Supreme Court was asked to determine to what extent a state could go to protect its young people from literature deemed morally offensive. Section 343 of the Michigan Penal Code made it a misdemeanor to sell or make available to the general reading public any book, magazine, newspaper, pamphlet, print or picture (among other things) containing "obscene, immoral, lewd, or lascivious language . . . tending to the corruption of the morals of youth." Appellant was charged with selling a book which the trial judge later characterized as "containing obscene, immoral, lewd, lascivious language, or descriptions, tending to incite minors to violent or depraved or immoral acts, manifestly tending to the corruption of the morals of youth." He was subsequently found guilty and fined one hundred dollars.

The peculiar facts of this controversy were such that the decision, no matter what the outcome, was bound to be of primary importance to the motion picture industry. While it was true that none of the states or cities which at that time were systematically censoring movies had statutory permission to deny a license to a film for the precise reason set forth in the Michigan law, the fact that several other states had similar subsequent punishment enactments on their books[159] illustrated the wide range of sentiment already mustered in support of such legislation. If the Court were to support the constitutionality of this law at least some communities would be emboldened to arm their motion picture censorship bureaus with authority to disallow the exhibition of films "tending to the corruption of the morals of youth." With the *Holmby* decision now "settled law" there were apparently very few, if any, standards that could be successfully invoked to keep "offensive" movies from being shown freely. A ruling upholding the Michigan statute would point the way to such a standard.

There were two other closely related reasons why this dispute might have been expected to have a substantial effect on the activities of movie companies. Even though the Court in the *Holmby* case had, at least in some measure, rejected the claim that a film could be banned if a duly constituted prior restraint agency labeled it "obscene," there was still a fair chance that the warning note sounded by Mr. Justice Clark in *Burstyn* v. *Wilson* might be reinforced by a majority of the judges. After all, since that decision the Court had always managed to dispense with similar issues by invoking a closely circumscribed, case-by-case analysis of the peculiar criteria contained in each enactment for

[159] Such states included Florida, Maine, and Rhode Island. For a complete list see William B. Lockhart and Robert C. McClure, "Censorship of Obscenity: The Developing Constitutional Standards," *Minnesota Law Review*, XLV (1960), 17-18.

gauging the suitability of films. The unhappiness with which Justices Black and Douglas viewed this procedure showed clearly that other members of the Court were certainly not as anxious to disallow all forms of movie censorship as they were. If the Court upheld the Michigan ordinance it would be going a long way toward upholding movie censorship laws based on the use of "obscenity" as a standard for judging the acceptability of a movie, although of course there was always a good chance that a distinction would eventually be drawn between obscenity as a proper guideline when used in a penal statute and its unconstitutionality when used in a prior restraint law.

Of equal importance, the Court's decision might have been expected to lay down certain clues for judging how sweeping in scope a law could be that guarded its citizens against the obscene. As was well known to all, the publication of obscene materials was considered a misdemeanor at common law and had been consistently treated as such in the courts of England. This doctrine was well known to early American legal scholars. Obscenity had long been a punishable offense under state laws which, in turn, had always been upheld in principle by local courts.[160]

However, most authorities agreed that there was a real problem in deciding exactly what constituted an obscene book or pamphlet. In 1868 Justice Cockburn in the English case of *Queen v. Hicklin* defined obscenity in a way which came to be generally accepted:

> I think the test of obscenity is this, whether the tendency of the matter charged as obscenity is to deprave and corrupt those whose minds are open to such immoral influences, and into whose hands a publication of this sort may fall.[161]

Though this standard for determining the nature of obscenity had been repudiated by Judge Augustus N. Hand in a notable 1934 decision handed down by a federal Court of Appeals,[162] the

[160] Philip M. Carden, "The Supreme Court and Obscenity," *Vanderbilt Law Review,* XI (1958), 585-86.

[161] 3 Queen's Bench 360.

[162] U. S. v. *One Book Entitled "Ulysses,"* 72 F. 2d 705 (1934).

Supreme Court itself had grappled with this vexing problem only once and then only in a most unsatisfactory manner. In that particular case, the New York Court of Appeals had unanimously upheld a conviction of Doubleday and Company for selling an obscene book, namely, Edmund Wilson's *Memoirs of Hecate County*.[163] The Court specifically rejected plaintiff's argument that the *Hicklin* test, which had been invoked by the trial judge to determine if the book were obscene, be turned aside because it did not take into account the effect such literature might have on the mind of the mature reader. Defendant had also contended that his right under the First Amendment had been ignored because the book presented no clear and present danger to the community. This claim was also ignored.

In pleading his case before the Supreme Court appellant relied chiefly on the second of these points, but again without success. By a vote of 4-4, with Justice Frankfurter abstaining, the Court, per curiam, upheld the position of the New York courts.[164] From the closeness of the vote, it was evident that the validity of the *Hicklin* rule from the standpoint of constitutionality was very much up in the air as was, perhaps, the entire question of under what conditions and to what extent freedom of speech immunity offered protection to authors and publishers of the obscene.

The upcoming case, based as it was on the working of the Michigan statute, would certainly give the Court a second opportunity to examine the *Hicklin* precedent. If the concept of obscenity as formulated by Justice Cockburn was upheld it would surely make it almost impossible for a movie maker to produce a picture any more challenging to the normal adult mind than the typical Walt Disney release,[165] once a locality saw fit to make it illegal to

[163] 297 N. Y. 687 (1947).

[164] *Doubleday and Co., Inc.* v. *New York*, 335 U. S. 848 (1948).

[165] This argument, of course, is based on the assumption that any principle laid down in the Court's holding would be applicable to motion pictures. Surely it would not be stretching the imagination to say that if the Court felt that books were to be classified as obscene in accordance with the dictates of *Hicklin*, then films would be at best "afforded" equal protection.

exhibit obscene motion picture film. And, to repeat, if the Court were also to find that obscene films could be censored the movie industry might just as well forget its "preferred" status as free speech for all the protection it would afford.

In a unanimous verdict, however, the Court swept the *Hicklin* doctrine aside.[166] In a concise statement of views, Mr. Justice Frankfurter found that the enforcement of Michigan's law amounted to "burning the house in order to roast the pig." Surely, he argued, "the incidence of this enactment is to reduce the adult population of Michigan to reading only what is fit for children."[167] Such a statute could not stand before liberties enshrined in the due process clause of the Fourteenth Amendment. Frankfurter did not find it necessary to discuss any other aspects of the "obscenity question" to dispense with the state's claim that its ordinance was constitutional; but motion picture companies and the other mass media as well could reasonably assume that what was acceptable book and film fare for children and adolescents would never affect the standard that would govern constitutionally protectable artistic and dramatic tastes for adults.

Shortly thereafter, the Court was given ample opportunity to pinpoint the essence of obscenity. In two cases argued before it in 1957, the fundamental issues in dispute were the constitutionality of the federal obscenity statute and the obscenity provisions of the California Penal Code. In the first of these controversies, Samuel Roth, who was a New York publisher of books and magazines, had used the mails to distribute circulars and advertising matter in order to solicit sales. He was convicted on several charges of violating the federal statute against mailing obscene books and advertisements. This law provided, in part, that:

> Every obscene, lewd, lascivious, or filthy book, pamphlet, picture, paper, letter . . . or other publication of an indecent character . . . is declared to be nonmailable matter and shall not be conveyed in the mails. . . .

[166] *Butler* v. *Michigan*, 352 U. S. 380 (1957).
[167] *Ibid.*, p. 383.

> Whoever knowingly deposits for mailing . . . anything de-
> clared by this section to be nonmailable . . . shall be fined not more
> than $5000 or imprisoned not more than five years, or both.[168]

The second case involved David S. Alberts, who conducted a
mail-order business in Los Angeles. He was convicted under a
complaint which charged that he had lewdly kept for sale obscene and indecent books, and with writing and publishing an
obscene advertisement in their behalf, contrary to the commands
of the California Penal Code. The law in question stated that:

> Every person who wilfully and lewdly either . . . writes, com-
> poses . . . publishes, sells, distributes, keeps for sale, or exhibits
> any obscene or indecent writing, paper, or book . . . or writes,
> composes or publishes any notice or advertisement of any such
> writing . . . is guilty of a misdemeanor.[169]

For purposes of convenience the Court decided to handle the
problems presented in these cases in one package.[170] As might
justifiably have been anticipated, the judges were far from a
meeting of the minds on any of the really complex questions at
hand.

For the Court, Mr. Justice Brennan commenced his argument
by noting that appellants had conceded from the start that the
objectionable materials they had dealt in were obscene. The key
question as he saw it then was whether or not the First Amendment protected such speech or writings. He found that, though
the Supreme Court had never faced this particular problem
squarely before, numerous past opinions indicated that obscene
speech and writings did not warrant such shelter. One of the
precedents he was able to single out, of course, was Chief Justice
Hughes's dictum in the *Near* decision. He was also able to point
to the fact that at the time of the adoption of the Bill of Rights,
obscenity was probably thought to have been outside the ambit
of free speech protection.[171] He summed up his feelings on the
matter in this way:

[168] 18 U. S. C., Sect. 1461.
[169] *West's Cal. Penal Code Ann.*, 1955, Sect. 311.
[170] *Roth* v. *U. S.* and *Alberts* v. *California,* 354 U. S. 476 (1957).
[171] *Ibid.*, pp. 481-83.

All ideas having even the slightest redeeming social importance—unorthodox ideas, controversial ideas, even ideas hateful to the prevailing climate of opinion—have the full protection of the guarantees, unless excludable because they encroach upon the limited area of more important interests. But implicit in the history of the First Amendment is the rejection of obscenity as utterly without redeeming social importance.[172]

He then addressed himself to the contention that no nexus could be established between obscene materials and antisocial conduct; in other words, that it was not demonstrable that the books or pamphlets proscribed created a clear and present danger that acts might be committed which a community had the power to guard against. This claim, of course, was predicated on the belief that obscenity was, in fact, speech and so Brennan had no difficulty in waiving it aside.[173] Likewise, the highly novel argument presented by Roth's attorneys that the federal obscenity statute usurped the rights of the states under the Tenth Amendment to punish speech and press where offensive to decency and morality was dismissed because it was also hinged upon the assumption that obscenity was protected within the sweep of the First Amendment. As obscenity could not be viewed in this light, Brennan thought that federal laws might reasonably be enacted to shield the mails from such matter in the exercise of the postal power delegated to Congress by Article I, Section 8.[174]

At this stage in the development of the Court's opinion, the train of thought becomes somewhat muddled. Rather than dealing directly with the only claim left open to appellants, which was simply that the laws being enforced against them were too nebulous and vague to apprise citizens properly of the kinds of literature being declared offensive, Brennan went to great lengths to explain the nature of obscenity itself. It was important to note, he began, that "sex and obscenity are not synonymous." Obscene materials were such that degraded sex by directing their appeal to prurient interests.[175] Furthermore, it would not do to judge a

[172] *Ibid.*, p. 484.
[173] *Ibid.*, p. 486.
[174] *Ibid.*, pp. 492-93.
[175] *Ibid.*, p. 487.

book or pamphlet by isolated passages contained therein or its effect upon "particularly susceptible persons." Though some American courts had adopted these standards as set forth in the *Hicklin* case, later decisions had invoked a formula much more in keeping with First Amendment guarantees: "whether to the average person, applying contemporary community standards, the dominant theme of the material taken as a whole appeals to prurient interest, i.e. a shameful or morbid interest in nudity, sex, or excretion and if it goes beyond customary limits of candor in description or representation of such matters."[176] Both trial courts below, however, had sufficiently complied with this definition as they sought to ascertain if the materials distributed by petitioners were obscene. Their assessment that the materials were obscene could not be constitutionally challenged, nor was it necessary for the Court to make any independent determination of the obscene character of the material.[177]

Brennan then went on to say that the Constitution did not require that the criteria utilized in these obscenity statutes be precise. All that was necessary to meet the demands of due process was that "the language conveys sufficiently definite warning as to the proscribed conduct when measured by common understanding and practices." These words, he found, when properly defined provided boundaries sufficiently lucid enough to be understood by the reasonable man. To be sure, it was mandatory in meeting defendants' assertions that the statutes were "void for vagueness" to show that the term "obscene" had some fairly discernible meaning and one way to do this was to analyze previous court decisions to see how they had construed the term. But if one reads carefully Brennan's argument relative to this point[178] in conjunction with his views on the nature of obscenity[179] it seems that he was, in effect, treat-

[176] *Ibid.,* p. 489.

[177] In *Alberts,* appellant had waived his right to a jury trial so that it was the judge who construed the obscenity laws to cover the objectionable literature in his possession. In the *Roth* case, the materials sent through the mail were found obscene by a jury.

[178] 354 U. S. 476 at p. 491.

[179] *Ibid.,* pp. 487-90.

ing the two as independent notions rather than using the latter to substantiate the former. His belief that obscenity gains clarity consistent with the Fourteenth Amendment when defined as the Court had suggested reads, in brief, like an afterthought.

It would appear that what Brennan had tried to do was to develop a ready test or formula that judges and attorneys could use in appraising speech and press so that they could discern with some measure of certainty if they were dealing with the obscene. The point is, however, that this effort was in a large sense totally unnecesary to resolving the litigation at hand because, as has already been mentioned, no issue was presented in either case concerning the obscenity of the paraphernalia that had been seized.

In a concurring statement, Chief Justice Warren expressed considerable doubt about the great heights he felt the Court's opinion had attempted to scale. He agreed that the dissemination of obscene materials created social problems which state and national governments had a constitutional right to legislate against, but this did not mean that all measures enacted to meet the issue were equally valid as Brennan had implied when he divorced obscenity from First Amendment coverage. The broad sweep of this assertion, he believed, could lead to the passage of laws that might be readily invoked against meritorious art or literature. Surely, however, state and federal governments could punish those engaged in selling or advertising written matter in a manner calculated to appeal to prurient sentiments. Appellant Alberts had been convicted of "wilfully" and "lewdly" distributing obscene materials while Roth had been found guilty of "wilfully" and "knowingly" mailing items "calculated" to debauch.

The key point presented in these controversies, then, according to the Chief Justice, was the conduct of petitioners rather than the nature of the books and pamphlets themselves, because most obscenity laws were hinged largely upon the effect such tracts might have upon those who received them. He summed up his view of the situation in this way:

> It is manifest that the same object may have a different impact, varying according to the part of the community it reached. But

there is more to these cases. It is not the book that is on trial; it is a person. The conduct of the defendant is the central issue, not the obscenity of a book or picture.[180]

Of course, he concluded, the nature of the materials being used to titillate the prurient interests of "customers" was a relevant fact in the proceedings but, again, must be viewed as secondary to the uses to which they were put. In short, "that is all that these cases present to us, and that is all we need to decide."

As one might have safely prophesied, Justices Douglas and Black dissented strongly from the Court's judgment. Basically, their position was that the statutes in question were not aimed at overt acts but at thoughts that might be provoked. If it could be averred with any degree of certainty that there was a relationship between the reading of obscene literature and substantial deviations from community norms then, perhaps, such enactments might be allowable, they believed; but without such evidence the Court's position could not be squared with the First Amendment. Nor could this issue be discounted by placing the obscene outside the spectrum of free speech and press coverage; for the question still remained, "What is the constitutional test of obscenity?"[181]

Given this assumption the definitions for obscenity approved by the Court could in no sense be deemed consistent with free speech guarantees. For example, the tests used to determine if convictions against Roth and Alberts were justified required only that sexual or prurient thoughts be aroused. Yet, sexual desires occur in the normal man or woman each day in countless ways. Or, to look at the matter from another perspective, obscenity was to be in part proven by ascertaining whether objectionable materials ran contrary to contemporary community standards.

Certainly that standard would not be an acceptable one if religion, economics, politics or philosophy were involved. . . . Under that test, juries can censor, suppress, and punish what they don't like, provided the matter relates to 'sexual impurity' or has a tendency 'to excite lustful thoughts.' This is a community censorship in one

180 *Ibid.*, p. 495.
181 *Ibid.*, p. 509.

of its worst forms. It creates a regime where in the battle between the literati and the Philistines, the Philistines are certain to win.[182]

In a most provocative statement of beliefs, Mr. Justice Harlan felt that the Court had made two drastic errors in its assessment of the constitutional problems at hand. First, it had under-emphasized the First Amendment rights of those wishing to distribute writings which courts had ruled obscene. The suppression of such tracts was, in every case, an individual matter and raised a unique free press problem which could only be resolved when a reviewing court decided for itself whether the attacked expression was proscribable within constitutional limits. In short, a jury might find James Joyce's *Ulysses* obscene, but the conviction of a defendant for selling this book would raise, for him, a serious constitutional dilemma. It was inconceivable that a work of this sort was "utterly without redeeming social importance."[183] It should be noted that this line of argument paralleled Mr. Justice Reed's train of thought in *Burstyn* v. *Wilson* which had led him to conclude that a state could not suppress *The Miracle* consistent with First Amendment rights.

The second fundamental difficulty Justice Harlan found in Justice Brennan's examination was that it had treated both cases before the Court as one. This, he felt, was grossly unsound. The remainder of his opinion was an attempt to show why the majority was correct in upholding the conviction of Alberts, but on dangerous ground in its adjudication of Roth's appeal.

His analysis of *Alberts* v. *California* is a study in the lucid and the logical. The role of the Supreme Court, he began, was not to determine if the public policies set forth in state legislative edicts were prudent or scientific. As local political bodies might reasonably find that there was a causal relationship between reading obscene matter and an upsurge in immoral or criminal acts, it was not the task of the federal courts to intervene. He agreed, also, that each book must be judged as a whole and in relation to the normal adult reader. In line with his initial and strongly worded contention, however, the disposition

[182] *Ibid.*, p. 512.
[183] *Ibid.*, pp. 497-98.

of this controversy turned on whether the Court felt the materials at issue to be objectionable. Thus, he was able to concur in petitioner's conviction because "upon an independent perusal of the material involved, and in light of the considerations discussed above, I cannot say that its suppression would so interfere with the communication of 'ideas' in any proper sense of that term that it would offend the Due Process Clause."[184]

In the *Roth* dispute, however, Harlan found it necessary to dissent sharply from the Court's sentiments, and it is here that the precision of his arguments appears to become somewhat less sharp. It was his feeling that the federal obscenity statute, as interpreted and applied in the instant case, had been unconstitutionally manipulated. To buttress this conclusion, he tried to distinguish between those areas of human conduct entrusted by the Constitution to federal control and those subject to the regulation of states. Obscenity statutes, he insisted, were primarily designed to deal with substantive interests under the aegis of local control whereas Congress had, at best, only an "incidental" prerogative in the general area of sexual morality derived, as it was, from its delegated authority to control postal affairs.

In the light of his circumscription of the federal interest in this field and the fear that there were real dangers of a "deadening uniformity" that could result from sweeping nation-wide obscenity laws, he would reverse in favor of appellant. To be sure, the trial court had decided that obscenity was not protected speech, but the judge's charge to the jury which had construed the applicable law as banning books that "tend to stir sexual impulses and lead to sexually impure thoughts" had defined obscenity so widely that it encompassed matters that might be protected speech. In his opinion, the only kind of matter which the statute could constitutionally proscribe was hard-core pornography. Nor did he think, disagreeing with Chief Justice Warren, that the law could be fairly interpreted to cover the activity of persons engaged in pandering to the prurient even though their "merchandise" fell short of hard-core pornography. Since

[184] *Ibid.*, pp. 500-503.

his own personal inspection of the pertinent materials led him to believe that they were not of this ilk, he would have dismissed the indictment.[185]

Though this entire argument sounds a convincing note, it appears to be laden with value assumptions rather than objective constitutional deduction. Without doubt, social problems resulting from the dissemination of the obscene are more amenable, under a federal system, to state action under its police power than to federal legislation. But if the peddlers of smut use the mails and other vehicles of interstate commerce to disperse their noxious wares, then why could not the Congress reasonably find that a problem national in scope had developed and, therefore, why could it not move to utilize one of its plenary powers granted in the Constitution to deal so far as it could with this objectionable business? In short, in as much as the Court had upheld federal legislation aimed at suppressing traffic in lottery tickets[186] and the transportation of goods produced under substandard labor conditions[187] in interstate commerce, why could the Congress not wield comparable power, either through the commerce clause or the postal power, to control the distribution of the obscene?

Yet, even Harlan was willing for the national government to be given some latitude in this area; for he would uphold a ban on hard-core pornography. But this leads to an evident ambiguity. On what constitutional grounds could he distinguish between this type of obscenity and other, more subtle, species? If Brennan's test for adjudicating the nature of obscenity was good enough for state courts to follow, then why was it not good enough for federal courts as well? It may be granted that the suppression of Miller's *Tropic of Cancer*, for instance, would be a far more serious thing if accomplished at the national level rather than by the states, if the courts had somehow mistakenly supposed it to be obscene. Nevertheless, the Court had decided, and with Harlan's approval, that obscenity was not protected speech. It would appear to follow, then, that Congress could

[185] *Ibid.*, pp. 507-8.
[186] *Champion* v. *Ames*, 188 U. S. 321 (1903).
[187] *U. S.* v. *Darby Lumber Co.*, 312 U. S. 100 (1941).

legitimately exercise its plenary powers to suppress all obscene materials, assuming of course, that it followed closely the Court's shorthand formula for determining what was obscene and that it did not run afoul of other constitutionally protected guarantees in choosing the means by which such items should be best restricted.

The arguments advanced by members of the Court in these two cases have been subjected to exhaustive scrutiny.[188] Little can be gained in trying to explore with a finely honed micrometer the nuances of each individual appraisal of the relevant issues. There are, however, certain essentials which must be underlined if one is to begin to grapple with the complexities of legal scholarship that these opinions have conjured up for constitutional lawyers.

Mr. Justice Brennan, in his analysis, divorced obscenity from First Amendment coverage and then went on to explain what obscenity was. Or, did he? Here are some questions that one might address to the majority about this definition as well as other related issues of significance:

1. If the dominant theme of the material taken as a whole must appeal to the prurient interests of the average person, does it necessarily follow that such material is always "utterly without redeeming social importance?"
2. What of material that is not prurient to the normal adult juror, but is highly salacious to other audiences such as the homosexual or other "deviant" adults?
3. Or, conversely, what if the material is prurient to the average person but is addressed to an audience of persons to whom the material would reasonably have no prurient appeal?
4. By "contemporary community standards" did the Court mean local standards, sectional standards, national standards, the standards of Western civilization, or world-wide standards?
5. Regardless of the dominant theme of the book or movie, could not some segments or sub-themes be so candid or pornographic as to, if not render the total work obscene, at least provide

---

[188] See, for example, James J. Kilpatrick, *The Smut Peddlers* (Garden City, N. Y.: Doubleday and Co., Inc., 1960), pp. 81-168, and especially Lockhart and McClure, *op. cit.*

a legitimate reason for passing criminal laws to protect the public against such objectionable portrayals?

6. If obscenity is not privileged speech, then is censorship of obscene books, pamphlets, picture postcards and motion pictures constitutional?

7. If the issue of the obscenity of the matter distributed by Roth and Alberts had been before the Court (Justice Harlan claimed it was *per force*), would a majority have made an independent determination of the objectionability of such materials under the applicable law?

8. If so, would the Court have found that obscenity is hard-core pornography and nothing more, or does it include other books, pictures and movies as well?[189]

This last question requires further elaboration. Justice Harlan used the term "hard-core pornography" in his dissent in the *Roth* case, but he made no attempt to isolate its meaning. In view of the fact that pornography has been defined as obscene "on its face" by students of psychology[190] and literature,[191] and, inferentially, can be shown to be at least partially what the Court had in mind when it characterized obscenity as utterly without content,[192] it might be useful to try to explain what the pornographic element is. One author, after making a thorough study of books and stories whose basic themes were closely linked to vivid and candid portrayals of sexual activities, drew a distinction between "erotic realism" and "hard-core pornography."

> Erotic realism . . . aims to show the sexual side of man's nature in terms that are psychologically based in reality, and on a scale

[189] These queries mark out only a beginning for the intelligent critic. See Lockhart and McClure, *op. cit.*, pp. 49ff.

[190] See Eberhard and Phyllis Kronhausen, *Pornography and the Law* (New York: Ballantine Books, Inc., 1959), pp. ix-xii. They did not distinguish between the obscene and the pornographic, but found instead that what is obscene is only what is pornographic.

[191] D. H. Lawrence, "Pornography and Obscenity," Anthony Beal (ed.), *Selected Literary Criticism* (New York: The Viking Press, 1955), p. 37.

[192] Lockhart and McClure, *op. cit.*, p. 60. By stating that the federal government could ban only the pornographic, Justice Harlan was apparently defining pornography as the most extreme example of the obscene. See also *Kahm v. U. S.*, 300 F. 2d 78 (1962) for an elaboration of this assessment.

that allows room to explore the anti-erotic impulses and circumstances in even the most erotic situations. Hard-core pornography, on the other hand, is invariably concerned with presenting a wish-fulfillment fantasy. The treatment deliberately omits real life considerations to present a steadily mounting excitation through the exclusive depiction of sexual acts arranged in a series according to the strength of the social taboo. . . .[193]

The main purpose of pornography then, indeed its only purpose, is to stimulate erotic responses. In order to act upon the reader as an aphrodisiac it must not tire him with character analysis, philosophical exposition, or artistic enlightenment. It is merely the crudest conceivable example of "dirt for dirt's sake."

This definition of pornography is important because it is objective. What was pornographic a decade ago is pornographic today. If it can be assumed that the Court's definition of obscenity is broad enough to encompass this smut (hardly a daring supposition), then at least one clear-cut, enduring touchstone for determining the limits of obscenity has been erected by Brennan's findings.[194] Whether obscenity meant any more than this, of course, would have incalculable repercussions on the motion picture industry, book publishing houses, and the arts in general.

During the past eight-year period (dating from 1957 through 1965), the Supreme Court has made use of but two occasions to answer the many questions critics have raised regarding *Roth-Alberts*. A study of these judgments leads irresistibly to the conclusion that the Justices have failed to evolve a consensus which clearly demarcates the nature of obscenity and that, therefore, there is currently much doubt as to the constitutionally permissible scope of any measure designed to discourage its dissemination.

Under federal law,[195] every "obscene, lewd, lascivious, inde-

[193] Kronhausen, *op. cit.*, p. xi.

[194] Some learned critics felt the Court had gone too far in placing even the pornographic outside the limits of free speech and press. See, for instance, Paul Goodman, "Pornography, Art and Censorship," *Commentary Magazine*, March 1961, pp. 203-12. Also, Kronhausen, *op. cit.*, p. 271 and pp. 285-86. Cf. the less extreme criticism posited by Leary and Noall, *op. cit.*, p. 353.

[195] 18 U. S. C., Sect. 1461.

cent, filthy or vile article, matter, thing, device, or substance . . . is declared to be nonmailable matter and shall not be conveyed in the mails or delivered from any post office. . . ." It will be recalled that the criminal penalties for using the mails to distribute such items had been upheld in *Roth* v. *U. S.* In the first of these cases, the Post Office Department had found that petitioners' magazines were obscene and so refused to accept them for delivery. A Departmental administrative board had held a hearing prior to its decision to bar the publications and had reached the following conclusions:

(1) The magazines, which consisted largely of photographs of nude, or near-nude, male models, were not physical culture or "body building" publications, but were composed solely for the benefit of homosexuals and had no literary or scientific merit.

(2) These photographs would appeal to the prurient interest of such sexual deviates, but would be of no interest to normal adults.

(3) The magazines were read almost exclusively by homosexuals; the average male adult would not buy them.

Based upon these findings the board construed the holding in the *Roth* case to mean that a magazine could be judged obscene if it appealed to the prurient interest of the audience it was designed to reach. It rejected plaintiff's claim that the prurient interest appeal of the publication should be judged in terms of their likely impact on the average person in the community.

The Supreme Court, by a vote of 6-1, reversed the Department's ruling,[196] but was widely split on the reasons for its decision. Speaking only for Justice Stewart and himself, Justice Harlan found that the fatal error in the board's review of the issues was that it had assumed that in the present context the only test for proving the obscenity of a volume was "whether to the average person, applying contemporary community standards, the dominant theme of the material taken as a whole appeals to prurient interest." He did not find it necessary to elaborate on the "average person" portion of the formula expostulated by the Court in the *Roth* case, for he found that the magazines in question lacked an

[196] *Manual Enterprises* v. *Day*, 370 U. S. 478 (1962).

element which was as essential as prurient interest to substantiate a finding of obscenity under Section 1461.

> These magazines cannot be deemed so offensive on their face as to affront current community standards of decency—a quality that we shall refer to as 'patent offensiveness' or 'indecency.' . . .
>
> The words of Section 1461, 'obscene, lewd, lascivious, indecent, filthy or vile,' connote something that is portrayed in a manner so offensive as to make it unacceptable under current community mores. While in common usage the words have different shades of meaning, the statute since its inception has always been taken as aimed at obnoxiously debasing portrayals of sex.[197]

Of course in most instances materials that were patently offensive would also appeal to prurient interests and vice versa, but on rare occasions, where the magazines at issue were aimed at a particular class of people, then a more rigorous examination of the volumes was in order. Thus, the public would not be denied access to worthwhile works of literature, science, or art whose dominant theme might appeal to the prurient but which was not patently offensive.

The key question to be decided, then, was whether or not these publications were offensive on their face, but first it was necessary to decide the relevant community in terms of whose standards of decency the issue must be judged. Here, he found that the proper test under this statute, since it had been enacted by the federal government with its jurisdiction extending to all parts of the country, was a national standard of decency. This being the case, his own independent examination of the pictures led him to conclude that while they might be uncouth and obnoxious, they certainly were not obscene. "Divorced from their prurient interest appeal to the unfortunate persons whose patronage they were aimed at capturing, these portrayals of the male nude cannot fairly be regarded as more objectionable than many portrayals of the female nude that society tolerates." In conclusion, it was important to emphasize that this case was being adjudicated within a particular statutory framework, and that his findings should in no way be taken as anticipating whether or not

[197] *Ibid.*, pp. 482-83.

Congress could bar the distribution of such matter through the mails by enacting a narrowly drawn statute that defined and punished "specific conduct as constituting a clear and present danger."[198]

Mr. Justice Black agreed silently in the result arrived at by Harlan, while Justice Brennan, joined by Chief Justice Warren and Justice Douglas, wrote a concurring opinion dealing with an entirely different aspect of the controversy. He believed that the order promulgated by the Post Office raised grave doubts about the constitutionality of the whole procedure which gave rise to its issuance, for the methods by which obscenity was condemned were as important as the standards to be used in assessing its content. As he saw it the Post Office had been practicing a form of administrative censorship of allegedly obscene materials for many years. The formal regulations currently in use, however, dated from 1957. In the instant case a postmaster in Alexandria, Virginia, suspecting that petitioners' magazines were obscene, forwarded samples to the General Counsel of the Post Office Department. He notified the petitioners that their publications were nonmailable and that no formal hearing would be held since an insufficient monetary value was involved. This order, however, was dissolved by his superiors and a hearing was granted to plaintiffs, but with no change of decision forthcoming.

The fundamental question at stake, therefore, in the dispute at hand, according to Brennan, was whether Congress, by its enactment of Section 1461, had authorized the Postmaster General to censor obscenity. To him the suggestion that Congress or any of its agencies might constitutionally institute any process other than a fully judicial one immediately raised the gravest doubts. Consequently, the provisions of the Act or its legislative history would have to be most explicit in this regard for him to assume that "Congress had made such a radical departure from our traditions and undertook to clothe the Postmaster General with the power to supervise the tastes of the reading public of

198 *Ibid.*, p. 491, footnote 14. Other questions of importance in determining the validity of plaintiff's contentions such as the application of the "scienter" rule to the probable state of mind of those disseminating these materials are of little significance for present purposes.

the country." He then found that the terms of the law were at best entirely vague on the matter of how obscene materials were to be kept out of the mails. The debates in Congress over the years on the passage of the original bill and several of its amendments indicated that postmasters were to remove offensive matter but only for the purpose of turning it over to appropriate authorities for possible criminal proceedings.

In a biting dissent Justice Clark evaluated the Court's holding as requiring the United States Post Office "to be the world's largest disseminator of smut and Grand Informer of the names and places where obscene material may be obtained." He treated with obvious disdain the position taken by Justice Brennan that Congress had not delegated censorship authority to the Postmaster General, pointing out that that issue was neither presented for examination below nor argued before the Supreme Court. Nonetheless he spent a few paragraphs in developing evidence to contradict Brennan's interpretation of the historical record. As for Justice Harlan's assertions, these, he believed, need not be considered at all because the magazines contained information on where obscene materials could be obtained, a clear violation of Section 1461. In other words, the Post Office Department operating under what he felt was a clear grant of power from the Congress to keep objectionable publications out of the mails, had properly banned these items on at least one specification defined in the law,[199] so that it was entirely unnecessary to determine if the magazines were themselves obscene.

The evident importance of this decision lies in the refinement of the *Roth* test advanced by Justices Harlan and Stewart. In order for a magazine, book, or, logically, a motion picture to be classified as obscene it must be shown to be patently offensive. This is a most important limitation on both the criminal law and censorship agencies because it means that more than mere speculation about the "average man's prurient interests" will be needed to establish obscenity. The inclusion of this new perspective may lessen to some extent, then, the subjectivity that seemed to inhere in the *Roth* formula and, further, should help restrain govern-

---

[199] Justice Harlan had rejected this argument because "scienter" was not clearly demonstrable.

mental agencies from overzealously suppressing expression whose dominant theme has to do with some aspect of sex. As Harlan himself noted, however, this decision cannot be read to confine communities from passing laws prohibiting expression that incites immoral sexual conduct. For this reason, one might legitimately ponder the question of whether the Court would uphold censorship policies aimed at movies that were guilty of such incitement. And, further, one might also wonder how binding for future courts Harlan's doctrine will be, approved as it was by only two of nine Supreme Court justices.

The cleavage that had made itself quite evident in the adjudication of *Roth-Alberts* appeared once again in 1964.[200] Nico Jacobellis, the manager of a Cleveland Heights, Ohio moving picture theater, was convicted of possessing and exhibiting an obscene movie entitled *The Lovers*, contrary to the Ohio penal code.[201] This verdict was upheld by that state's highest court.[202] While six members of the Supreme Court agreed that the conviction must be reversed, no three of them could agree to the same opinion.

Speaking for himself and for Mr. Justice Goldberg, Justice Brennan began by examining the vital problem of delimiting the Court's role in enforcing obscenity laws. He found that it was the duty of the Justices themselves to evaluate in a de novo proceeding any allegation of obscenity that a state might levy against a "work of expression." Since only obscenity was without First Amendment protection, it was inherent in the scope of constitutional law that guidelines spelling out the difference between the two be applied to particular cases. Juries, he implied, might err in applying judicial standards to fact situations and so could stifle the dissemination of free speech.[203]

---

[200] *Jacobellis* v. *Ohio,* 12 L. Ed. 793.

[201] *Ohio Rev. Code,* Sect. 2905.34.

[202] 173 Ohio St. 22 (1963).

[203] Clearly this reasoning cannot be squared with Brennan's earlier opinion in the *Roth* case or his dissent in the *Kingsley Books* case (discussed in this section, *infra*). As will be seen, however, the view first expressed by Mr. Justice Reed in *Burstyn* v. *Wilson* and reinforced by Justice Harlan in *Roth* had since become the Court's "official" position.

Next, Brennan attempted to dispel any doubts that the suppression of obscenity might threaten First Amendment liberties. It must be remembered, he stated, that obscenity was "utterly without redeeming social importance" and that the material must go "substantially beyond customary limits of candor in describing or representing such matters" (sex, nudity, or excretion).[204] Thus, the constitutional status of books or movies could not be judged by "weighing" their artistic merit or social importance against their appeal to prurient interest.

But what contemporary community standards were to be used in evaluating the nature of the obscene? He found that guidelines reflecting "society at large" must be utilized for "it is, after all, a national Constitution we are expounding."[205] Of course, local communities might be somewhat diverse in their notions of obscenity but such differences, like other disparities in social norms, have never been a bar to the application of a supreme federal law.

As to *The Lovers* itself, the Court found that the allegations presented by Ohio were based almost entirely on an explicit love scene in the last reel of the movie which was thought to "infect" the entire production. Having viewed the picture, Brennan merely found it appropriate to note that it did not come within the purview of *Roth-Alberts*.

Four judges, while sharing in the reversal of plaintiff's conviction, could not support the Court's reasoning. Mr. Justice White, for one, concurred separately but also silently, while Justices Black and Douglas, building upon their dissent in *Roth-Alberts*, argued that a state could not arrest and convict anyone for exhibiting a motion picture regardless of mitigating circumstances.

A second concurrence, strange yet provocative in its import, was filed by Mr. Justice Stewart. It was his belief that the Court had not spelled out as clearly as it might have done in prior cases the meaning of obscenity. He could only surmise from a reading of decisions such as *Roth-Alberts, Manual Enterprises,* and *Jaco-*

---

[204] 12 L. Ed. 793 at p. 800.
[205] *Ibid.*, p. 802.

*bellis* that what the Court viewed as obscenity could only be that which was usually termed "hard-core pornography." At this point, however, Stewart side-stepped his own invitation to pinpoint precisely the kind of presentation he had in mind, preferring to say only that, "I know it when I see it, and the motion picture involved in this case is not that."

One may defensibly criticize labeling proscribable speech as hard-core pornography without attempting to describe this phenomenon except by the subjectivities of judges. A far more complex question, however, was raised when Stewart asserted that the Court, in fact, had established an alleged congruence between obscenity and pornography. At best, Mr. Justice Brennan is vague on the point. It is true that in *Jacobellis* he stressed the notion that obscenity was an appeal to prurient interest that is utterly without social importance and goes beyond customary limits of frankness. It could be argued therefore that this is simply using other language (as Justice Harlan had, it could similarly be argued, used the phrase "patently offensive") to denote pornography. And yet Brennan also stated, in rebutting the notion that local juries could successfully apply the Court's definition of obscenity, that this standard would have "'a varying meaning from time to time'—not from county to county, or town to town."[206] How can pornography vary from time to time and still meet the "dirt for dirt's sake" criterion set down by the Kronhausens?[207] The point is that the Court has a long way to go before it can be said that it has deduced a definition of *either* obscenity or pornography much less decided if the two are as one.

In dissent, Mr. Justice Harlan generally hewed to the doctrine he had espoused in the *Alberts* ruling. States, he claimed, have greater discretion than the federal government in suppressing obscenity and so might proscribe any material that could be rationally found to fall within this category. To be sure, the Supreme Court justice must exercise some measure of independent judgment in such cases, but in the enforcement of state laws his sole task should be to see that the *Roth-Manual Enterprises* test had been applied in a rational manner. Having viewed the

[206] 12 L. Ed. 793 at p. 801.
[207] Cf. their definition relevant to footnote 193, *supra*.

film in question, he was unwilling to say that Ohio had acted in an arbitrary or capricious way in labeling it as obscenity.

Chief Justice Warren, joined by Mr. Justice Clark, filed a second dissent but generally their position was much the same as Judge Harlan's. They did, however, directly assail the Court's belief that obscenity could only be constitutionally delimited through the use of a "national community standard"; in their judgment no such criterion in fact existed. The "contemporary community standard" facet of *Roth-Alberts* could plausibly refer only to *community* criteria as set forth by appropriate state and federal courts. Such decisions would merely require "sufficient evidence" as opposed to "substantial evidence" to be upheld in appellate courts and, like Harlan, they believed *The Lovers* to be legitimately proscribable. They also pointed out, however, in a statement to have much significance for future censorship cases, that all criminal *and civil* suits involving the suppression of obscene materials must meet minimal standards of due process. What these guidelines might consist of in a hearing before a censorship tribunal remained an open question.[208]


## Motion Pictures, Literature, and Censorship: The Present State of the Law

On the same day that the *Roth-Alberts* decision was decided, the Court also handed down a vital judgment relating to censorship itself. Under a New York State statute,[209] the chief legal officer of any city or town in which a person was trying to sell or would try to sell written material believed by this officer to be obscene, could maintain an action for an injunction against such a person so as to prevent its dissemination. The person or corporation sought to be enjoined was to be granted a trial of the issue within one day after joinder, but if the materials in question were, in fact, ruled objectionable they were to be surrendered to the police and destroyed.

By a vote of five to four, the Court upheld the terms of the

---

[208] 12 L. Ed. 793 at p. 806.
[209] *New York Code of Criminal Procedure,* Sect. 22-a.

statute[210] against the challenge of a book dealer whose distribution of a paper-covered booklet entitled *Nights of Horror* had
been restrained when the book was declared obscene by the
courts of New York. Mr. Justice Frankfurter, speaking for the
slender majority, began his discussion of the issues by reiterating
the Court's view in *Alberts* that a state might protect its citizens
from obscene literature. The sole issue, then, rested on a state's
right to utilize a prior restraint technique to help it solve the
problem at hand.

Here, Frankfurter returned to the famous *Near* precedent
which appellant claimed should be invoked to nullify New York's
injunctive "censorship" remedy. While he readily agreed that the
statute was indeed a form of prior restraint, he refused to concede
that such a designation automatically doomed it to constitutional
rebuff. Even in the *Near* decision, he argued, Chief Justice
Hughes had made it painfully clear that "the protection even as
to previous restraint is not absolutely unlimited" and that, furthermore, one of the exceptions noted by the Court at that time
was the right to suppress obscene publications.

Over and above this assertion, however, was the fact that
the majority believed the statute at issue to be as equitable in its
adherence to due process as the usual penal law. In *Near* a court
had tried to enjoin future issues of a newspaper because its past
issues had been found to be offensive rather than obscene. Here,
a court had enjoined the circulation of material already published, which had been found to be obscene in a judicial proceeding where all the rules of procedural due process were observed.
To the contention advanced by Justice Brennan, in dissent, that
petitioner was not afforded a trial by jury, Frankfurter replied that
at no time was such a trial requested nor was that issue even
raised in oral argument before any of the appellate courts that
had heard the controversy including the Supreme Court.[211]

Three dissenting statements were filed in opposition to these
contentions. Reiterating the position he had taken in *Roth-Alberts*,

[210] *Kingsley Books, Inc.* v. *Brown*, 354 U. S. 436 (1957).
[211] At no time did petitioner challenge the trial court's finding that the
book was in fact obscene. Lockhart and McClure concluded that the matter
was "clearly hard-core pornography." See *op. cit.*, p. 30.

Chief Justice Warren believed that total emphasis should be placed on the defendant's actions and not on an abstract discussion of the book being distributed. Unlike the federal obscenity statute and the California penal law upheld in those verdicts the New York enactment took no account of appellant's behavior but, instead, placed the book itself on trial. Obscenity could only be judged by understanding the manner in which the materials had been used and, as the personal element so fundamental to the criminal law was an unknown quantity, the statute was in reality little better than "book burning."

Justice Douglas, with Justice Black approving, felt that to restrain the distribution of literature before a hearing even though a trial of the issue was mandatory within one day was an imposition on plaintiff's right of free speech. This, they believed, was "censorship at its worst." Furthermore, they were concerned about the fact that one conviction would serve as the basis for a state-wide decree against the particular publication. They thought that each attempt to distribute a copy of such material was a separate offense which entitled the accused to a trial of his own, for juries and judges might differ in their opinions, community by community, case by case.

In a final dissent, Justice Brennan stated that the law offended due process because it did not guarantee defendant a jury trial. In *Roth-Alberts* the Court had fashioned a test for determining the nature of obscenity predicated on the beliefs of the "average person." As the statutes upheld in those cases allowed a jury trial by right, the Court had not decided if such a provision was necessary for securing the freedoms of speech and press for material not obscene. It was his belief that a jury represented a cross-section of the community and possessed a special aptitude for reflecting the view of the average person. This point was so basic, he believed, that it should be included in all enactments where a finding of obscenity would eventually be necessary in their enforcement.

The importance of the *Kingsley Books* holding cannot be stressed too greatly. This decision marked the first and, indeed, the only time the Court has condoned a prior restraint on books. Of course, this was not "censorship at its worst" as Douglas and

Black had dubbed it. The tribunal imposing the restraint was a court of law where witnesses could be called by either side and questioned by either side in an attempt to probe the matter of obscenity. The trial was open to the public and records were kept of the proceedings. The Court had certainly gone a long way in accepting Professor Freund's view that prior restraint in and of itself is not the tool of the Devil. Still the question nagged: Would the courts confine constitutional censorship of movies to such narrow contours?

This important question was not the subject, however, of the Supreme Court's next attempt to further spell out the constitutional liberties of the motion picture medium. Six months later a case arrived from the Seventh Circuit Court of Appeals which for the first time required the application of principles set forth in *Roth-Alberts* to film productions. Plaintiff, a New York corporation, had filed a complaint in federal district court, on grounds of diversity of citizenship, against the censorship bureau of the City of Chicago because it had refused to license a film entitled *The Game of Love.* This movie had been submitted to the bureau in accordance with city law but was found to be "immoral and obscene" because "it is not acceptable to standards of decency, with immorality featured and dialogue unfit."[212] The district court subsequently viewed the film and agreed that it was obscene and immoral and that the ordinance did not violate the First and Fourteenth Amendments of the Constitution.[213]

By a unanimous vote, the Circuit Court, by Justice Schnackenberg, upheld these results.[214] He examined the Supreme Court's rulings in *Near* and *Burstyn* and concluded that it was perfectly constitutional for a city to bar the public exhibition of obscene films. Further, the Illinois Supreme Court had held that the words "obscene" and "immoral" as used in the statute were synonymous and that they were to be construed as meaning that a movie could be banned if "when considered as a whole, its

212 Under the terms of Sect. 155-4 of the relevant ordinance a film could be denied a license if believed to be "immoral or obscene." See *Times Film Corp.* v. *Chicago,* 244 F. 2d 432 at p. 434.

213 139 F. Supp. 837 (1956).

214 *Times Film Corp.* v. *Chicago,* 244 F. 2d 432 (1957).

calculated purpose or dominant effect is substantially to arouse sexual desires, and if the probability of this effect is so great as to outweigh whatever artistic or other merits the film may possess. In making this determination the film must be tested with reference to its effect upon the normal, average person." With such a precise interpretation of the pertinent words of the ordinance to guide the censorship board, Schnackenberg could not countenance appellant's belief that the law was void for vagueness.

Unlike the state supreme court judges who had upheld, for example, the Kansas State Board of Review's suppression of *The Moon is Blue* or the Ohio film censorship agency's proscription of the movie *M,* the federal appellate court justices felt it incumbent upon themselves to see the movie itself so as to be sure the judgment of the district court had not been erroneous. They found that, from beginning to end, the thread of the story was "supercharged with a current of lewdness generated by a series of illicit sexual intimacies and acts." Their conclusion was that:

> We do not hesitate to say that the calculated purpose of the producers of this film and its dominant effect are substantially to arouse sexual desires. We are of the opinion that the probability of this effect is so great as to outweigh whatever artistic or other merits the film may possess. We think these determinations are supported by the effect which this film would have upon the normal, average person.[215]

There were several nice issues presented to the Supreme Court by this controversy. First of all, it is worth noting that although the Circuit Court's opinion had been written prior to the Supreme Court's decision in *Roth-Alberts,* nonetheless the test for obscenity utilized by the lower court was very much like the one fashioned by Justice Brennan. The Justices had viewed *The Game of Love* as a total production, had pinpointed what they thought was its dominant theme, and had taken into account the movie's influence on the average person. However, the test invoked made no mention of "contemporary community standards" and the Supreme Court might also feel that "substantially to arouse sexual

---

[215] *Ibid.,* p. 436.

desires" was not quite the same as "appealing to prurient interest," though this was not likely.[216] Finally, and perhaps of greatest magnitude, the weighing of the dominant theme as against any artistic values the film might possess flew in the face of Brennan's dictum in *Roth-Alberts* that obscenity was "utterly without redeeming social importance."[217] In the event the criteria used by the court were not believed to be adequate, the Supreme Court very likely might reverse and remand with an order to put *Roth-Alberts* to use.

Then again the Court quite conceivably might see no problem at that level. If so, the Justices could either accept the findings of the Circuit Court that the film was, in fact, obscene or it could analyze the contents of the movie on its own to see that the lower court had done its job wisely. Which procedure would be followed was, of course, an open question for only two of the judges had found it necessary to grapple with this problem before. Justice Harlan had insisted, in *Roth-Alberts*, that as a matter of law each judge should examine for himself the contents of materials deemed offensive while Justice Brennan, in *Kingsley Books*, had come to the opposite conclusion that a jury trial was required under the Constitution to make the "average person" test a reality.[218] If the Court, regardless of which of these paths it chose to follow, eventually supported the views of Justice Schnackenberg it would then have an opportunity to judge the constitutionality of the Chicago law itself.

One other approach to the case at hand, however, seemed even more likely to win the approval of a majority than any of the alternatives arising out of *Roth-Alberts*. In previous disputes that

---

216 Brennan had, at one point in his opinion, defined material that dealt with sex in a manner appealing to the prurient as that which had a "tendency to excite lustful thoughts." *Roth* v. *U. S.*, 354 U. S. 476 (1957) at p. 487.

217 The Court, of course, has since resolved this discrepancy in its *Jacobellis* decision.

218 In the instant case the movie was declared obscene by a district court judge, 139 F. Supp. 837 (1956), so that petitioner did not have the benefit of a jury trial. Unlike *Kingsley Books, Inc.* v. *Brown*, the key issue in this controversy was whether the matter deemed offensive was indeed obscene.

had dealt with the prior censorship of movies the Court had
always been able to strike down the particular standard used by
censorship agencies to suppress movies and in the *Holmby* case,
the last of this group to be decided, the guidelines "obscene and
immoral" had been voided as inhibitions on free speech. Why
could not the Court, then, simply declare these criteria null as set
forth in the instant controversy? It will be recalled that one of the
obscurities of *Holmby* was whether the Court was dealing with
the term "obscene" when narrowly defined (as Justice Clark in
*Burstyn* had certainly thought it could be) or with "obscene" as
defined by the censorship board itself. If the Justices had been dissatisfied with the way in which the term had been manipulated in
gauging the permissibility of *The Moon is Blue* then, quite likely,
it would be unhappy over the reasons advanced by Chicago for
finding that *The Game of Love* was "immoral and obscene."

By per curiam opinion the high Court reversed the judgment
of the Court of Appeals citing only the *Alberts* decision.[219] As
Lockhart and McClure have pointed out, the judges themselves
must have made an independent examination of the film and
found that its censorship on the ground of obscenity was a violation of First Amendment rights, for by reversing the lower
court "it thus terminated the litigation and gave final protection
to the materials in question."[220] The Court had thus gone on
record as adopting Justice Harlan's position that whether a book
or movie was obscene or not was a matter of First Amendment
construction and so was a task reserved for judges themselves.
Indeed, Justices Burton and Clark were of the opinion that
certiorari should not have been granted. They must have believed
that the *Roth-Alberts* formula covered a movie like *The Game of
Love*.[221]

Motion picture producers and writers must have been elated
that the Supreme Court had not included under the obscenity
doctrine of *Alberts* v. *California* a film whose only objectionable
feature was that it did not indict illicit sex relationships as

[219] *Times Film Corp.* v. *Chicago*, 355 U. S. 35 (1957).

[220] Lockhart and McClure, *op. cit.*, p. 34.

[221] I have seen this motion picture and believe it to be of high merit
and clearly not obscene.

reprehensible conduct. This movie, simply stated, had done nothing more than depict the story of a boy who has had an affair with an older woman and has discovered that he has been awakened to something so full of meaning that he believes he ought to share its secret with his inquisitive teen-age girl friend.[222] Yet, the fact that the high Court did not throw out the applicable section of the Chicago ordinance as unconstitutional even with *Holmby* v. *Vaughn* already on the books was more than just an indication that that case was sui generis and that film censorship laws requiring the suppression of the obscene were far from dead.

The evolution of constitutional rights for the motion picture medium under the First Amendment which the Supreme Court had been advancing since the *Burstyn* decision moved toward a new climax with its consideration of the *Kingsley Pictures* controversy in 1959.[223] The State of New York had amended its film censorship law following the *La Ronde* decision to provide that the term "immoral" and the phrase "of such a character that its exhibition would tend to corrupt morals" would be applicable to movies "the dominant purpose or effect of which is erotic or pornographic; or which portrays acts of sexual immorality, perversion, or lewdness, or which expressly or impliedly presents such acts as desirable, acceptable or proper patterns of behavior."[224]

As the distributor of a motion picture entitled *Lady Chatterley's Lover*, petitioner submitted that film to the state's motion picture censorship body for a license. The bureau found that three of the scenes contained within this production were "immoral" and directed that they be deleted before commercial presentation.[225] The distributor appealed to the Regents of the University

[222] A reading of the opinions advanced by both lower courts conveys the impression that if an attempt had been made somewhere during the course of the film to show that the characters in this triangle were immoral, depraved, irreligious, or just improper in their actions then there would have been grounds for reversal.

[223] *Kingsley Pictures* v. *Regents*, 360 U. S. 684 (1959).

[224] *McKinney's N. Y. Laws*, 1953 (Cum. Supp. 1958), Education Law, Sect. 122-a.

[225] The order was as follows:

(1) Eliminate all views of Mellors and Lady Chatterley in cabin from point where they are seen lying on cot together, in a state of undress, to end of sequence.

of the State of New York for a review of that ruling. The Regents upheld the denial of a license, but on the broader ground that "the whole theme of this motion picture is immoral under said law, for that theme is the presentation of adultery as a desirable, acceptable and proper pattern of behavior." This appraisal was upheld in the New York Court of Appeals.

The facts of the case raised a novel issue for the Supreme Court and so, for the first time since *Burstyn* v. *Wilson*, the per curiam format was dispensed with. Like all of the preceding cases, however, the judges unanimously agreed that New York had overstepped constitutional limits. Mr. Justice Stewart, who spoke for the Court as a whole, began by stating that it was unnecessary to consider if *Lady Chatterley's Lover* was obscene because the New York Court of Appeals had unanimously and explicitly rejected any such notion. Nor was it suggested that the movie would incite to illegal action. Rather, he found, the censorship board had banned the film because New York law had required that no movie could be granted a license which approvingly dealt with an adulterous relationship.

> What New York has done, therefore, is to prevent the exhibition of a motion picture because that picture advocates an idea that adultery under certain circumstances may be proper behavior. Yet the First Amendment's basic guarantee is of freedom to advocate ideas. The State, quite simply, has struck at the very heart of constitutionally protected liberty.[226]

---

(2) Eliminate all views of Mellors caressing Lady Chatterley's buttock and all views of him unzipping her dress and caressing her bare back. Eliminate following spoken (in French) dialogue accompanying these actions:

"But you're nude . . .
You're nude under your dress, and you didn't say so . . .
What is it?"

Eliminate accompanying English superimposed titles:

"You have nothing on . . .
And you didn't say so . . .
What is it?"

(3) Eliminate entire sequence in Mellors' bedroom, showing Lady Chatterley and Mellors in bed, in a state of undress.

[226] 360 U. S. 684 at p. 688.

If the grounds upon which the state had acted to suppress this film were themselves inconsistent with the First Amendment then Stewart saw no reason to consider appellant's contention that the state had no power whatever to license movies prior to exhibition. Nor was it appropriate to determine if the controls which a state might impose upon this medium of expression were "precisely coextensive" with those allowable for the regulation of books, newspapers, or speech "despite problems peculiar to motion pictures."

Though the eight other justices adhered to Stewart's conclusions five of them found it necessary to write concurring opinions offering their own modes of reasoning as a substitute for the Court's. The most important of these was drafted by Justice Harlan for himself and Justices Frankfurter and Whittaker. He agreed that public discussion or advocacy of adultery, "unaccompanied by obscene portrayal or actual incitement to such behavior," might not be constitutionally proscribed, but he felt that the New York Court had construed the statute narrowly to apply only to obscenity or incitement. So construed, he believed the statute clearly constitutional.[227] The application of the law, however, was a different matter. He had seen the movie and regarded it as merely "a somewhat unusual, and rather pathetic, love triangle." In no sense could it be considered obscene or an incitement to commit any illegal act. The movie, then, was entitled to First Amendment protection.

Justice Frankfurter wrote a separate opinion which agreed thoroughly with Harlan's approach to the problem. Of special importance, however, was his strong statement that previous decisions of the Court "had left no doubt that a motion picture licensing law is not inherently outside the scope of the regulatory powers of a state" and that even D. H. Lawrence had favored the censorship of pornography. He also stressed his conception of the role of appellate court judges in handling cases of this kind, claiming that it was impossible to escape an instance-by-instance, case-by-case application of the due process clause in order to mark out constitutional bounds for state and local regulatory policies.

[227] *Ibid.*, pp. 706-7.

Justice Clark was of the opinion that the Court should dispense with the law in question as it had with the standard of "sacrilegious" in the *Burstyn* case. Frankfurter and Harlan, in his view, had twisted the meaning of the enactment put upon it in no fewer than fifteen places in the majority statement of the appeals court as well as in the report of the Board of Regents. The only limits on the censor's discretion was his perception of what was "desirable, acceptable or proper" and this no more closely confined him in his work than did terms like "sacrilegious" or "immoral." The heavy burden of the state in justifying a prior restraint on speech had not been satisfied. He saw no reason, however, why a narrowly drawn censorship law banning "pornographic" films, or those that "portray acts of sexual immorality" would not be consistent with due process.

Justices Douglas and Black each filed separate statements joining in the Court's trend of thought, but again urged that the censorship of movies be declared unconstitutional on its face. Black, however, went on to criticize sharply the Harlan-Frankfurter axis with its emphasis on the individual scrutiny of motion pictures by each judge. Judicial officers possessed no special competency for judging what was or was not obscene, he believed, and the result would be that the subjective moral beliefs of judges would be the determining factor in deciding if motion pictures could be viewed in communities around the country. Such policy controversies, he concluded, were a thicket that had little in common with lawsuits.

Given the Court's construction of the New York law it hardly appears surprising that a majority of the judges were able to strike it down as a violation of the First Amendment either because of the reasons set forth in Stewart's eminently logical argument or because of the similarity of the facts with those presented in the *Burstyn* precedent, as Clark had believed. Indeed, Harlan had readily conceded in his analysis that the findings of the majority followed inevitably from its original assumption as to the meaning of the statute. And, if the New York enactment said what the concurring minority of three said it did, then it must have again been reassuring to film executives and personnel to see a movie like *Lady Chatterley's Lover*, so closely modeled after the expurgated version of the novel, qualify as free speech.[228] But this judgment was no victory for the motion picture industry. Four judges, Frankfurter, Whittaker, Harlan, and Clark had for the first time stated their unequivocal support of some kind of movie censorship. How precisely stringent it would have to be in the eyes of each of them to satisfy the demands of the First Amendment and whether they could carry another member of the Court with them was still a matter of conjecture.

The fundamental constitutional question of the permissibility of local censorship of motion pictures finally reached the Supreme Court in 1961 in the case of *Times Film Corporation* v. *Chicago*.[229] Petitioner was a New York corporation owning the exclusive right to exhibit publicly in the City of Chicago the film *Don Juan*. It applied for a permit, as required by city law, and tendered the mandatory license fee but refused to submit the movie for examination prior to exhibition.[230] The appropriate city official refused to allow the license to issue and petitioner brought suit in federal court asking that Chicago be restrained from interfering with the exhibition of the movie on the ground that the provision of the ordinance requiring censorship of films was void on its face as contrary to the First and Fourteenth Amendments. Both the district court and the court of appeals dismissed the complaint on the grounds that the case presented merely an abstract question of law since neither the film nor evidence of its content was involved in the proceedings.

Speaking for a slim majority of five, Justice Clark began his inquiry into the delicate question of law at stake in this controversy by holding that a justiciable dispute clearly existed. The section of Chicago's ordinance in question provided that films must be examined by the city censorship board prior to public showing and violation of that stipulation carried certain concrete punishments. Admittedly, this section of the law was a prior restraint and the legal issue at stake, therefore, was whether or not the

[228] Having also seen this film, I frankly cannot understand how it could be said to appeal to prurient interest when gauged by the demands of *Roth-Alberts*.

[229] 365 U. S. 43.

[230] See *Municipal Code of Chicago*, Sect. 155-4 (1939 as amended).

*Burstyn* rule precluded the enforcement of this kind of licensing scheme.

Having overruled the lower courts on this point he then went on to try to set in its proper frame of reference the complaint that had been advanced by appellant. He found that the nature of this attack upon the ordinance did not require that any consideration be given to the validity of the standards set out therein. Unlike other cases that had been decided by the Court, the criteria used by the local censorship bureau had not been challenged. Further, the nature of the movie itself was an unknown quantity; indeed, not a word as to its content could be found in the record. In short, Clark held that what petitioner was saying was that the nature of the film was irrelevant, and that:

> Even if this film contains the basest type of pornography, or incitement to riot, or forceful overthrow of orderly government, it may nonetheless be shown without prior submission for examination. (Or to put it another way) . . . the broad justiciable issue is therefore present as to whether the ambit of constitutional protection includes complete and absolute freedom to exhibit, at least once, any and every kind of motion picture.[231]

This principle, he felt, was contrary to the Court's interpretation of First Amendment guarantees expressed in *Near* v. *Minnesota* where several types of permissible prior restraints had been suggested by the majority. To emphasize the fallacy in petitioner's argument he noted that one of the purposes of the Chicago ordinance was to protect the public against "obscene" films which was, according to the scope of the *Near* precedent, one of the "exceptional cases" justifying the use of prior restraint. Furthermore, the Court had held in *Roth* v. *U. S.* that obscenity was not within the area of constitutionally protected speech. To this argument, he found that appellant's only rejoinder was that regardless of the capacity for evil a movie might possess, previous restraints could not be justified to deal with the problem. Clark's answer to this rebuttal was to state that "capacity for evil may be relevant in determining the permissible scope of community control" and that motion pictures were not "necessarily subject to the precise

[231] 365 U. S. 43 at pp. 46-47.

rules governing any other particular method of expression."[232] It was not for the Court to strip a state of the most effective means at its disposal for dealing with the problem of obscene or incendiary films.

In a long and rambling dissent Chief Justice Warren, joined by Justices Black, Douglas, and Brennan, vigorously attacked the Court's holding on a number of counts. Because his opinion was so diffuse and yet so important in its criticism of the majority's position it might be well to try to list in some detail the major points of his argument. They were as follows:

(1) The decision in this case, he found, was contrary to each and every precedent the Court had handed down relative to censorship. In the *Near* case, for example, the statute under attack was not as noxious to personal liberties as the Chicago ordinance because it did not require that all publications be approved before distribution. Or, in *Cantwell* v. *Connecticut* the law in question was aimed at a specific evil, namely, fraudulent solicitation. Of course, it constituted an unconstitutional abridgment of freedom of religion because the public official could refuse to license representatives of a certain faith if he felt the sect they represented was not truly a religion. But, constitutionally, where was the difference between the danger of obscene films and fraudulent solicitation?

(2) Of course, *Near* v. *Minnesota* had clearly stated that prior restraints against the publication of "obscene and indecent" materials were justifiable. But there were prior restraints and prior restraints. The Court had certainly miscast the issue when it claimed that what was at stake was petitioner's right to exhibit a movie at least once. The real question was whether a city could command *all* motion picture owners to present their films for licensing and censorship. There was certainly nothing in the record to indicate the slightest suspicion that *Don Juan* was objectionable for any legitimate reason. The point, then, was that Chicago had strayed from a fundamental principle of constitutional law. It had not demonstrated that its prior censorship board had been instituted to deal with "exceptional cases" and it had not rebutted the "heavy burden" of proof required in previous

[232] *Ibid.*, p. 49.

Court rulings to sustain such a program.[233] "Clearly, this is neither an exceptional case nor has Chicago sustained any burden."[234]

(3) In the case at hand the Court had approved the invocation of the most dangerous form of prior restraint, the censorship bureau. But certainly other remedies were available. In the *Kingsley Books* controversy the Court had allowed a state to use a limited injunctive procedure closely guarded by procedural safeguards to deal with books deemed offensive. But the Chicago scheme contained no procedural ground-rules for the benefit of the film-maker; there was no trial of the issue before the blanket proscription became effective. The *Kingsley Books* statute had required the existence of some belief that the publication was obscene before it was put on trial. The Chicago ordinance required no such showing.

(4) But to understand the evil of the Chicago law it was necessary to understand what censorship really can do to a medium of expression. The Court was correct in assuming that censorship boards constituted the most effective means of stifling speech. The snip of the censor's scissors mitigates the contemplation that will mark the prosecutor's judgment in preparing a criminal indictment. The standards of proof, the judicial safeguards afforded a defendant, and the consequences of bringing such charges will all provoke mature deliberation. None of these things hinder the censor. His decisions are insulated from public pressures because the public knows almost nothing about what the censor has stifled. There are no rules of evidence in his domain, nor may the film owner always have the opportunity even to defend his product.[235]

But this is by no means the extent of the damage. In order to

[233] Compare the statement of Justice Clark in *Burstyn* v. *Wilson*, 343 U. S. 495 at pp. 503-4.

[234] *Times Film Corp.* v. *Chicago*, 365 U. S. 43 at pp. 55, 64.

[235] The Chief Justice's dissent contains some revealing comments made by members of the Chicago censorship board about the tasks they perform. Some of these remarks are worth noting to understand his objection to censorship. For instance, a police sergeant attached to the board said, "coarse language or anything that would be derogatory to the government— propaganda" is ruled out of foreign films. "Nothing pink or red is allowed," he added. The police sergeant in charge of the censor unit said: "Children

achieve a redress of grievances the courts must be brought into play. Yet, the delays in adjudication might well result in irreparable damage to the film producer. The instant litigation had already consumed almost three years. Moreover, the exhibitor very likely will not pursue judicial remedies. His inclination will simply be to capitulate rather than to spend the time and money on litigation. This is especially true for moviemakers because of the large financial burden that they must assume to create a salable product.

(5) The Court's opinion was largely predicated on the belief that each medium of expression is subject to differing standards of community control because each presents its own peculiar problems. But this is surely only a truism. The point is that the Court had not even attempted to justify why moving pictures should be treated differently from other media to the extent that they should be denied protection from censorship—"a form of infringement upon freedom of expression to be especially condemned." Because of the obvious weakness in the majority's argument the decision presented a real danger of eventual censorship for every form of communication.

Over and above the differences between censorship and procedures under the penal law which the Chief Justice placed great emphasis on in his dissent and which have been discussed in some detail heretofore, there are two other arguments he presented which deserve further enlargement. He carefully noted that Justice Clark's statement had assumed that the fundamental issue was whether or not petitioner had a constitutional right to be free from all community prior restraint.[236] As he pointed out, of course, this was a non sequitur. The facts of the case were such that the Court was called upon to examine the workings of the Chicago inspection system and that system alone. Though the standards used by Chicago were not germane because *Don Juan*

---

should be allowed to see any movie that plays in Chicago. If a picture is objectionable for a child, it is objectionable period." See *ibid.*, pp. 70-72. Compare these views with the terms of the Chicago ordinance, *supra,* footnote 230.

[236] This line of reasoning seems to have captivated some critics as well. See McAnany, *op. cit.*, pp. 442-43.

had not been submitted for examination and clearance, certainly
the nature of the censorship program itself was of relevance because that was the substance of the regulatory scheme which appellant had sought to avoid. As the Chief Justice maintained, the
Court could have struck down Chicago's censorship program on
the authority of *Near* v. *Minnesota, Lovell* v. *Griffin,* etc., and still
left that city with an effective arsenal of weapons to use in stifling
obscene and incendiary movies over and above subsequent
punishment laws. The decision reached in *Kingsley Books, Inc.* v.
*Brown* attests to this.[237]

This discussion leads irresistibly to a second problem. Chief
Justice Warren could not understand, evidently, why it was that
censorship of movies was to be countenanced while the censorship of virtually all other forms of written and spoken speech
that the Court had had the opportunity to pass upon was to be
considered prima facie unconstitutional. At one point in his
remarks he did imply that the Court was of the view that "the
impact of the motion picture is greater than that of some other
media"[238] and Justice Clark had, of course, specifically mentioned that "capacity for evil" was a definite factor in measuring
the limits of community regulation.[239] This basic supposition concerning the power of the screen to affect the behavior of viewers

---

[237] Definitions become a matter of importance at this point. Up until
*Kingsley Books, Inc.* v. *Brown* every prior restraint ordinance that has
been discussed above was enforced by what the Chief Justice would
term a censorship board with the exception of the Alabama law voided in
*Thornhill* v. *Alabama* and, possibly, the laws at issue in *Cox* v. *New
Hampshire, Lovell* v. *Griffin,* and *Thomas* v. *Collins.* The *Kingsley Books*
decision, however, introduced a new factor, the use of a judicial hearing.
Though the New York statute was a previous restraint at least in form, its
substance was such as to bring it closer to the penal law than to the
"censorship" Blackstone had impugned. In understanding the correlative
rights of the various mass media under the First and Fourteenth Amendments, then, it is important to note which forms of expression are susceptible
to censorship and which are susceptible only to more refined previous
restraint techniques. It should be noted that each prior restraint program
for movies to be analyzed has been, and is currently, enforced almost
completely by censorship boards.

[238] 365 U. S. 43 (1961) at p. 77.

[239] *Ibid.,* p. 49.

coupled with "a respect for the federal system and the separation of powers" were apparently what had prompted the Court to allow localities the greatest degree of leeway in dealing with the possible "evil consequences" of films.

The tragic flaw in this type of reasoning is that it treats the motion picture like a textbook abstraction, or like an integer on some sort of graph designed to compute "community control of capacities for evil." Movies have been found to be part of the speech and press that is guaranteed protection by the First Amendment. A great film like *Citizen Kane* can teach more about American political and social thought than most treatises on American culture. Ingmar Bergman's *Wild Strawberries* is as artistically and dramatically significant as most books that reach the best-seller list. Should cities and states be given the constitutional power to rip these productions apart in the privacy of their censorship chambers while books, pamphlets and newspapers may only be held accountable in the courtroom for what they say? Or, to turn the Court's test fashioned in *Times Film* around, is the proper rule of law in such cases to be that the more effectively a medium of speech moves men's minds and hearts then the more power the community possesses to limit what it has to say?

In gaining a full understanding of the purport of this holding it is essential to keep in mind the many cases decided in the past which carefully excluded censorship as a weapon to be used by communities in protecting their citizens from offensive speech. In only two decisions handed down by the Court had it upheld a form of prior restraint granting any discretion at all to those exercising that restraint. One of these judgments, of course, was the *Kingsley Books* controversy. But the New York law under examination in that case was far different from the censorship ordinance of *Times Film*. There, a book could not be found obscene unless a full-dress hearing in a court of law was granted and, further, city officials could only ask for an injunction to limit the distribution of the specific matter believed to be obscene prior to such hearing. In short, the law did not apply to all books being circulated in a given community but only to those as to which officials were sure to possess at least a modicum of evidence to substantiate their claims. Indeed, the substance of the New York law, as Justice Frankfurter tried to point out, was such as to make its enforcement procedures almost a replica of subsequent punishment laws aimed against the dissemination of the obscene.

The second case where some aspect of previous restraint was affirmed was the New Hampshire parade decision. But here again the facts were far different from those presented in the Chicago case. In *Cox* there was no showing that the law in question had ever been used against any group wishing to stage a parade. Further, the clear purpose of the statute was not to regulate the content of the message being circulated by the procession but to protect the public from the confusion such proceedings might cause. Needless to say the entire raison d'être of the Chicago statute was to control the content of motion pictures and to decide which films could or could not be exhibited. Nor can one ignore the important fact that movies are shown in special "film houses" constructed solely for that particular purpose. The audio portion of the presentation cannot disturb persons on the streets or in private houses. Even the blare of the sound truck when used *on public property* was shielded from censorship in *Saia* v. *New York*.[240]

One final word about *Times Film Corporation* v. *Chicago*. Because a majority of the judges on the Supreme Court believed the controlling issue to be whether any form of prior restraint against motion pictures was constitutional there is still a very definite question as to what standards may be used by local censorship boards in judging the acceptability of movies. In his opinion for the Court, Justice Clark had relied heavily on the fact that one of the purposes of Chicago's ordinance was to shield its citizens from the obscene, a justification for prior restraint

[240] The assertion that censorship of films is more plausible than censorship of other media because a movie is before the licensing official in its complete form so that his judgment as to what will be presented is not based on conjecture (see McAnany, *op. cit.*, p. 453), does not seem to come to grips with the objections to censorship voiced by the Chief Justice in his dissent. Nor, of course, does it explain why such laws are constitutional when applied to movies but void when used to inhibit books. See *Bantam Books, Inc.* v. *Sullivan,* 372 U. S. 58 (1963).

which had initially been advanced in the *Near* holding. In his concurring statement in the *Lady Chatterley's Lover* decision, however, he had unequivocally stated the view that narrowly drawn previous restraints banning "pornographic" movies or those that "portray acts of sexual immorality" would be consistent with free speech guarantees. Pornography may or may not be all that obscenity encompasses from the legal standpoint (the Court has yet to settle this point), but a serious constitutional question is raised when one talks of proscribing motion pictures that "portray acts of sexual immorality." What is an act of sexual immorality in the first place? And, secondly, does not the use of such a test presuppose judging a film by some of its parts rather than as a whole?

Justice Frankfurter had implied in the same case that a licensing act of this sort could be used to sift out the pornographic while Justice Stewart had implied that prior restraint laws might be utilized to suppress both obscene movies and films that incited to illegal action. On the other hand, Mr. Justice Harlan had specifically stipulated that motion picture censorship boards could suppress not only the obscene but also any presentation that incited to sexual immorality which he considered to be an integral part of obscene conduct. It seems clear that a majority of the Justices would uphold a censorship law aimed at the banning of obscene or pornographic movies, but whether they would agree with Justice Clark's opinion regarding movies depicting sexual immorality or whether they would stretch a community's power to censor films that incited to illegal or sexually immoral action, and, indeed, what test they would use to determine incitement if they did so, are matters of conjecture.[241]

The broad brush strokes used in deciding the *Times Film*

[241] One critic thinks it "almost inevitable" that film censorship based on anything but obscenity is null. For example, he thinks it settled law that ordinances providing for the banning of movies that "incite to crime" are void on authority of *Winters* v. *New York* (see footnote 135, *supra*, and the relevant discussion). An attempt by the New York Court of Appeals to limit the scope of the New York law to articles which incited violent or depraved crimes was to no avail. See Melville B. Nimmer, "The Constitutionality of Official Censorship of Motion Pictures," *University of Chicago Law Review*, XXV (1958), 639-40.

controversy are clearly illuminated when contrasted with the Court's painstaking analysis and subsequent voiding of two state prior restraint enactments aimed at the distribution of books. In the first of these recent disputes, the Rhode Island legislature had created a Commission "to educate the public concerning any book . . . containing obscene, indecent or impure language, or manifestly tending to the corruption of the youth . . . and to investigate and recommend the prosecution of all violations (of said provision)." The Commission's practice was to notify a book distributor that certain works being handled by his firm had been found by the Commission to be objectionable for sale, distribution or display to youths under 18 years of age. Such notices requested the distributor's "cooperation" and advised him that copies of this list of objectionable publications had been given to local police departments and that it was the duty of the Commission to recommend prosecution against those who circulated such volumes. Four New York publishers whose works were widely distributed throughout Rhode Island sued in the courts of that state for injunctive relief on the grounds that the Commission had intimidated their chief distributors into "blacklisting" several of their books. The Rhode Island Supreme Court denied petitioners' plea, but by an 8-1 vote, the United States Supreme Court reversed.[242]

Speaking for this lopsided majority Mr. Justice Brennan first reiterated his argument presented in the *Alberts* case that while a state may restrict the dissemination of the obscene, nonetheless the line between materials that appeal to prurient interest and those that do not is often thin and imprecise so that communities must be on their guard to protect literature that is sheltered by the First Amendment. It followed, then, that a state was not free to adopt whatever procedures it pleased for dealing with obscenity and that such practices must be consistent with due process.

One of the chief grounds upon which counsel for Rhode Island had rested his case, however, was that this principle was not applicable to the activities of the Commission because it in

[242] *Bantam Books, Inc., v. Sullivan,* 372 U. S. 58 (1963).

no way regulated or suppressed obscenity but simply "exhorts book-sellers and advises them of their legal rights." But Justice Brennan had a ready answer:

> Though the Commission is limited to informal sanctions—the threat of invoking legal sanctions and other means of coercion, persuasion, and intimidation—the record amply demonstrates that the Commission deliberately set about to achieve the suppression of publications deemed objectionable and succeeded in its aim. We are not the first court to look through forms to the substance and recognize that informal censorship may sufficiently inhibit the circulation of publications to warrant injunctive relief.[243]

Furthermore, the behavior of the Commission was performed under color of state law and the distributors' compliance with the received "directive" could hardly be called voluntary. People do not lightly disregard threats of prosecution from public officials if they do not do as they are told.

But there was another important argument against Rhode Island's procedures that Brennan felt must be discussed. The primary "vice of the system" was that the work of the Commission eliminated in large measure the need for criminal sanctions against distributing the obscene and, hence, the safeguards of the criminal process. Indeed, the Commission's practices provided no protection at all against the suppression of legitimate speech. As proof of this assertion he pointed to the fact that the Attorney General had conceded in oral argument that several of the books condemned by the Commission were not obscene when measured in terms of previous Supreme Court rulings.

What the state had done, in short, was to subject book distributors to a system of censorship, for the Commission was not a judicial body and its decisions did not follow judicial findings that such volumes listed as objectionable might lawfully be banned. Any system of prior restraint must be presumed to be unconstitutional, he felt. He noted that the Court had upheld such a system only in the *Kingsley Books* case where the role of the judiciary was of prime importance in the implementation of the statute there in question. So far as the law at issue in this

[243] *Ibid.*, p. 67.

case was concerned there was no provision whatever for judicial superintendence before notices issued nor even for judicial review of the Commission's findings. The distributor was not even entitled to notice and hearing before his publications were deemed offensive. Such a system of censorship was in clear violation of the Fourteenth Amendment.

But what of the *Times Film* precedent? Justice Brennan's rejoinder to its relevance could be found in a footnote. Adopting Justice Clark's premise that that decision was concerned only with whether the prior restraint of films was necessarily unconstitutional under all circumstances, he went on to mention that the Court in that case did not uphold the constitutionality of any specific such restraint. Furthermore, the holding in *Times Film* was expressly confined to motion pictures.[244]

This attempt to distinguish the embarrassing Chicago case from the controversy at hand clearly leaves much to be desired, but as Brennan had dissented in the former decision he should in no way be blamed for essaying a most difficult task. Obviously, if Clark's initial assumption about the nature of the basic issue in *Times Film* be granted, the Court would certainly have thrown out the Chicago ordinance if it could not have justified the fact that *some element* of censorship of movies was constitutionally valid. If none was permissible then why not strike down the law and dispense with a case-by-case, standard-by-standard approach? Although the statement that *Times Film* was applicable only to movies was certainly one of the chief conclusions reached by the Court, it does nothing to enlighten one as to why censorship of books is less obnoxious than censorship of movies. It merely echoes the talismanic phrase contained in Clark's opinion that each medium of expression presents its own peculiar problems (whatever they are) and may be regulated accordingly.

In a concurring statement of some interest Justice Clark found that Brennan's opinion was not clear enough in advising Rhode Island how it should alter its policies in limiting the distribution of the obscene to conform with due process. He felt that all the majority had really said was that the Commission

<hr>

[244] *Ibid.*, p. 70, footnote 10.

should cease its "thinly veiled threats" against book distributors
and leave such matters to prosecuting attorneys. If so, then the
Court should have been more lucid in saying so and should have
also made clear that there was nothing wrong with the Commission making assessments as to the obscene character of any book
and then furnishing law enforcement officials with their recommendations.

Justice Harlan, in a dissent that reads at times like a concurring opinion, agreed that the Commission had indulged in
"overbearing utterances" and actions that "might tend to give
any person an erroneous impression either as to the extent of the
Commission's authority or the consequences of a failure to heed
its warnings." But he also agreed with Justice Clark that the
majority's "opaque pronouncements" might leave the Commission
in the dark about its constitutional rights which certainly included
reading books to test them for obscenity and then reporting the
conclusions to police officials.

What bothered Harlan more than anything else was the
Court's "broadside attack," which resembled the pleas of the
plaintiff in the *Times Film* case, on the Commission's procedures.
Any affected distributor wishing to stand his ground on a particular publication need only test the Commission's views simply
by refusing to accept its opinions and by awaiting criminal prosecution. In short, so long as the state had placed no roadblocks
in the way of plaintiff's recourse to the courts to test the validity
of the Commission's determinations or so long as the purpose of
the Commission's procedures was not to stifle freedom of expression, then due process had been satisfied. This rule of thumb, he
believed, could even stand up against the claim, conceded to be
accurate, that several distributors had withdrawn books from
circulation out of fear of prosecution. This in spite of the fact
that he himself felt the Commission deserved to be warned to
cease and desist.

Though this assertion was clearly unacceptable to the other
members of the Court, including Justice Clark, the consistency
of thought which marked Harlan's appraisal of the problem at
least saved him from the arduous duty of distinguishing the
*Times Film* precedent. He could see little difference from a con-

stitutional standpoint between Rhode Island's law and Chicago's film censorship ordinance, for the findings of the bureaus created by both could be tested in the courts. If there was any difference at all in the statutes it lay in the fact that the Rhode Island Commission's advisory condemnation of books did not create as great a danger of restraint on expression as that involved in *Times Film,* where exhibition of a film without a license was made a crime.

Nothing is more illustrative of the second-class citizenship motion pictures enjoyed while under the leash of the *Times Film* doctrine than Justice Brennan's remarks in *Bantam Books.* Censorship of books, he had said, when carried out by nonjudicial agencies was to be frowned upon even if its sole purpose was to suppress the obscene. To be sure, the activities of the Commission established by the state legislature were extralegal, but the Court could look behind the superficialities of the matter to see the real pressures being exerted on distributors all over the community. Contrast this vigilance with the Court's refusal to examine the nature of the Chicago film censorship law with *its* total lack of judicial protections. Contrast it further with Brennan's naive assertion that *Times Film* in no way served as a precedent for Rhode Island's policies because movies were movies and books were books.

But what of prior restraints enforced by *judicial* agencies aimed at inhibiting the free flow of written matter? The Court had, of course, opened the door to this type of inhibition in the *Kingsley Books* case but to what extent would states be given a free hand in experimenting with other kinds of in rem procedures aimed at accomplishing a similar purpose? Kansas had on its books a law[245] giving the State Attorney General the power to go before a judge and obtain a warrant allowing him to seize books he believed to be obscene. The judge was under an obligation to issue the necessary warrant if the Attorney General "signed and verified" his allegation. A hearing was to be held at a time not less than ten days after seizure during which the judge was to determine whether the literature might be suppressed and thence destroyed.

[245] *Kan. Gen. Stat.,* Sect. 21-1102.

In the case at hand, however, the Attorney General had listed in his initial complaint fifty-nine specific books he thought ought to be seized and, furthermore, supplied copies of several of these so that the judge might glance them over. Although also not expressly required by the statute, a forty-five minute ex parte inquiry was then held by the magistrate at the conclusion of which he found that "reasonable grounds" existed for believing that all of the materials mentioned in the affidavit (they were all "original Night Stand books") were obscene. He therefore issued a warrant giving the sheriff power to seize these volumes. While only thirty-one of them were later found on plaintiff's property each of these was held to be bannable.[246]

By a margin of seven votes to two, the Court found against the state. Speaking for Justices White, Goldberg, Chief Justice Warren, and himself, Justice Brennan concluded that the procedure leading to the initial seizure order did not adequately safeguard the rights of those whose nonobscene books might be impounded.[247] He carefully distinguished the *Kingsley Books* precedent from the instant dispute. The New York law at issue there merely postponed all injunctive relief abating the initial court order until both sides could state their positions before a judge. Kansas, on the other hand, had been more repressive in its actions because it had seized all copies of particular titles. Thus, any opportunity to circulate these volumes and then raise a claim of nonobscenity by way of defense to a prosecution for doing so was lost. A temporary impounding order of this type could only stem from a formal adversary proceeding. Nor did the fact that a hearing conforming to due process was held shortly after the confiscation save Kansas' enactment because of "the right of the public in a free society to unobstructed circulation of nonobscene books."[248]

[246] A unanimous court had found, of course, that a statute giving a law enforcement officer the right to seize *any* book he thought obscene under the terms of a general warrant issued by a judge was unconstitutional. See *Marcus* v. *Search Warrant*, 367 U. S. 717 (1961). In that case the judge was told only that appellant was suspected of having obscene literature. No titles were enumerated and, of course, no ex parte hearing was held.

[247] *A Quantity of Books* v. *Kansas*, 12 L. Ed. 2d 809 (1964).

[248] *Ibid.*, p. 814.

As might have been expected, the Black-Douglas tandem joined in a concurring opinion which labeled "the burning of these books . . . in plain violation of the unequivocal prohibition of the First Amendment. . . ."[249] Mr. Justice Stewart, however, was willing to join in the majority's judgment in full measure only because he could not find appellant's books to be hard-core pornography. Thus, they could no more be subjected to the Kansas in rem procedure than could the exhibition of *The Lovers* be inhibited by Ohio penal law. While reserving judgment on the seizure of materials which the judge had been unable to "scrutinize," he believed a state could constitutionally impound hard-core pornography that had been screened in an ex parte hearing.

In a carefully drafted dissent, Mr. Justice Harlan, joined by Justice Clark, reiterated his view that a state could proscribe obscenity if "reasonably found in state judicial proceedings to treat with sex in a fundamentally offensive manner."[250] In the case at hand, the judge had not gone too far, he believed, in ruling against appellant. More to the point of Brennan's objections, however, Harlan found it mandatory to compare various kinds of prior restraints. Censorship, to him, involved the matter-of-course prepublication screening of material, which is usually followed by granting a license to that material which meets minimal statutory standards. The original burden is on the citizen to bring the book or movie before a state official. Thus, the state is not compelled to make an initial decision to pursue a course of action. Furthermore, the censor is part of the executive structure while in a criminal proceeding the decision-maker is a judicial agent (judge or juror). In neither case does the censor or the decision-maker have a personal interest in perpetuating censorship. In all of these respects the Kansas law, like the New York in rem procedure sustained in *Kingsley Books,* resembled the operation of a penal rather than a licensing law.

But to see the striking similarity in the two sets of procedures one must descend to the level of the practical. First of all, each required some independent judicial examination of allegedly obscene materials before seizure. Harlan found it of secondary

---

[249] *Ibid.*
[250] *Ibid.*, p. 815.

importance that the judge in the instant case had not held a full-dress hearing at that point nor did he think the First Amendment demanded an inspection of each volume prior to confiscation. Secondly, the police could seize only specifically designated books. Thirdly, each scheme involved some restraint of relevant materials prior to an adversary confrontation. In the case of New York this restraint took the form of a temporary injunction since it was unrealistic to suppose that those accused of possessing obscene literature could prepare a defense in four days, the hiatus between the issuance of the complaint and the application of the injunction. While the Court was uncertain in *Kingsley Books* whether New York could punish someone who distributed a book contrary to this injunction even if the volume was later found to be nonobscene, it could hardly have ignored the fact that a court order would have a stifling effect on the marketability of any such work. Indeed, even bringing a criminal charge might result in a corresponding cessation of distribution during litigation since the accused would perhaps not wish to incur additional penalties if he tried to outguess the court. And, finally, Kansas had shown good faith by moving quickly to establish the obscenity of appellant's books. While the state statute itself lacked the safeguards for speedy disposition found in the New York law, the Court was bound to assume that Kansas would continue to construe its law according to judicially defined restraints.

The *Bantam Books* and *Quantity of Books* judgments, taken together, are of tremendous significance because they show that the Supreme Court will countenance the prior restraint of written material only under the most unusual circumstances. While the *Kingsley Books* opinion had seemed to provide an entering wedge for such action, that decision had been in a few short years distinguished and redistinguished so much that only a law which read like a carbon copy of the New York enactment would seemingly pass constitutional muster. And the censorship of literature by an agency with licensing prerogatives was clearly out of the question.

This discussion serves as an important backdrop to the Supreme Court's latest excursions into the realm of motion picture censorship. Ronald L. Freedman, a Baltimore, Maryland theater owner, refused to submit a movie entitled *Revenge at Daybreak* to the State Board of Censors. While this tribunal went on record as conceding it would have issued the necessary permit, appellant was nonetheless found guilty of exhibiting the picture without obtaining prior approval. The Court of Appeals of Maryland affirmed this conviction.[251]

It is clear that the facts of this case bear a striking resemblance to those of the 1961 *Times Film* judgment. As in that controversy, the constitutional issue hinged not on the nature of the statutory standards set up to guide the censors in their work, but on the more basic question of whether a licensing tribunal could be invested with the authority to pre-screen all movies to be exhibited. Indeed, the highest court of the State of Maryland had patterned its judgment on precisely this supposition when it said that "the Maryland censorship law must be held to be not void on its face. . . ."[252]

Here now was an opportunity for the Supreme Court to strike down *Times Film* and to place state regulatory practices for spoken, written, and filmed speech (at least that shown in movie houses rather than over television) on the same constitutional footing.[253] In fact changes in the makeup of the Court's constituency seemed to assure that this would be done. In the preceding four years two of the five judges who had voted to affirm in the Chicago case had been replaced while the four dissenters remained. Perhaps the choice of Byron White to succeed the ailing Charles E. Whittaker might not be crucial, but surely the retirement of Felix Frankfurter and his replacement by Arthur Goldberg would be. Mr. Justice Goldberg's short tenure on the Court had already provided strong evidence that he was not willing to grant to the states the discretion Justice Frankfurter had in construing civil and political rights set out in the Consti-

[251] 233 Md. 498 (1964).

[252] *Ibid.,* p. 505.

[253] The Court has never specifically included radio and television within the terms of the First and Fourteenth Amendments, but they are protected against state and local censorship policies by federal law. See Paul C. Bartholomew, "Movie Censorship and the Supreme Court," *Michigan State Bar Journal,* August 1961, p. 16, and Note, "Motion Pictures and the First Amendment," *op. cit.,* p. 700.

tution.[254] Or, perhaps the Court would put its final stamp of approval on the *Times Film* doctrine by upholding the Maryland Supreme Court. Faced with this choice of alternatives, however, the Justices proceeded to do neither.

Speaking for a unanimous Court, Mr. Justice Brennan found that appellant's conviction must be overturned.[255] The Maryland court's reliance on *Times Film* had been "misplaced." In that case the only question to be decided was whether censorship of movies was necessarily unconstitutional under all circumstances. But appellant in the instant controversy had been less sweeping in his allegations. His claim, said Brennan, was that the Maryland prior restraint was invalid because the total context of the statutory mechanism indicated that it presented a danger of unduly suppressing protected expression. Nor had appellant, by not submitting his film for licensing, confined himself to challenging only the prepublication feature of the program. The teaching of such cases as *Thornhill, Saia, Hague,* and *Lovell,* Brennan believed, was that a person who could have a permit for the asking might question the entire program of licensing when prosecuted for refusal to procure it. One must never forget, he reminded, that censorship is "always fraught with danger and viewed with suspicion."

But what was it about this restraint's "statutory context" that threatened rights guaranteed by the First Amendment? Under the law, the censorship bureau could take as much time as it desired in examining motion pictures. While the Board was bound to hear all appeals taken from adverse rulings and to dispose of these "promptly," it was the duty of the distributor or exhibitor to initiate any subsequent judicial action. Indeed, no censored movie could be shown until a court had found against the state. These procedures flew in the face of what Brennan believed to be the Court's findings in *Bantam Books, Quantity of Books,* and *Manual Enterprises* v. *Day.* Had the Court now held that movies were entitled to all of the constitutional pro-

[254] Compare Frankfurter's impassioned dissent in *Baker* v. *Carr,* 369 U. S. 186 (1962) with Goldberg's reliance on "one-man, one-vote" in *Reynolds* v. *Sims,* 377 U. S. 533 (1964).

[255] *Freedman* v. *Maryland,* No. 69, October Term, 1964.

tection afforded written matter, this assertion would have followed logically enough. But Brennan was not willing to go this far since under the *Times Film* doctrine it had been decided that "films differ from other forms of expression" and that some type of movie censorship was therefore valid.

What the Court found it necessary to do then was to spell out those procedural safeguards implicit in these aforementioned "book cases" that were so essential that they must also bind movie censors. Brennan was equal to the challenge. First, the burden of proving a movie bannable must rest on these officials and not on the exhibitor. Secondly, only a procedure requiring a judicial pronouncement can "lend an effect of finality to the censor's determination" of unacceptability. In short, the censorship bureau must go to court to obtain a permanent restraining order. And lastly, the entire process should be expeditious so as to avoid long and arduous court entanglements.

Of course, the Court did not mean to tell Maryland how to run its legislative shop. But, hinted Brennan, if it wished to be sure it was inaugurating a constitutionally permissible program, it could use as a model the New York injunctive mechanism upheld in *Kingsley Books*. The only difference between the two, he noted, would be that a board of censors could still be commissioned to check initially on each and every movie before it was exhibited commercially.

Only the irreconcilables, Black and Douglas, found it necessary to take issue with Brennan's arguments. If censors were banned from screening books, religious sermons, and political speeches, what were they doing regulating theater fare? The "full literal meaning" of the First Amendment meant that all forms of speech were on a par and that every kind of prior restraint, including the *Kingsley Books* ilk, was unconstitutional.

A discussion of the *Freedman* case and its future impact on state and local movie censorship policies might well begin by noting an observation of the concurring justices. In a footnote statement that sounds a note of triumph, they declared that the Chicago censorship system, "upheld by the narrowest of margins in *Times Film* . . . ," could not meet one of the criteria set out by the Court in *Freedman* as being constitutionally binding.[256] While Mr. Justice Brennan could answer with some effectiveness that the Court did not uphold *any* of the provisions of the Chicago censorship law in that case, the Black-Douglas observation is not without its utility. The Court might well have taken the facts given to it in *Times Film* and construed them in much the same fashion it had utilized in interpreting the facts given to it in *Freedman;* consequently these same procedural standards would have been old-hat by now. Mr. Justice Brennan's attempts to distinguish the two cases sound a hollow note especially in view of the fact that he concurred in Chief Justice Warren's vehement dissent in the 1961 decision. What has happened, to put it bluntly, is that a new consensus has developed on the Court regarding the means a state can use to censor movies and those Justices whose greater permissiveness was once the order of the day are now more than happy to effectuate a compromise. How else can one square Mr. Justice Harlan's silent concurrence in *Freedman* with his scathing dissent in *Bantam Books* which had explicitly averred the constitutionality of Chicago's procedural guarantees? And, if the Court has not altered its position, why had Brennan in the very same dispute been forced to distinguish the holding in *Times Film* on the grounds that "movies were movies and books were books."

It would be a grave mistake to believe that the *Freedman* decision automatically gives to the motion picture-maker the same constitutional liberties accorded the pamphleteer or book publisher. As already noted, the Supreme Court will allow a state or city to pre-screen all films before their entrance into the "market place" and to reject those that fail to meet minimal standards. Nor does it follow that this power is nugatory because of the judicial supervision guaranteed in *Freedman.* For one thing, it is by no means clear that only obscene films can be

[256] A reading of the entire footnote implies that Justices Black and Douglas believe that the Court is countenancing censorship of movies only for the purpose of isolating obscenity. Thus, in enumerating the safeguards guaranteed by *Freedman* they state that "a prompt judicial determination of obscenity must be assured." There is, however, nothing in Mr. Justice Brennan's opinion to indicate that this might be the case.

suppressed. It is quite conceivable that movies which *incite* to conduct contrary to the public morals or to illegal action may also be censored. It may take years before the Court spells out for the benefit of local officials, no matter what branch of government they represent, how far they may go in restraining movies for these reasons. Of greater practical importance, however, is the fact that a mass of empirical evidence (to be presented in succeeding chapters) shows that most moving pictures are denied licenses because *specific portions* are considered unacceptable usually for reasons of obscenity. The Supreme Court, of course, has confined itself to definitions of obscenity that are grounded on the dominant theme of the presentation. In other words, films can only be banned if the underlying motif *taken as a whole* appeals to salacious instincts. This practice, then, flies in the face of the *Roth* test. Furthermore, censorship bureaus and lower courts have no definitions or guidelines to help them decide what constitutes an obscene word or filmed segment assuming, for the moment, that such items even exist from the standpoint of constitutional law. Of course, procedural due process will be helpful in checking censors, but the point is that difficulties of this sort exist *only* for movies and for no other medium of speech or press.

But these are not the only problems that result from the prepublication licensing of all movies within a particular jurisdiction. A majority of the censorship agencies extant charge a fee for their services. There is nothing in *Freedman* which mitigates this constitutionally suspect inhibition; indeed, Mr. Justice Brennan specifically stated as much at one point in his opinion. Nor can one forget that the Court merely *suggested* that states substitute a version of the New York injunctive approach for their present procedural practices. It is possible that these communities will try other, perhaps more stringent, measures to cope with the Court's pronouncements set out in *Freedman*. If these are contrary to the supreme law it may once again take years before the Supreme Court so decides. Perhaps the Justices will even approve such procedures.[257]

257 See the recent amendments to their censorship laws adopted by the state of Maryland and the city of Chicago discussed in Chapter III, in

But who can say that this decision will be taken under advisement by each of the affected localities? Perhaps only a few will make a good faith attempt to comply. A study of New York State's reaction to the *Freedman* judgment indicates that it is a hazardous business indeed to try to predict how various communities will respond. Shortly after Mr. Justice Brennan's opinion was announced, Charles A. Brind, Counsel for the New York State Education Department which governs movie censorship, stated that:

> (the holding has) no bearing on New York's film censorship procedures. We feel our statutes are fair and adequately provide for fast procedural reviews of films brought before us . . . we intend to continue just as we have in the past.[258]

The Supreme Court, however, thought otherwise. In its most recent foray into this constitutional thicket, it reversed a finding by the New York Court of Appeals that the Danish picture *A Stranger Knocks* could be proscribed because two of its scenes depicted sexual intercourse and, hence, were obscene.[259] This movie had followed the usual statutory path laid out for distributors whose films were denied licenses. After the initial censorship order, an appeal had been lodged with the Board of Regents of the State of New York which was given an unspecified amount of time to inspect the picture and render a verdict. Following an adverse ruling there, a second appeal was taken to the State Supreme Court within the allotted twenty days. In due course, this tribunal found in favor of the appellant, but the censors won a reversal from the state's highest court. The U. S. Supreme Court's binding reprieve did not come until two years after the original request for a permit. This exhausting process must have posed no trouble for the Justices for they reversed per curiam, citing only *Freedman* v. *Maryland*.

In paving the way for the implementation of its ruling, the

---

"Movie Censorship in Maryland," and Chapter IV in "Movie Censorship in Chicago," *infra*.

258 A. H. Weiler, "Movie Censorship Seen in New Light," *The New York Times*, March 3, 1965, p. 35.

259 *Trans-Lux Distributing Corp.* v. *Regents*, No. 314, October Term, 1965.

Court appended the usual order directing the applicable state court to dispose of the controversy in proceedings not inconsistent with its decision. It should not have surprised anyone, therefore, when the New York Court of Appeals, in finalizing this directive, declared the entire state censorship law violative of the Fourteenth Amendment's due process clause. But what was not anticipated was that the Court would specifically say that it was declaring the statute null and void over and above the procedures utilized. To some, this reasoning seems to mean that the law was being invalidated because it was a prior restraint.[260] This plausible interpretation, if valid, would place New York's highest court in direct conflict with the landmark *Times Film* judgment of 1961.

However, another factor of significance in this dispute is that the Board of Regents, shortly after the Supreme Court's *Trans-Lux* decision, had issued a directive speeding up the entire licensing procedure. Under its terms, the Motion Picture Division (the board of censors) would have only five days to consider a picture while the Regents themselves would be given a maximum of seven days to dispose of appeals taken from an adverse Division ruling. If the Regents concurred in the Division's finding, it would have to obtain "forthwith" a court order permanently enjoining the film's exhibition.

It is probable, therefore, that what the New York court was really saying was that these new procedural safeguards were not sufficient because they were not approved by the state legislature. Of course, it is common judicial practice to construe statutes so as to read into them the various attributes of an equitable appeals system and, in the instant case, the Regents seemingly had shown good faith by streamlining the law's enforcement provisions. One might have anticipated that the Court of Appeals would have given due consideration to this shift in policy. By failing to do so, however, an order voiding the entire censorship mechanism was pro forma in implementing the Supreme Court's decision. This interpretation may be open to counterclaim but surely it

[260] John Sibley, "Film Censorship in State is Ended," *The New York Times*, June 11, 1965, pp. 33, 61. No citation is as yet available for this latest New York court opinion.

has more merit than does the presumption that the Court of Appeals is not cognizant of *Times Film.* It will not be surprising if the New York legislature responds, as Maryland and Chicago have done, by providing for motion picture censorship hedged about by more stringent courtroom checks.

It seems to follow inevitably from these several observations that movie censorship tribunals are still—even after the Court's declamations in *Freedman*—key links in the decision-making process, with responsibilities for enforcing the supreme law which will remain a facet of community control for some time to come.

*Chapter III*

# State Censorship of Motion Pictures

Up until the present decade eight states had provided by statute for the creation of censorship boards to judge the acceptability of movies. These were New York, Pennsylvania, Maryland, Ohio, Massachusetts, Virginia, Louisiana, and Kansas. The past ten years, however, have seen state supreme courts declare the film censorship laws of Ohio, Massachusetts, and Pennsylvania unconstitutional in the wake of *Burstyn* v. *Wilson* (1952). Meanwhile, in 1961 the state of Florida inaugurated the first new state movie censorship operation since 1935. The reluctance of Louisiana to enforce its statute and the rather unorthodox procedures of the Florida law, however, make it clear that the only systematic movie censorship programs now in use at the state level are found in New York, Maryland, Virginia, and Kansas.[261] This chapter will, in large measure, be a detailed examination of the censorship mechanisms of these four states.

Three preliminary areas of relevance need to be explored. First of all, the censorship laws of Louisiana and Florida and their enforcement will be diagrammed in general terms even though their practical significance is quite limited. Secondly, the key state supreme court holdings which have upset the movie censorship acts of Ohio, Massachusetts, and Pennsylvania will be reviewed. There is much in these decisions that is revealing about both state movie censorship practices in general and the various constitutional questions inherent in the overall controversy cen-

[261] Letter of December 3, 1962, received from Barbara Scott, attorney for the Motion Picture Association of America. See also Leary and Noall, *op. cit.*, p. 328.

tering around censorship. Thirdly, the questionnaire used to interrogate members of the boards still extant will be examined at some length so that its purposes can be clearly set forth.


## Movie Censorship in Louisiana and Florida

In 1935, the state of Louisiana drafted a statute setting up a state board of censors.[262] This board was to consist of three members appointed by the governor and removable at his discretion when their staggered three-year terms expired. Each board member was to receive compensation of five dollars for each meeting attended plus an extra twenty-five cents for each one thousand feet of film previewed.

Under the terms of this law all movies for which public exhibition was sought were to be previewed. Furthermore, no parish or municipal film censorship was permissible, so that judgments handed down by the state agency could not be altered at the local level. Only movies that were deemed to be of a "moral, educational, or amusing and harmless character" could be approved[263] and the bureau was to issue a certificate for each picture stipulating whether it had been rejected, accepted, or accepted with eliminations. The board was to charge a fee of four dollars per thousand feet of film inspected. Finally, a first offense committed in violation of this act was to be punishable by a fine of from twenty-five to three hundred dollars, while any subsequent misdemeanor could lead to a fine of between three hundred and five hundred dollars.

It can be readily seen that the standards to be used by the Louisiana board for evaluating movies were identical to those set forth in the Ohio law which, of course, had been declared constitutional by the Supreme Court in 1915,[264] but whose very same criteria were rejected by the Court in 1954.[265] There can be little doubt, then, that the guidelines provided in this enactment

---

262 *La. Rev. Stat.*, Sects. 4:301–4:307 (1950).

263 *Ibid.*, Sect. 4:304.

264 *Mutual Film Corporation* v. *Industrial Commission of Ohio*, 236 U. S. 230.

265 *Superior Films, Inc.* v. *Dept. of Education of Ohio*, 346 U. S. 587.

are also unconstitutional under the *Burstyn* doctrine. The question is largely academic, however, because the Louisiana law has never been enforced.[266]

The movie censorship situation in Florida is bizarre indeed. In 1921, that state passed a law empowering the governor to "appoint three competent persons from the state of Florida to be members of the National Board of Review" and prohibiting the commercial exhibition of "any motion picture . . . that has not been approved by the National Board of Review, its appointees or successors or by the State Censorship Board of the State of New York."[267] The National Board of Review is an independent agency operating out of New York City which was employed by motion picture producers from approximately 1910 to 1920 to pre-screen films to be shown commercially in that city. Because it was accused of being too lax, the National Board lost its job as official movie reviewer and, since that time, it has confined its activities mostly to publishing a booklet called *Films in Review* which evaluates movies much as a film critic might. How a governor could ever appoint anyone to the membership of an independent agency with residence in some other state is baffling and it is probable that this power was never exercised.[268]

A second unusual feature of the 1921 law was that it vested power to censor movies within its area of jurisdiction in two out-of-state agencies, namely, another state censorship board and an independent reviewing bureau. No other state has ever passed such a statute in this area of legislation. This sweeping delegation of power led to the downfall of the enactment when a state circuit court in 1937 ruled it in violation of the Florida Constitution.[269] In spite of this holding, the law remained on the books for twenty-four years though, of course, it was entirely without force or effect.

In 1961 Florida passed a new law which substantially amended the old regulations,[270] without, however, clarifying any

[266] Leary and Noall, *op. cit.*, p. 328, footnote 14.

[267] *Fla. Stat.*, Sects. 521.01-.03 (1955).

[268] Interview with Barbara Scott.

[269] *State ex rel. Cummins v. Coleman*, Circ. Ct., 11th Jud. Circ., May 1, 1937.

[270] *Fla. Stat.*, Sects. 521.01-.04 (1962).

of its evident weaknesses. The statute reiterates that it is unlawful to exhibit commercially any movie unless it has been "reviewed and approved by the National Board of Review . . . or licensed by the State Department of Education of the State of New York (the movie censorship agency of that state)." It adds the further stipulation that a film can be shown if it is approved by the Film Estimate Board of National Organizations (the so-called "Green Sheet"). Furthermore, the enactment continues to vest authority in the governor to appoint three members to the National Board of Review.

Some of the enforcement provisions of the new law are worth noting. Under the 1921 enactment any violation was punishable by a fine of up to five hundred dollars or by no more than a six-month jail sentence. The new statute metes out these two penalties *or both* for a first offense. It then goes on to declare any subsequent violation to be a felony punishable by a prison term of up to three years, a fine of up to five thousand dollars, or both. These penalties are extraordinarily harsh when compared with those of other states. The statute also stipulates that a state circuit court has jurisdiction to enjoin the threatened exhibition of any film in violation of the terms of the law upon complaint filed by a state attorney and that a defendant shall be entitled to a trial of the issues within one day after joinder.

The provisions of this law were discussed in detail by the writer with Barbara Scott of the Motion Picture Association of America. In her opinion the statute is simply "absurd." She pointed out that the National Board of Review is practically moribund and that there are countless films released each year that it does not see. Furthermore, neither the National Board nor the "Green Sheet" are in the business of "approving" pictures. Generally they comment upon how worthwhile certain films are, but they are in no sense involved in censorship. Miss Scott also could not understand how the Florida legislature could have enacted such a law when its basic provisions had been voided by a state court more than twenty years earlier. It seemed inconceivable to her that a state could delegate any authority it might have to censor movies to another state or to two private organizations. She made it clear, however, that there was no censorship board

in Florida and that what movie distributors and exhibitors probably did to steer clear of the statute's ambit was to present to
state authorities a certificate of approval from the New York
Board of Regents.

Of course, this system could not have evolved but for the
fact that New York is one of the most important distribution
centers for domestically produced films. New York City is also,
of course, the chief port of entry for foreign movies. Consequently
motion pictures are released there well before they find their way
to Florida. The fact is that the censorship policies of a state situ-
ated in relation to the movie industry as is New York, can reach
well beyond its own borders and, in the ordinary course of events,
have a marked effect on the film fare of out-of-state audiences.
This is largely because the movie industry divides the nation into
multi-state geographical areas for purposes of distribution so that
each of these sectors is serviced by one exchange center. If deletions are ordered by a state censorship board the distributor,
motivated by his natural desire to seek maximum revenue by not
being excluded from this more closely regulated market place,
will simply alter the particular movie as ordered and send it along
to all exhibitors within the total exchange area in its expurgated
condition. Thus, before the demise of the Ohio law West Virginia
and Kentucky saw movies that had been censored in Ohio while
Massachusetts' requirements carried over into Rhode Island,
Vermont, and New Hampshire. Missouri is today entirely depend-
ent upon the decisions of the Kansas State Board of Review because both states are serviced by the same exchange center whose
distributors see no reason why they should take the time and
money to rent purified movies to one state and uncut versions of
the same pictures to another.[271]

### The Voiding of Three State Censorship Laws

Except for adoption of the new Florida film censorship law in
1961, noted above, the last decade has seen a definite retardation
in the activities of state movie prior restraint agencies. This is
largely because several state supreme courts have interpreted

[271] Harris, *op. cit.*, pp. 124-25.

*Burstyn* v. *Wilson* and subsequent Supreme Court per curiam judgments to be binding upon the jurisdiction of censorship agencies within their respective states.

The first of these bureaus to fall by the wayside was the Ohio censorship board. The United States Supreme Court, of course, laid the groundwork for this when in the *Superior Films* case it summarily reversed that agency's banning of the movie *M*. Nonetheless that holding alone did little to alter the decision-making processes of the bureau as could be seen by its subsequent actions with regard to various movies, *e.g.*, its treatment in 1954 of *Son of Sinbad*, where eliminations were ordered because "certain dance scenes have no conceivable purpose except to be sensually stimulating and lust provoking"; of *Mom and Dad*, which it decreed could not be shown unless cuts of a baby being born of Caesarian section and by "natural childbirth" were made; and in its evaluation of *The French Line*, where "obscene movements of body of the dancer . . . accompanying lust-provoking words of her song—all deliberately sexually suggestive," were proscribed.

On appeal, these orders were voided on the ground that in the light of the Supreme Court's judgment in the *M* case the Ohio censorship board could no longer restrain exhibition of any motion picture.[272] Mr. Justice Lamneck's basic contention was that the Supreme Court had invalidated use of the term "sacrilegious" as a standard for gauging the acceptability of films in *Burstyn*, and had reversed the Ohio court's belief that *M* could be suppressed on authority of that precedent. It followed, then, that the guidelines in the Ohio law—"moral, educational, or amusing and harmless character"—were equally invalid. Thus, while he readily admitted that a censorship law based on obscenity might be constitutional, as indicated by Justice Clark in *Burstyn*, he was sure that the criteria set forward in Ohio's enactment rendered the statute unenforceable.

In an interesting dissent, Justice Hart claimed that what the Supreme Court had meant in citing *Burstyn* as a reason for its

---

[272] *R. K. O. Radio Pictures, Inc.* v. *Dept. of Education of Ohio*, 162 Ohio St. 263 (1954).

overturning Ohio's judgment that *M* could be banned was that
*that particular* film did not fall into the class of movies that were
proscribable. The conclusion he drew was that the clarity of the
statute needed to be sharpened accordingly. This, he believed,
still left Ohio enough latitude to censor movies under the present
law if they were found to be obscene and immoral.

The aforementioned Supreme Court holdings also proved to
be the undoing of the highly unique Massachusetts censorship
law. Under the terms of that enactment[273] the mayor of any city
had the power to grant permits for public entertainments on
Sundays provided, however, that such licenses first received clearance from the Massachusetts Commission of Public Safety "as
being in keeping with the character of the day and not inconsistent with its due observance." So far as movies were concerned,
the Commissioner insisted upon pre-screening each film to see
if it was in keeping "with the character" of the Lord's Day. If he
ruled that a film was offensive in some way, then it could not be
shown on that day unless the necessary eliminations were made.
The result was that since motion picture exhibitors could not, for
economic reasons, alter their movies so as to show different versions on different days, the Commissioner of Public Safety's decisions carried over to the other six days of the week as well.

The constitutionality of this enactment was tested before the
Supreme Judicial Court of Massachusetts as a result of the Commissioner's refusal to allow the film *Miss Julie* to be shown on
Sundays. By unanimous vote, this tribunal found the law in question "void on its face as a prior restraint on the freedom of speech
and of the press guaranteed by the First and Fourteenth Amendments."[274] The state's basic assertion was that the Commissioner's
statutory power extended only to his previewing movies to be
shown on the Lord's Day. This, it contended, was a proper exercise of its police power. To this, Mr. Justice Wilkins retorted that
"it is unthinkable that there is a power, absent as to secular days,
to require the submission to advance scrutiny by governmental
authority of newspapers to be published on Sundays, of sermons

---

[273] *Mass. Ann. Laws*, Ch. 136, Sects. 3-4 (1949).
[274] *Brattle Films* v. *Commissioner of Public Safety*, 333 Mass. 58 (1955).

to be preached on Sundays, or public addresses to be made on Sunday."[275]

Several months later, the Supreme Court of Pennsylvania was asked to declare that state's prior restraint law invalid because of the sweep of *Burstyn* and related rulings. This particular enactment empowered the state board of censors to approve films that were "moral and proper" and to disapprove those that were "sacrilegious, obscene, indecent or immoral, or such as tend, in the judgment of the board, to debase or corrupt morals."[276] The Hallmark Production Company had submitted a movie entitled *She Should'a Said No* to the bureau for approval. Evidently the theme of this film centered around the activities of a dope peddler and the manner in which he attempts to entice innocent people in the use and sale of marijuana. It also apparently contained some risqué scenes of sexual behavior by those under the influence of drugs. At any rate, the Pennsylvania board concluded that the picture was "indecent and immoral and . . . tended to debase and corrupt morals."

By a vote of five to one, the state supreme court threw out the entire Pennsylvania law.[277] Speaking for the majority, Chief Justice Stern made a careful review of each Supreme Court judgment that had been rendered in the wake of *Burstyn* v. *Wilson* as

[275] Nimmer has contended that this decision followed necessarily from *Burstyn* v. *Wilson* because vesting a censorship official with the power to determine what movies can be shown consistent with the due observance of the Lord's Day is no different than allowing him to decide what films are sacrilegious. See Nimmer, *op. cit.*, p. 638. However, the argument that the *Brattle Films* holding threatens the constitutional basis underlying the myriad of state and local Sunday closing laws which now place limitations on movies shown on that day is probably dubious given the fact that these statutes are generally of a subsequent punishment nature. In this regard is the Supreme Court's recent ruling in *Braunfeld* v. *Brown*, 366 U. S. 599 (1961). For a complete list of such ordinances as well as other "blue laws" applicable to the showing of motion pictures see *The 1962 International Motion Picture Almanac* (New York: Quigley Publications), pp. 736 ff.

[276] Act of May 15, 1915, P. L. 534, as amended by the Act of May 8, 1929, P. L. 1655; 4 P. S., Sect. 41, *et seq.*

[277] *Hallmark Productions* v. *Carroll*, 384 Pa. 348 (1956).

well as of the conclusions of the supreme courts of Massachusetts and Ohio as each had assessed the constitutionality of the movie censorship laws in its state. He concluded that "there exists a marked difference of viewpoint as to the exact import of the rulings of the Supreme Court." Did the *Burstyn* case mean to strike down all censorship of movies because of the scope of the First Amendment (Massachusetts) or did it mean to void only certain guidelines for judging films as incapable of precise definition (Ohio)? It was his belief that the Court's judgments at least meant that criteria such as "sacrilegious," "prejudicial to the best interests of the people," "moral, educational or amusing or harmless," "immoral," "tend to corrupt morals," and "obscene and immoral" were offensive to the due process clause of the Fourteenth Amendment because of vagueness. That the latter phrase—"obscene and immoral"—was too indefinite to be valid he deduced from the Court's rather slippery per curiam judgment in *Holmby Productions* v. *Vaughn* (the *Moon is Blue* case). Of course, this evaluation was formulated a year prior to *Roth* v. *U. S.* where the Court held that the term "obscene" was clear enough to be used as a legislative standard.

In refusing to license *She Should'a Said No* the board of censors of Pennsylvania had found that that movie was "indecent and immoral" and "tended to debase and corrupt morals." With the exception of the word "indecent" each of the other criteria had already been voided by the Supreme Court. Surely, thought the Chief Justice, the Pennsylvania law could not stand against such overriding evidence. The Supreme Court's ban, he believed, necessarily included the terms "obscene" (not invoked by the bureau in this case) and "indecent," which in his estimation were evidently no less vague than any of the other guidelines that had been utilized.

Mr. Justice Michael Musmanno dissented "at the top of his lungs." To him, *She Should'a Said No* was "a monstrosity of a motion picture" filled with portrayals of immoral sexual conduct resulting from the constant use of habit-forming drugs. The film had been previewed not only by the board of censors but also by several members of the federal and state bureaus of narcotics and by two clergymen. All agreed that it was in the public interest to ban this movie.

In Musmanno's judgment the Supreme Court had on only one occasion struck down even a portion of a prior restraint enactment. This was in the *Burstyn* decision where it had voided the standard "sacrilegious." As each of the other opinions cited by the majority had been delivered per curiam, he could not believe that the highest court of a state should nullify such an important law "only on an inference" as to the motivations for the holdings. Indeed, it was his feeling that in these cases the Supreme Court had examined all films involved in litigation before it and cleared each film because it had been incorrectly proscribed. In summing up, Musmanno found that the Pennsylvania board typically viewed over one thousand pictures a year. In 1953 it had passed on 1144 subjects, rejecting ten of these outright while from thirty-four others it had deleted eighty-four scenes. Each producer, distributor, or exhibitor who felt aggrieved was guaranteed due process because he had a right of appeal to the courts on any censorship board ruling. While Musmanno acknowledged that censorship officials were fallible, this check on their authority more than removed any impediment that could constitutionally block a state from invoking its police power to suppress the obscene, indecent, and immoral.[278]

This decision by the Pennsylvania Supreme Court by no means convinced the state legislature that it should not attempt carefully to regulate commercially exhibited motion pictures. Three years later, it passed by an overwhelming majority what came to be known as the Motion Picture Control Act of 1959. There can be little doubt that one factor leading to the adoption of this law was that two months before, Pennsylvania's highest judicial tribunal, in a ruling of questionable soundness, had voided on grounds of vagueness the 1939 subsequent punishment statute making it a crime to exhibit obscene movies. This judgment had been rendered even though the Supreme Court had, two years earlier, formulated its famous *Roth-Alberts* doctrine freeing such

[278] Justice Musmanno's stirring defense, which is included in this dissent, of movie censorship from a normative standpoint is discussed in Chapter V, in "Should Motion Picture Censorship Be Abolished?" *infra.*

laws from First and Fourteenth Amendment challenge.[279] The Pennsylvania court's decision had had the effect of removing the last statutory barrier aimed at impeding the exhibition of offensive films.

What were the provisions of this new enactment? It provided that any person in the business of exhibiting motion pictures on a commercial basis must register with a newly established Pennsylvania movie screening board. Upon request of this agency, such person was to present to the bureau for inspection any movie he was currently showing. Each registrant was to pay an annual fee of one dollar plus fifty cents for every twelve hundred lineal feet of film examined. The board was given authority to inspect any film which had been shown publicly at least once in Pennsylvania and to disapprove any movie deemed by a majority of its members to be obscene. If a majority was of the opinion that a motion picture was "unsuitable for children," admittance to such films for anyone under seventeen years was to be denied. The act stipulated that a picture was to be ruled obscene "if to the average person applying contemporary community standards its dominant theme, taken as a whole, appeals to prurient interest." A movie was to be judged as "unsuitable for children" if it was obscene or "incites to crime." The latter phrase was defined to include that "which represents or portrays as acceptable conduct or as conduct worthy of emulation the commission of any crime, or the manifesting of contempt for law." The statute excluded from its purview all newsreels or current events films as well as all movies to be shown purely for "educational, charitable, fraternal, family

[279] *Commonwealth* v. *Blumenstein,* 396 Pa. 417 (1959). The nub of Justice Bok's majority statement was his belief that the Supreme Court in the first *Times Film* holding (355 U. S. 35, 1957) had reversed the Chicago censorship board's finding that the movie *The Game of Love* was obscene because it felt the Chicago statutory scheme too arbitrary. It will be recalled that the Supreme Court had rendered a per curiam opinion in that decision, citing only *Alberts* v. *California.* It seems evident that the Supreme Court meant by its ruling that *The Game of Love* was not obscene under the *Alberts* definition, not that the term "obscene," as found in Chicago's law and interpreted by a lower federal court (see 244 F. 2d 432) to cover almost the same ground as the *Roth-Alberts* definition, was void for vagueness. See footnote 219, *supra,* and the relevant analysis of *The Game of Love* holding.

or religious purposes." A record was to be made public of any movie found to be either obscene or unsuitable for children. All judgments rendered by the bureau were to be promptly reexamined by at least two of its members in the presence of any aggrieved registrant lodging an appeal. Further appeals might be taken to appropriate courts. Any violation of this law was to be punishable by a fine of from four hundred dollars to one thousand dollars or a prison term not to exceed six months, or both.[280]

By a slender vote of four to three, the Supreme Court of Pennsylvania supported the claim of the Goldman Theatre Chain and others that a permanent injunction should issue preventing the Pennsylvania State Board of Motion Picture Control from enforcing any of the provisions of this statute and relieving plaintiffs from any obligation to register or otherwise comply with the law. In an opinion that might have been drafted by a Hugo Black or a William O. Douglas, Chief Justice Charles A. Jones found the enactment "invalid on its face" as a violation of several commands of both the United States and Pennsylvania Constitutions.[281] Starting from the premise that "when a restrictive statute is made to operate in the area of individual liberty, the usual presumption supporting legislation is balanced by the preferred place given in our scheme to the great, the indispensable democratic freedoms secured by the First Amendment," the Chief Justice began by at once characterizing the 1959 law as a prior restraint. To be sure, the board could not review a particular film until after a first showing, but at no time during either the inspection or appeal hearings before the bureau was a registrant entitled to introduce any evidence on his own as to the character of the movie or to challenge the standards to be applied in judging it. Furthermore, a person could be punished under the terms of the statute not because he had exhibited an obscene film or one that was unsuitable for children, but simply because he had shown a picture that had been "restrained." While the statement for the majority did not mention that a verdict of guilty on this count probably would have to survive a challenge to the bureau's initial ruling, what obviously rankled the Chief Justice was that

[280] Act of September 17, 1959, P. L. 902; 4 P. S., Sect. 70.1 et seq.
[281] Goldman Theatres v. Dana, 405 Pa. 83 (1961).

the burden of proof rested squarely on the shoulders of the motion picture exhibitor throughout the entire course of proceedings.

Granted that the enactment smacked of movie censorship, the majority still could not invoke the First Amendment to nullify its provisions because of the Supreme Court's *Don Juan* decision. In spite of this holding, however, Chief Justice Jones felt that it in no way limited the scope of Article I, Section 7, of the Pennsylvania Constitution which stated that "the free communication of thoughts and opinions is one of the invaluable rights of man, and any citizen may freely speak, write and print on any subject, being responsible for the abuse of that liberty." This provision, he claimed, was a direct inhibition on all previous restraints and had been promulgated by men well versed in and greatly influenced by Blackstone's anticensorship sentiments.

But the statute ran afoul of a whole host of other constitutional limitations as well, according to the majority opinion. These infirmities might be summarized as follows:

1. Article I, Sections 6 and 9 of the Pennsylvania Constitution guaranteed a trial by jury to anyone accused of violating the criminal law. The distribution of obscene materials was a crime at common law. Yet, under the provisions of the 1959 statute a finding of obscenity was not to be determined by any cross-section of a defendant's peers—as was guaranteed by use of the jury system—but by a three-man censorship board. And, if an exhibitor was arrested for showing a movie contrary to the law's specifications the sole task of a jury would be to determine only if defendant had shown an unauthorized motion picture. It would not be asked whether or not the film itself was obscene or unsuitable for children.

2. The enactment's "defective censorial standards" violated procedural due process of law guaranteed by the Fourteenth Amendment in two important respects. The so-called *Roth* definition of obscenity invoked by the authors of this act had been approved by the Supreme Court only in the context of a criminal proceeding where a jury would have a special aptitude for reflecting the view of the "average person" of the community. As used by any other trier of fact this conception of obscenity was void for vagueness. Secondly, the definition provided for films "inciting to crime," which clearly constituted the major class of movies that those

under seventeen would not be allowed to see, was so broad as to include "a large portion of films depicting historical, including Biblical, events."

3. The fees to be paid to the state control commission were, to the majority, nothing more than a plain attempt to tax the exercise of the right of free speech directly contrary to the constitutional doctrine expressed in *Murdock* v. *Pennsylvania.*

Justices Musmanno, Eagen, and Bell dissented from this holding. Justice Musmanno was especially concerned that Pennsylvania was being deprived of what he felt was its basic right to protect children from deleterious motion pictures. The statute books of every state, he insisted, "glow with special laws shielding tender minds and bodies from inhuman treatment and cruelty, injurious labor conditions, and (harmful) environments." Certainly Pennsylvania, in the light of these precedents, should be allotted maximum flexibility in giving her youth the type of "moral and legal" guidance implicit in this law.

Mr. Justice Eagen, with Justice Bell in agreement, struck hard at other phases of the majority's decision. The 1959 statute was not a previous restraint in its application but a subsequent punishment law, because an exhibitor was not required to submit any film to the board in advance of its commercial presentation. Furthermore, the *Roth-Alberts* doctrine had clearly established that obscenity was not within the ambit of protection of the First Amendment. If this was true then by what logic was it protected by Article I, Section 7 of the Pennsylvania Constitution which differed only in language, but certainly not intent, from the coverage of free speech and press set out in the Bill of Rights. As proof of this assertion, he pointed to the fact that the very men who drafted this Article for the Pennsylvania Constitution in 1790 were fully cognizant of the terms of the national Constitution written three years earlier and, more importantly, of the meaning of the First Amendment which was ratified by Pennsylvania only six months prior to the adoption of the new state constitution.

It was true that the fundamental law of Pennsylvania required a trial by jury in criminal cases. But the statute in question was not a penal law at all. Its purpose was to establish a system of administrative control to the end that obscene movies could not reach the open market. The opinion rendered by the majority could jeopardize the functioning of the many other administrative tribunals that the legislature had seen fit to create. As for the objection that the law contained no provision for a hearing, it was the Court's task to save state statutes, not to strike them down; and the record was replete with instances where courts had construed enactments lacking this guarantee as nevertheless requiring such protection under the principles of due process.[282]

## The Questionnaire

Examination of the relevant statutes and court decisions governing procedures and policies of the eight state and local film censorship agencies under analysis yields only relatively superficial data. Meaningful evaluation of those practices in the light of constitutional limitations declared applicable to them by the Supreme Court necessitates their examination in greater depth. A questionnaire designed to elicit critical information regarding not only each bureau's policies but also its division of labor and the attitudes of its personnel was prepared. The questionnaire, with the exception of minor adjustments necessitated by the statutory idiosyncracies of certain of these boards, needed to be one that could be used in all of the interviews that had been scheduled. Thus, interviewees representing each censorship department would be responding to the same set of questions which, if properly framed, would facilitate "inter-bureau" and "inter-personnel" comparison. Indeed, the use of a "master questionnaire" would seem mandatory if comparative research involving individual decision-making is to be conducted with any rigor.[283]

Much of the explanation of the purposes of each of the questions asked is self-evident and need not be explored in any

[282] This decision is worthy of careful scrutiny because it is the only instance at this writing of a state age classification statute relative to movie exhibitions having been adjudicated in the courts.

[283] The questionnaire may be found in Appendix I. For an interesting discussion of some of the theoretical problems involved in comparative political analysis see Gabriel Almond, "Comparative Analysis of Political Systems," S. J. Eldersveld *et al* (eds.), *Political Behavior* (Glencoe, Ill.: The Free Press, 1956), pp. 34-42.

detail here. Suffice it to say that it was deemed of paramount importance to probe the activities of each board, the movies it has restricted, its decision-making processes (as much as is possible), and its relationship to pressure interests and other censorship bodies. At the individual level an attempt was made to discern something about the censor's background, his opinions about censorship, and his views on and his knowledge of judicial decisions that should affect his responsibilities. Of course, the questionnaire was intended to explore other informational areas as well, but in all cases it was to be hoped that each response, in its most general application, would provide meaningful data about how the censorship board or the interviewee had been performing assigned duties and would afford insight into the personality, knowledgeability, and attitude of each respondent.

Some of the questions need further justification and comment. An example might be Question 5. While it is true that several of the statutes creating censorship bureaus are silent about the matter of "cutting" movies, it is common knowledge, as has been mentioned earlier, that each board requests alterations in far more movies than it suppresses. A distributor will do almost anything rather than be deprived of marketing rights in a large city like Detroit or Chicago or in some state and, of course, a censorship board has little objection to the exhibition of most movies if it can exercise the right of emasculation. Indeed, so few movies are proscribed in toto that I soon came to have no compunction in asking about films that had been banned over the preceding five years. Question 11, which has to do with the number of requested alterations, was found to involve so many that it was felt advisable to slice the number of years to three lest the interviewee feel that he was being "overworked" in excavating too much data. When one is utilizing a questionnaire that takes well over an hour to cover it is best to pace the interview in such a way as not to allow respondent's attention to lag even if it means being satisfied only with basics. Otherwise his "cooperation level" will also begin to rapidly descend.

Questions 8 and 20 are other good instances where deliberate attempts were made to surmount inherent difficulties involved in this kind of interview. At first glance the former (does the board consider banning a movie necessary) seems redundant; why not simply ask how many pictures have been banned recently and what these movies were? The problem is that censorship boards have so often been bombarded with criticism in their banning activities that this is a sensitive area. Question 8, hopefully, lays a foundation for Question 10 and so cushions what otherwise might appear to be a threatening, but necessary, question. With Question 20 (division of votes in restricting a particular film) the problem is one of self-restraint. It would be valuable to know the votes of each board member if they were recorded, but again it would take too much time away from the interview to copy out such data. Furthermore, this is the type of information that a censor might be reluctant to divulge to an outsider. It was deemed important to discover whether such votes could be at all publicized, or if they, as a matter of policy, were kept under lock and key except when passed on to other governmental officials. As can be seen, the wording of the question also carries with it a request from the interviewer to look at such records. The intent, if this was permitted, was to find out by cursory examination to what extent the board was unanimous in its decisions and to make a general assessment of what board members seemed most often to take a minority view.

A final methodological notation might be made, viz., that certain items, such as Question 11, were divided into two parts because it was thought that the entire question, taken together, would be asking too much at one time. Other inquiries, such as Question 14, consist, also, of two smaller interrogations; but with this group it was felt that the two "went together" more appropriately so that they could be read as one, almost without a pause. This is more a matter of phrasing than anything else, but the important consideration constantly kept in mind was to make each question as simplified and as natural, but also as pointed, as possible.

## Movie Censorship in New York State

Motion picture censorship came to the state of New York in 1921 with the creation of a politically appointed commission whose task it was to pre-screen all films prior to their public exhibition.[284] In 1927, this agency was superseded by a statutory scheme[285] which has since remained relatively unchanged.[286] This law vests full authority in a Motion Picture Division which is to be lodged in the State Department of Education to preview each movie to be shown commercially in New York. The idea that movie censorship authority is to be affiliated with, indeed, subordinate to, those who regulate public education within a community is unique. This chain of command is, however, clearly set forth in the statute. The head of the Motion Picture Division is to be appointed by the Board of Regents of the Education Department upon the recommendation of the Commissioner of Education and it is this Board, and not the Division Director, that is allotted the responsibilities of appointing "such officers and employees" as the Division may need, prescribing the powers and duties of these members including those of the Director and fixing their compensation, all upon the recommendation of the Commissioner of Education. Furthermore, the Board of Regents is empowered to hear all appeals from adverse rulings by the Motion Picture Division. The Regents, however, are given the discretion of delegating this duty to a special Regents' subcommittee, the Commissioner of Education, the Deputy Commissioner of Education, or an assistant commissioner of education.

The key provision in the law is Section 122. It states that the Director of the Motion Picture Division shall be in charge of examining all films proposed for commercial presentation and that each such movie shall be granted a license unless such picture "or a part thereof is obscene, indecent, immoral, inhuman, sacrilegious, or is of such a character that its exhibition would tend to corrupt morals or incite to crime." It is also incumbent upon the Director to furnish a written report to a person who has filed for application on behalf of a rejected movie stipulating either the

---

[284] *L. 1921*, Ch. 715.

[285] See *McKinney's Con. Laws of New York*, Education Law, Book 16, Sects. 120-32 (1953).

[286] The only amendments of consequence to be appended were drafted in 1954 and 1961 and are discussed, *infra*.

reasons why the board of censors could not permit a license to issue, or, a description of each rejected part of a film when that movie was not rejected in toto.

As is the case with most movie censorship laws, certain motion pictures of an unusual type are purposely omitted from the sweep of censorship coverage. Thus, so-called "current events films" or newsreels may be exhibited without inspection. Furthermore, the Director is to issue licenses without pre-screening for "every motion picture film of a strictly scientific character intended for use by the learned professions" provided that such films are never to be shown at any public or private place of amusement. Finally, the Director, in his discretion, may issue licenses without the usual previewing for any motion picture "intended solely for educational, charitable or religious purposes" provided that the owner files a statement with the board which includes a description of the movie.

Section 126 of the New York law is important because it commands the Director to collect a fee from each applicant for a permit, ostensibly to finance the overall censorship operation. Up until 1961 the charge had been three dollars for each one thousand feet of any original movie submitted and also included an assessment of two dollars for every additional copy that the picture owner wished to circulate in New York State. A recent amendment to the law, however, has lowered these fees considerably; the board now charges three dollars for an original, plus fifty cents for every one thousand feet of such film, and then goes on to require a payment of three dollars per copy and one dollar for every one thousand feet of each such duplicate. No payment has ever been required for films that may be exhibited without prior inspection.

Two other sections of the statute are of importance. No person or corporation is permitted to exhibit any poster, banner, or other advertising matter in connection with any movie which is "obscene, indecent, immoral, inhuman, sacrilegious or of such a character that its exhibition would tend to corrupt morals or incite to crime." The exhibition of any material of this kind is to be sufficient grounds for the revocation of the license that had been issued for the particular movie involved. Secondly, the Board of Regents is given authority to enforce all of the provisions and purposes of the statute and a violation of any provision of the enactment is to be considered a misdemeanor.

More court cases have resulted from decisions handed down by New York State movie censors than from judgments rendered by censors in Maryland, Virginia, and Kansas combined. For example, it was a 1936 ruling by the Motion Picture Division proscribing the showing of the well-known Czechoslovakian import *Ecstasy* which led the federal courts to pass on the fundamental question of whether this action was constitutionally allowable, given the fact that customs officials operating under federal law had previously allowed the film to enter the country. In answering plaintiff's contention that censorship in this circumstance was an impingement on national control of foreign commerce, a federal district court found that the state statute was a proper exercise of its police power applying equally to both foreign and domestic productions. The court went on to point out that if censorship did not constitute an encroachment on interstate commerce, as Justice McKenna had said it did not in the *Mutual Film Corporation* case of 1915, then certainly the same rule was applicable to foreign commerce.[287]

The courts of New York have, on the other hand, also established certain precedents regarding the right of city officials to censor movies even after they had been cleared by the state board. In 1947, the Division passed a movie entitled *The Outlaw*. When it was announced that a New York City movie house intended to exhibit this picture the Commissioner of Police announced that he would prosecute anyone who showed the film under a section of the New York Penal Code (Section 1140-a) which made the exhibition of an immoral film a crime. As justification for his edict he noted the provision in the censorship law which stated that none of its terms should be construed so as to "relieve any state or local peace officer from the duty otherwise imposed of detecting and prosecuting violations" of state law. In its decision the Supreme Court for New York County accepted

[287] *Eureka Productions* v. *Lehman,* 17 F. Supp. 259 (1936), *affirmed by memo.,* 302 U. S. 634 (1937).

this line of argument[288] and found that these two laws were in no sense inconsistent. The statute authorizing censorship made no mention of taking appeals to the courts, it found, and defendant's proposed action was nothing more than the initiation of such a proceeding. This avenue, then, "is one possible and not unreasonable method of accomplishing the purpose of reviewing this question" as guaranteed by due process. This section of the criminal law was repealed shortly thereafter. Under ordinary circumstances any conflict that exists between the licensing of movies by the New York board and decisions reached by any city censorship bureau must be resolved in favor of the action of the state agency.[289] Thus, local film censorship cannot, as a matter of law, subsist within the state.

The early view taken by the New York courts which, indeed, held sway until the 1950's was that only an arbitrary or capricious ruling by the censorship bureau could be voided by judicial fiat. One of many instances that could be cited to illustrate this position was the adverse judgment rendered by the board which resulted in the banning of *The Naked Truth* in 1928. This film "traces the lives of three young men from boyhood to manhood, and is intended to portray the dangers and results of association with lewd women" by discussing venereal diseases and the effects thereof. Upholding the bureau's ruling that this movie was indecent and obscene, a lower New York court found that there was only a difference of opinion as to the character of the picture and that such questions of fact were for the censorship board to adjudicate.[290] Indeed, the court did not even feel obligated to view the picture to see if the agency's opinion was at all justified.

In an important 1939 decision,[291] the courts upheld the view that the movie *Remous* would tend to corrupt morals but took the important step of seeing the film before assessing the legal questions involved. While the picture merely depicted a wife's infidelity following a crippling accident suffered by her husband,

---

[288] *Hughes Tool Co.* v. *Fielding*, 73 N.Y.S. 2d 98, *affirmed* 75 N.Y.S. 2d 287 (1947), *affirmed* 297 N.Y.S. 2d 1024 (1948).

[289] *Monroe Amusements* v. *Rochester*, 75 N.Y.S. 2d 807 (1947).

[290] *Public Welfare Pictures Corp.* v. *Lord*, 230 N.Y.S. 137 (1928).

[291] *Mayer* v. *Byrne*, 10 N.Y.S. 2d 794 (1939).

and her eventual realization of her wrong-doing—a somewhat pedestrian plot by 1966 standards—the courts agreed that the censors might reasonably have found that the movie, because it portrayed immorality, might corrupt others. To quote the court's evaluation: "Such is not the subject matter for screen display." The courts of New York were, as late as 1947, respectful enough of the board's determinations to concur in its holding that the movie *Amok* was "indecent, immoral, tends to corrupt morals, and tends to incite to crime" simply because "it is understandable . . . that some reviewing bodies would think this film offended, thus, there doubtless is some evidence to sustain the finding. . . ."[292]

Beginning in 1952, however, the Supreme Court of the United States began to intervene directly in the movie censorship policies of both the state board and the New York courts. The first blow, of course, was *Burstyn* v. *Wilson* which voided the use of the term "sacrilegious" as a criterion of acceptability.[293] Two years later the Court overruled the New York Court of Appeals holding that had branded the movie *La Ronde* "immoral" and "tending to corrupt morals."[294] Actually the first "liberalizing" decision handed down by the New York courts might very well have been rendered even if the Supreme Court had not injected itself into the picture.[295] The Motion Picture Division had banned the film *Teenage Menace* on the grounds that it would, if exhibited, "tend to corrupt morals" and "incite to crime." The movie depicted the brief life span of a youth who becomes a drug addict, lives only for the gratification of his need and eventually pays with his life because of his awful mistakes. The courts, first of all, rejected the finding that the movie tended to corrupt morals on the ground that the New York Court of Appeals, in the *La Ronde* case, had construed

[292] *Distinguished Films* v. *Stoddard,* 68 N.Y.S. 2d 737, *appeal denied,* 71 N.Y.S. 2d 728 (1947). The pamphlet *What Shocked the Censors* issued by the American Civil Liberties Union in 1933 is instructive in that it lists many of the cuts demanded by the Motion Picture Division at that time.

[293] 303 N. Y. 242 (1951), *reversed,* 343 U. S. 495 (1952). Yet, this standard still remains in the law having never been formally deleted by the state legislature.

[294] *Commercial Pictures Corp.* v. *Regents,* 305 N. Y. 336 (1952), *reversed* per curiam, 356 U. S. 587 (1954).

[295] *Broadway Angels* v. *Wilson,* 125 N.Y.S. 2d 546 (1953).

this phrase as relevant only to standards of sexual morality, an issue which was of no consequence in this controversy. Nor did *Teenage Menace* incite to crime, for the entire movie did nothing more than portray "a sordid and dismaying picture of mental and physical misery. . . ." In short, there was nothing in the film which could support the allegation that the picture might prompt anyone to emulate the conduct of its main character.

Two more recent decisions reflect clearly the effect of Supreme Court holdings. In 1956 the censorship board refused to license *Mom and Dad* because it showed a human birth. This sequence was believed to be proscribable on the grounds of being "indecent." By this time, of course, the Supreme Court had gone so far as to overrule Kansas' ban on *The Moon is Blue* even though that picture had been found, among other things, to be obscene. In a memorandum holding a lower New York tribunal dismissed the bureau's ruling by noting that a prior restraint of movies could only be constitutionally justified in the rarest of circumstances and that no "heavy burden" of proof had been met by the broad sweep the Motion Picture Division was allotting to the term "indecent."[296]

The second of these holdings revolved around the controversial *Garden of Eden* which was a fictionalized depiction of the activities of the members of a Florida nudist camp. The censorship agency agreed that the film was not obscene because there was no appeal to prurient interest (the *Roth* decision had been handed down a few months earlier), but insisted that it was indecent because it showed nude men and women together even though the movie itself did not include a full exposure of any adult nude body. To buttress its argument, the board pointed to Section 1140-b of the state penal laws making it illegal for men and women to expose their private parts to one another publicly. This provision, it felt, could be properly carried over to the work of the board through the word "indecent." In overriding this train of thought the New York Appeals Court found, by a vote of four to three, that Supreme Court decisions had struck down, either directly or indirectly, all standards contained in the New York law, with the exception of obscenity, that could be used to deny

[296] *Capitol Enterprises, Inc.* v. *Regents*, 149 N.Y.S. 2d 920 (1956).

this particular movie a license.[297] The term "indecent," then, could only survive if its scope was interpreted to cover only that which was obscene. Thus, if *Garden of Eden* was not obscene then it could not be classified as indecent. Furthermore, the court saw no analogy between the criminal law provision aimed at indecent exposure and any movie. After all, it pointed out, to say that picturing criminal behavior is in itself criminal was to "abolish the drama and the novel in one stroke."

On only two occasions since the Supreme Court began to encroach upon state and local movie censorship authority have the courts of New York upheld an agency ruling against a film. The first of these revolved around the *Commercial Pictures* decision by the high Court which had reversed the ban on *La Ronde* because it had been deemed "immoral" and "of such a character that its exhibition would tend to corrupt morals." The state legislature, it will be recalled, had responded to this judgment by amending the censorship statute so as to redefine these two standards. This new provision (Section 122-a) was added in 1954 and stipulated that these two criteria were to be applicable to any movie or part thereof "the dominant purpose or effect of which is erotic or pornographic; or which portrays acts of sexual immorality, perversion, or lewdness, or which expressly or impliedly presents such acts as desirable, acceptable or proper patterns of behavior." It should be noted that this 1954 amendment also defined the phrase "incite to crime" to apply to any motion picture "the dominant purpose or effect of which is to suggest that the commission of criminal acts or contempt for law is profitable, desirable, acceptable, or respectable behavior, or which advocates or teaches the use of, or the methods of use of, narcotics or habit-forming drugs." While the latter provision has never been litigated the New York Court of Appeals, as has been recounted, agreed with the finding of the New York Board of Regents that the movie *Lady Chatterley's Lover* violated the first section of the 1954 alteration in that it depicted adultery as a desirable and acceptable pattern of behavior.[298] The Supreme Court, for the third time in

[297] *Excelsior Pictures Corp.* v. *Regents*, 3 N. Y. 2d 237 (1957).

[298] *Kingsley Pictures* v. *Regents*, 4 N. Y. 2d 349 (1958).

recent years, reversed the New York courts in their assessment of a film by holding that this segment of the law was a clear violation of the First Amendment.[299]

In still another recent opinion of import the New York courts handed down what might be termed the most liberal holding they have drafted to date when one of their number dismissed a finding by the Board of Regents that the movie *The Connection* could not be licensed even though the word "shit" was used with great frequency throughout the production.[300] In a memorandum order, a lower court noted that this word was not used in its usual connotation but as a synonym for narcotics, and that while such slang might be classified as vulgar language its use did not justify the belief that the movie was obscene as had been determined by the Division. Petitioner also challenged, for the first time in a New York court, the fee that he had been forced to pay under Section 126 of the state law. Here he was summarily rebuffed; the court dismissed his claim that this fee was, in fact, a tax by curtly noting that in 1961 the legislature had reduced such assessments so that "we must assume, as of now, that the present charges are fair and reasonable."

As has been described, New York's highest court supported both the Censorship Division and the Board of Regents in its most recent opinion on the subject when it ruled that *A Stranger Knocks* might be denied a license for exhibition in its uncut version. While the United States Supreme Court reversed on procedural grounds,[301] this holding by the New York tribunal shows that courts in the Empire State will probably be loath in future

---

[299] 360 U. S. 648 (1959). Like the word "sacrilegious" this provision of the law still remains on the statute books as a vestigial organ.

[300] *Connection Co.* v. *Regents,* 230 N.Y.S. 2d 103 (1962).

[301] See footnote 259 and the relevant discussion. As of the moment, the impact of this holding has caused a cessation in the licensing of movies by the Division pending corrective legislative action. In the judgment of one noted authority, ". . . there undoubtedly will be efforts made to introduce some sort of legislation at the next session, . . . (but) I doubt very much that . . . (it) will be passed. . . . It is my private understanding that the Board of Regents is not too anxious to have censorship resumed." Letter of October 12, 1965, received from Bosley Crowther, motion picture critic for *The New York Times.*

cases to abet the distributor who desires to market a film which overtly depicts unusually intimate sex acts.

These statutory requirements of the New York law and the trend of thought of the New York courts serve as background for an analysis of an interview obtained in April of 1963 with Mr. Louis Pesce, the Chairman of the Motion Picture Division in charge of movie censorship.[302] First of all, some general impressions—which cannot be captured through the question-answer technique—should be given regarding this interview. Movie censorship is treated with high regard in New York State, and Mr. Pesce's office is plush compared to those of others who were questioned. Furthermore, his salary far exceeds that of anyone in a comparable position in another city or state while his level of knowledge is also of a high order. This is a man not readily susceptible to the dogmatisms which might color a censor's thinking. Indeed, it has been said that the interviewee and the bureau he administers are more cooperative and easier to work with than any other movie censorship group.[303]

The use of interviewing as a substitute for mere "statute reading" is at once justified in this instance by the confession, in response to Questions 9 and 15 (among other items), that only the standard that calls for the banning of the obscene is being enforced today. Thus, even that part of the enactment (Section 122-a passed in 1954) that defines incitement to crime with greater precision than any similar law used by other state and local censorship bureaus, with the exception of Maryland, is of no

[302] See Appendix II for the text of this discussion. This interview might be profitably compared with an enlightening discussion between a well-known movie critic and Dr. Hugh M. Flick, former Director of the New York Censorship Division, which was published in a prominent literary magazine eleven years earlier. See Hollis Alpert, "Talk with a Movie Censor," *Saturday Review*, Nov. 22, 1952, pp. 21, 50-54.

[303] Interview with Barbara Scott. The fact that the chairman must have a mastery of at least one foreign language, a qualification unknown to any other board of censors that was investigated, may reflect the fact that most foreign films enter the country via New York City and that these films cause many difficult problems. See Leary and Noall, *op. cit.*, footnote 18.

force and effect even though it has never been subject to judicial examination.[304]

Yet, what of Mr. Pesce's answer to Question 18? When asked to pinpoint the particular standards that domestic motion pictures violate he unequivocally stated that their biggest infirmity is that they are too violent. This would seem to indicate that the New York board is censoring films for reasons other than their appeal to prurient interest. One must note carefully, however, his answers to Questions 19 and 27, both of which certainly imply that the law as it is now being enforced is too weak to allow the bureau the discretion needed to check movies featuring unusual violence or those that dwell morbidly on terror for its own sake. The point, of course, is that any attempt to determine what this agency is doing in this regard would be conjectural because there is no way of ascertaining, except in exceptional cases, what movies have been banned or altered and, if cut, in what ways this has been done.

Mr. Pesce, in Question 8, went out of his way to defend the Division's policy of not divulging this information unless the licensee either publicizes the facts himself or gives his assent. His argument, boiled down to its basics, is grounded on the judgment that the Board of Regents owes it to the applicant to protect him from disadvantageous economic consequences that might result if inhibiting censorship orders were disclosed. Just how this argument is applicable to movies that are proscribed in toto is not clear since a ban would obviously destroy a distributor's entire market. But over and above this, a more pressing value question looms large. Is it the business of only the distributor or the exhibitor that he must submit to censorship orders or, on the other

---

[304] Though the board certainly has the constitutional power under the doctrine of the second *Times Film* decision to license obscene movies, compare the present state of affairs with the claim made by Dr. Flick in 1952 that the bureau altered motion pictures mostly because of either indecency or immorality (both are no longer utilized as criteria) and that obscenity "is one of the least of our problems" because the Bureau of Customs does not allow such films to enter the country. See Alpert, *op. cit.*, p. 52. It is more than a bare possibility that what the board thought was "indecent" or even "immoral" in 1952 is being called "obscene" in 1966.

hand, is it the public's business when a government official exercises a prior restraint on speech? Whether these orders are constitutional or unconstitutional, good public policy or dubious public policy, it would appear that the interested citizen ought to have the right to know what kinds of decisions these agencies make. Even Mr. Pesce (Question 22) recognized the strength of this contention.

In listening to Mr. Pesce's explanation of the activities of the Censorship Division he directs, it was not difficult to observe his familiarity with *Roth* v. *U. S.* This, of course, should not be surprising, but it is a curious fact that not once during the course of the discussion did he mention the *Don Juan* holding which justifies the very existence of his agency while, without doubt, he could have recited Mr. Justice Brennan's so-called formula for obscenity by heart. It is interesting to see how he attempted to square his concern for the *Roth* standards with the fact that the board cuts certain passages from motion pictures. At first, in answering Question 4, Mr. Pesce pointed with approval to the grant of power contained in Section 122 of the state law as a rationale for such alterations. This, of course, is an accurate statement of the ambit of the statute, but it also leaves the door ajar relative to its constitutionality. Later on, in responding to Questions 9 and 16, he attempted to create a greater discretion for the board than the *Roth* criteria allow by trying to remove motion pictures from the scope of this decision. In any event, such argumentation should leave little doubt that it is no easy thing to use a judicial test that stresses "the dominant theme taken as a whole" to justify the deletion of particularly offensive or obnoxious scenes or dialogue.

A final point of special interest is Mr. Pesce's liberal orientation toward censorship in general. His answer to Question 20, which places him in opposition to the prior restraint of movies shown solely to adults, is a really remarkable example of self-restraint. As an alternative to the present law, he advocated, in his replies to Questions 10, 19 and 20, a two-fold age classification scheme that would work as follows: (1) children could be admitted to certain "safe" films unaccompanied by an adult, but in order to qualify for such status, an exhibitor would have to submit

his product to the board for licensing; (2) children (the maximum age limit is not specified) might be admitted to all other
movies if accompanied by an adult and such fare would be
shown in unexpurgated form subject only to the usual subsequent
punishment rules of the game. Actually, Section 484 of the New
York Penal Code prohibits the admission of boys and girls under
sixteen to any theater where public entertainment is being shown
unless accompanied by a parent or guardian. This law, however,
is rarely enforced and, furthermore, is not at all concerned with
the content of such entertainment but was, on the other hand,
apparently drafted in the hope of providing greater protection
and supervision of minors from the standpoint of personal
safety.[305] In spite of the relatively liberal outlook inherent in this
proposal, however, the enforcement of the New York statute as
it now reads promises to present to both the courts of that state
and the nation many new and basic questions for constitutional
adjudication.

## Movie Censorship in Maryland

Movie censorship came to the state of Maryland in the year
1916.[306] Between that time and the present this statute has been
altered in great detail on two occasions. The first of these occur-
ences was in 1955 when it became necessary for the legislature
to respond to a liberalizing lower state court decision which had
challenged the validity of several of the criteria for censorship
then being administered under the law.[307] The second such alteration grew out of the Supreme Court's *Freedman* holding which,
of course, had had the effect of throwing the entire censorship
operation into a state of turmoil.

The enactment specifies, first of all, that no movie can be
shown for commercial purposes within the state unless it has
been approved by the Maryland State Board of Censors. However,

[305] Note, " 'For Adults Only': The Constitutionality of Governmental Film
Censorship by Age Classification," *Yale Law Journal*, LXIX (1959), 143.
Hereinafter cited as Note, "For Adults Only. . . ."

[306] *Laws of Maryland* 1916, Ch. 209.

[307] This statute can be found in the *Md. Code Ann.*, Article 66A (1957).

it exempts from examination and fee, in terms somewhat more specific than its New York counterpart, any film to be used for noncommercial purposes such as those to be exhibited for purely educational, charitable, fraternal, or religious reasons. The Board is to consist of three citizens of Maryland who are "well qualified by education and experience to act as censors." One member of the group is to serve as Chairman, another Vice-Chairman, and the third is to act as Secretary. All are to be appointed by the Governor with the advice and consent of the State Senate and are to serve three-year terms. If vacancies occur, the Governor is empowered to appoint new members to fill the unexpired terms of their predecessors.

The key provision in this statute is Section 6. It stipulates that the Board is to approve and license such films which are "moral and proper, and shall disapprove such as are obscene, or such as tend, in the judgment of the Board, to debase or corrupt morals or incite to crimes." Prior to 1955 the bureau could also proscribe a movie if it was "sacrilegious, indecent, inhuman or immoral." This change in the scope of the statute was only one of several important alterations drafted in that year. Not only did this amendment provide for the exemption, in the discretion of the censors, of all newsreel films from inspection or fee, but also it carefully defined the three standards which could be used to deny a movie a license—obscenity, corruption of morals, and incitement to crime. This change in the guidelines to be administered by the bureau stemmed from a decision handed down by the Baltimore City Court declaring the entire censorship law void because it contained "no fixed standards by which to interpret what is indecent, obscene and immoral."[308] This case arose out of the Board's refusal to license *The Moon is Blue*. Appellant was able to win a reversal of this ruling in a hearing before the Baltimore tribunal and the Board was unable to take a further appeal into the higher state courts because the 1916 law did not provide for such relief. Thus, the state legislature found it necessary to adopt clarifying definitions for the more controversial

[308] *United Artists Corp.* v. *Maryland State Board of Censors,* Baltimore City Court, Docket 16, Folio 295 (1955).

criteria if these were to be applied to prospective Maryland film fare by the bureau.

The law defines a movie as obscene "when considered as a whole, its calculated purpose or dominant effect is substantially to arouse sexual desires, and if the probability of this effect is so great as to outweigh whatever other merits the film may possess." While this provision was inserted into the Maryland enactment two years prior to *Roth* v. *U. S.* it can readily be seen that it approximates Mr. Justice Brennan's definition of obscenity in that case. The standard focuses on the movie as a whole and its dominant effect. At the same time, however, it runs afoul of Brennan's declaration in the *Jacobellis* holding that an obscene movie must be devoid of ideological or aesthetic value.[309] One might also ponder the question as to whether arousing sexual desires is exactly the same thing as appealing to prurient interest. If, for example, a book was written so as to deal with a love affair largely through the use of the words and style which characterize several of the controversial passages in *Lady Chatterley's Lover*, could it be said to be obscene? It could hardly be denied that the dominant effect of this writing would be to arouse the sexual desires of the average person; but, again, is this an appeal to prurient interest? Apposite to this hypothetical situation is Mr. Justice Brennan's succinct, "sex and obscenity are not synonymous."

The statute goes on to define a film that debases or corrupts morals as one whose "dominant purpose or effect is erotic or pornographic; or if it portrays acts of sexual immorality, lust or lewdness, or if it expressly or impliedly presents such acts as desirable, acceptable or proper patterns of behavior." This provision, of course, is a carbon copy of the first part of Section 122-a of the New York law which had been added to the censorship statute of that state one year earlier. That part of the amendment which calls for the banning of movies which depict certain acts or ideas as proper patterns of conduct is certainly unconstitutional under the *Kingsley Pictures* doctrine and, for this reason, the

---

[309] Compare the definition of obscenity utilized by lower federal courts to ban *The Game of Love* in Chicago relevant to footnote 212, *supra*.

State Attorney General advised the Board in 1959 to discontinue employment of this guideline in its enforcement activities. At the same time, a movie whose dominant purpose is pornographic would be obscene on its face and would, just as evidently, be proscribable. Whether or not a film that contained specific "acts of sexual immorality, lust or lewdness" could be suppressed is, at least, an open question.[310]

Finally, this part of the law defines a movie that incites to crime as one "where the theme or manner of its presentation presents the commission of criminal acts or contempt for law as constituting profitable, desirable, acceptable, respectable or commonly accepted behavior, or if it advocates or teaches the use of, or the methods of use of, narcotics or habit-forming drugs." This section merely reiterates the command of the second half of Section 122-a of the New York censorship law. Indeed, it is fairly evident that both this definition and the one which spells out the meaning of "corruption of morals" were taken directly from the New York enactment, in view of the interaction that Mr. Pesce said existed between his agency and other state boards.

Under the terms of the Maryland statute the Board must keep a record of each movie it examines, noting carefully which were approved, which were rejected and why any film could not qualify for licensing. Furthermore, the Board is required to submit an annual report, in writing, to the Governor. The report, among other things, includes a record of its meetings and a summary of the proceedings at such meetings, a numerical tabulation of films accepted, rejected and altered, a statement of all prosecutions for violations of Article 66A, and a record of all expenses and incomes made in behalf of the Board. Such reports, indeed, are made readily available to the public as a matter of course. On the other hand, these pamphlets do not specify which movies were rejected or altered nor do they attempt to describe objectionable material which was censored.

The schedule of fees to be paid by movie distributors to the Board is somewhat complicated. If a particular picture averages

---

[310] This problem is part of the overall comparison that will be made in the concluding chapter between Supreme Court decisions and state and local laws that provide standards and guidelines for the censorship of movies.

sixteen frames or less for each foot of film the Board is to charge three dollars for each one thousand feet the picture contains as well as one dollar per one thousand feet of every copy. However, a movie that averages more than sixteen frames per foot is to be taxed at the rate of four dollars for every one thousand feet of film, while each copy of such film is to be charged a fee of two dollars per thousand.

Like its New York counterpart, the Maryland statute provides that the use of any poster, banner or other advertisement that is "obscene, indecent, immoral, inhuman, or sacrilegious" to promote any film will be proper grounds for the revocation of any license already granted. Furthermore, a fine of not less than fifty dollars nor more than one hundred dollars or imprisonment for a maximum of thirty days, or both, may be assessed. An interesting peculiarity in this section of the law stipulates that if advertising matter "of such character that its exhibition would tend to corrupt morals or incite to crime" is used in connection with a specific film it will lead to the suppression of that movie; but use of such advertising is not a crime in and of itself. On the other hand, the exhibition of any such matter that "tends to unduly excite or deceive the public" is punishable as a misdemeanor but, curiously, is not grounds for banning any picture being promoted through its use.[311] As is also the case in New York, this statute is to be enforced by the Board itself, which is empowered to make such reasonable rules, consistent with state law, as are necessary to accomplish its purpose. Over and above any penalty to be meted out for displaying offensive advertising matter, the law provides that a person who violates any other provision of the censorship statute is subject to a fine of between twenty-five and fifty dollars. For any subsequent offense a fine of between fifty and one hundred dollars may be levied.

As the result of the revision of 1955, the law clearly specified an appeal process which the distributor was free to pursue. If the Board found it necessary to suppress a movie in toto or to order certain eliminations the person who had made application for a license had the right, first of all, to be given immediate notice of

---

[311] Compare Sections 15 and 21 of Article 66A.

such ruling. If an appeal was lodged the film had to be promptly reviewed in the presence of the claimant by two or more members of the Board. If his contentions were again rejected he was then given the prerogative of appealing first to the local courts and, ultimately, to the highest court in the state.

It was the foregoing appeals procedure that fell in the wake of the *Freedman* decision. The Maryland legislature, however, responded to this reversal with celerity. It passed a law requiring the three-man bureau to pre-screen each film within five days after its submission. If it finds fault with the production under the guidelines previously set out, it has three days in which to bring a complaint before the Baltimore Circuit Court. This tribunal must, in turn, inspect the picture and hold a hearing within five days and reach a decision within two days after this proceeding. In short, a binding order must be issued after, at the most, a fifteen-day interim.[312]

While it is true that the amount of time afforded for an initial judicial determination far exceeds that which circumscribes New York's in rem procedure affirmed in *Kingsley Books,* the Maryland legislature has certainly been more stringent in its enforcement of *Freedman* than has the City Council of Chicago.[313] The new provision also lays down the command, in keeping with the spirit of current Supreme Court doctrine, that "the burden of proving that the film should not be approved and licensed shall rest on the Board." It must be remembered, however, that the courts of Maryland were bound to observe the exhibitor's presumption of innocence in any event given the criteria set out in *Freedman.* Furthermore, the new law in no way alters the standards that censors are to apply to each and every movie before it is afforded the privilege of entry into the "market place."

In 1959 the legislature of the State of Maryland passed another highly novel statute relating to the exhibition of motion pictures. While this enactment is clearly not a prior restraint, the

---

[312] "Arbitrary Movie-Censorship Invalidated by Supreme Court," *Weekly Bulletin* #2232, published by the American Civil Liberties Union, May 10, 1965, p. 2.

[313] Cf. the recent change in the censorship ordinance of that city discussed in Chapter IV in "Movie Censorship in Chicago," *infra.*

fact that it was adopted in a state that already utilizes a systematic film censorship program makes it of great importance to an understanding of the regulation of motion pictures in this particular jurisdiction. This law makes it illegal for anyone to knowingly exhibit a motion picture to a minor under the age of 18 "which for such minor would be: (1) obscene, indecent or immoral or, (2) of such character that its exhibition would tend to debase or corrupt the morals of such minor." Any person found guilty of committing an act contrary to these specifications is subject to a maximum fine of two hundred dollars or a prison term of at most one year, or both fine and imprisonment at the discretion of the court.[314] The terms of this enactment are unique because they require a motion picture exhibitor, under the duress of extraordinarily harsh penalties, to make judgments as to what films would be, for example, indecent or immoral for a minor to view. It will be recalled that the defunct Pennsylvania age classification system set up a board of censors whose job it was to make evaluations of this kind. The latter scheme has been used recently in Chicago and is presently being tried in Atlanta. To impose a responsibility involving such legal niceties in the hands of a movie house owner when so expert a body as the Supreme Court of New York erred in holding *La Ronde* immoral seems to be, at the very least, unreasonable. Such legislation, if properly enforced, will tend to cause exhibitors to decide every close case in favor of censorship for minors and so force the motion picture industry to accept a state-wide curtailment of both attendance and profits as long as the statute is on the books.

Under the appeal procedure set out in the 1955 amendment three cases have found their way to the Maryland Court of Appeals relative to the meaning of the censorship statute. In each instance the Court found against the Board.

The first involved an order issued by the bureau deleting a scene from *The Man With the Golden Arm* which showed in great detail the male lead, a drug addict, preparing an injection of heroin for himself. The elimination covered about two minutes of the film's running time. In its statement before the Court, the

314 *Md. Code Ann.* (Cum. Supp. 1962), Article 27, Sect. 419 B.

Chairman of the censorship agency claimed that the law required this alteration because the deleted portion "teaches the use of, or methods of use of, narcotics or habit-forming drugs." Appellant, on the other hand, argued that if the word "teach" contained in the statute was to be given its ordinary meaning, then the applicable provision of the law was unconstitutional. The Court's position in this dispute[315] was that the key word in this section of the law was "advocates." A movie did not violate this provision unless it "advocates or teaches the use of. . . ." The word "advocates," it stated, must be construed as controlling upon the word "teaches" so that this part of the law did not condemn discussion of a particular theme, but only "teaching with the purpose of inducing or encouraging." Viewed in this light, the proposed elimination was unwarranted because the evidence strongly favored the assumption that the movie, if anything, would deter the use of narcotics.

A second decision, handed down a year later, involved the film *Naked Amazon*.[316] This movie was an attempt to photograph a factual account of the everyday lives of savages living in the heart of Brazil. The Board of Censors held that all scenes in the picture which showed the nude bodies of the primitives below the waist had to be removed even though intimate parts of the body were at no time exposed and the wearing of clothing was an unknown custom among these tribes. The Board based its holding on two grounds. First, those parts of the movie that had been denied approval were obscene because their dominant effect, when contrasted with whatever artistic merits were to be found in such scenes, was to arouse sexual desires. Secondly, it contended that the public would find these excerpts shocking and tending to arouse lustful desires in "irresponsible numbers of people."

The Court of Appeals rejected each of these assertions. The Board, it said, had misread the statute. It had failed to weigh each objectionable scene in relation to the picture as a whole to

---

[315] *United Artists Corp.* v. *Maryland State Board of Censors,* 210 Md. 586 (1956).

[316] *State Board of Censors* v. *Times Film Corp.,* 212 Md. 454 (1957).

determine whether overall worth more than counterbalanced possibly obscene sequences. A determination of obscenity could only be made after the whole purpose and effect of the movie had been assessed. As for the bureau's concern for the irresponsible members of the community, the Court merely noted the Supreme Court's finding in *Butler* v. *Michigan* that the tastes of the immature and unstable could not be made binding on the average person through the censorship of everything that might provoke the thoughts and actions of such unfortunates.

In its most recent holding in the area of movie censorship, the Court of Appeals once again found that the Censor Board had gone too far in eliminating nudity.[317] The picture involved was *Have Figure—Will Travel* which portrayed the story of three girls, two of whom are confirmed nudists, who launch a vacation cruise by boat which takes them from New York to Florida. While the bureau passed several scenes showing naked men and women in nudist camps, it refused to sanction scenes of the nude girls, unclothed above the waist, on shipboard. The censors justified this distinction on the ground that nudity on the ship did not constitute a normal pattern of behavior and that the sole purpose of this portrayal was to arouse the sexual desires of theater-goers. The Court, in unanimously reversing, found that nudity per se was not obscenity no matter what the locale. Mr. Justice Hammond left for another day, however, the question whether such segments could be rejected if "sexual activity or awareness was presented."

It can be seen that the Maryland judiciary has not gone quite so far as New York did in *Trans-Lux,* but that both the *Naked Amazon* decision and the instant case provide it with enough leeway to approve the suppression of highly objectionable scenes and script. It must also be noted that the *Naked Amazon* test stresses a comparison between the movie as a whole and particular segments, whereas the Court's judgment in the *Have Figure* controversy concerned itself with these scenes in and of themselves. These are clearly different approaches to a difficult prob-

[317] *Fanfare Films, Inc.* v. *Motion Picture Censor Board,* 234 Md. 10 (1964).

lem and it must be remembered, as Mr. Pesce so clearly pointed out, that the Supreme Court of the United States has, at this writing, done nothing to encourage the validity of either.

In April of 1963 I arranged for a meeting with Mr. Elwood L. Gebhart, the Executive Assistant to the Motion Picture Censor Board of Maryland. Mr. Gebhart is a professional accountant by training and is not a member of the Board per se. He is, however, in charge of the censorship office, its day-to-day work load, its relations with other agencies of state government, and all records that are kept by the Board.[318]

The first general area for discussion that necessarily arises from an examination of this interview centers around Mr. Gebhart's status vis-à-vis the Maryland Board of Censors. Does the fact that he is not a member of this bureau render the information obtained less valuable than data that might have been gathered if, for example, the Chairman had been interrogated? Clearly, this does not necessarily follow. It is undoubtedly true that his answers to Questions 18 (difficulties in interpreting the standards set out in the state law) and 29 (negative attitudes toward court decisions),[319] for instance, do not reveal important aspects of the decision-making process that might have come to light had he been a Board member. But there is another side of this coin, also. Surely, no member of the Board would have been as candid as Mr. Gebhart was in his answer to Question 17 (disagreements among the censors). Comparisons between the points

[318] See Appendix III for the substance of this interview. One of the difficulties inherent in this kind of project is that there is no way of knowing, in advance, the man (or men) whom it would be of most value to interview in a given community. For the sake of consistency, it would be highly desirable, lacking such data, to talk with officials who are performing like tasks, preferably as chairmen of censorship bureaus. But in setting up appointments with board representatives, an interviewer operates largely at the whim of those he wishes to see. In this case, the Chairman of the Maryland Board was unavailable nor was it possible to talk with other censors. The interview with Mr. Gebhart developed into at least as fruitful a meeting as one could reasonably hope to anticipate.

[319] These numbers, of course, refer to the order of questions asked of respondent and not to the order of items as assembled in the master questionnaire.

of view of the three censors crop up throughout the entire discussion. Furthermore, more cooperation was obtained from Maryland in obtaining the names of movies altered or banned than from any other censorship agency. Whether such assistance could have been obtained from a bureau member is problematical.

Actually, this whole problem is related to the somewhat unique function of movie censorship in Maryland. This agency is the only one examined which employs an executive assistant with responsibilities that even approach those of the interviewee. One of the reasons for this is because Maryland's censors are part-time workers who are often away from their duties; note, for example, respondent's reply to Question 25. The Chairman of the Board (Mr. Mason) lives in a town that is 147 miles from Baltimore so that he rarely is in his office more than twice a week.

Two incidents that occurred while the interview was in progress should highlight this point. The Board had received notification to the effect that the distributor of the Bardot film entitled *Please, Not Now* intended to launch a lawsuit against the agency if a license was not issued at once. In a telephone conversation Mr. Gebhart advised Mr. Mason to let the distributor spend his time and money in court if he wanted to. The nature of this interchange left little doubt that the executive assistant, an officer not mentioned in the relevant Maryland statute, plays a significant role in deciding questions of even this magnitude. In another interesting aside, an exhibitor walked boldly into the censorship office while our conversation was in progress and demanded, as a taxpayer, the right to see how much expense money the Board had allotted to Mr. Mason for traveling to the city where his movie-house was located to check on whether he was showing expurgated movies as ordered by the Board. Again, the decision to give the exhibitor this information was made by Mr. Gebhart.

These instances seemed to be, in fact, only conspicuous examples of a somewhat subdued anarchy that pervaded the censorship office. From comments made by Mr. Gebhart to Mrs. Holland, Mr. Vaughan, and Mrs. Avara (members of the censorship "team") who, on separate occasions, passed through the room where the interview was being conducted it was evident that protests about the Board's decisions were coming from several sources. That Mr. Gebhart's answer to Question 23 calls for a tightening of the state law because of numerous violations seems to justify this conclusion. It can be seen, then, that the number of cases that have reached the Maryland Supreme Court is no criterion by which to measure citizen resistance. The New York Court has decided far more cases than have been adjudicated in Maryland, but the relative lack of stability in the latter state, caused basically by the part-time efforts of a Board lacking in legal expertise until the State Attorney General is consulted (Questions 3, 19, and 25), characterizes a situation which could probably never develop in New York.[320]

This interview proved to be fruitful not only because of the unexpected revelation of how day-to-day powers were wielded by Gebhart especially in the area of line activities, but also because of the frankness with which he was willing to discuss what the Board had been doing and the beliefs of its various members. Mr. Gebhart is an aggressive, opinionated person well suited to be a controlling force in situations in which informality is a byword and the duties of personnel are not clearly defined. He is the sort of man, if indications are reliable, who would sit in on censorship meetings (which he does) because he thought he ought to and not because he had been asked; he has offered numerous suggestions to the Board about policy matters, *e.g.*, how the Maryland law could be revised. Thus, the censorship office is, in

[320] In 1962, however, the Baltimore City Court did decide two controversies dealing with movie censorship. On March 23 it upheld the Board's belief that *The Immoral Mr. Teas* was obscene in that its calculated purpose was to arouse sexual desires. On May 11 it reversed a bureau ruling that two scenes be eliminated from *The Lovers*. The Court found that this film was not obscene, erotic, or pornographic. See *Forty-Sixth Annual Report of the Motion Picture Censor Board of Maryland* (1962), p. 4. Given the fact that no dispute had reached the courts prior to these decisions since the *Naked Amazon* holding, these cases seemed to indicate that a more frequent use of the state judicial appeal system was in the offing. The *Freedman* and *Fanfare* holdings, of course, have vindicated this expectation and many more decisions will probably be forthcoming in the near future as well.

part, what Mr. Gebhart has made it through the exercise of his personality and the free-wheeling discretion inherent in his job. With the exception of basic organizational policies regarding restrictions on particular films, in large measure his decisions are those which seem to affect the bureau's relations with other people. It is obvious that in New York the situation is of a far different order; there Mr. Pesce holds complete control over Board activities.

Mr. Gebhart's reply to Question 37 is of tremendous importance. A reading of the Maryland law certainly implies that all pre-screening is to be done by the Board of Censors, who are to be chosen by the Governor. In point of fact, two underlings in the department have been vested with the authority to preview all movies and to make recommendations to the Board regarding movies *they* think are likely to be objectionable. Only then (according to Gebhart's response to Question 17) will a member of the bureau step in and make a judgment. It is a curious thing indeed that the lower level echelon in this procedure should have to know "film law," while the policy-makers may be hardware dealers and bondswomen by vocational training. While it is perhaps true that rephrasing the final few questions asked of Mr. Gebhart violated the letter of the laws of good empirical research, how was it possible to anticipate the fact that such important decision-makers were at work behind the scenes?

It is of more than passing interest to note the avenues of communication that exist between Maryland and other cities and states as stipulated by Mr. Gebhart. There is a strong link, for instance, between Baltimore and New York while somewhat weaker ties exist between Baltimore, Virginia, and Kansas. But, whereas the bureau can keep in touch with Chicago because its decisions seem always to be challenged in the courts, there appears to be no hook-up with Detroit and Memphis, whose decisions are rarely disputed or, strangely, with Atlanta, whose censorship law was recently voided by the courts.

Mr. Gebhart's comments in regard to Questions 8, 16, and 17 are fascinating. Any scene that shows naked private parts is cut out unless, as was the case with the Academy Award winning

*The Sky Above, the Mud Below,* they are exhibited simply because unclothed natives have been photographed in their natural habitat. One Board member is tough on all nudity simply because of nudity; another Board member is very strict with foreign films such as Ingmar Bergman's *The Virgin Spring* because of her belief that children should not be exposed to items of this type (contra the Supreme Court ruling in *Butler* v. *Michigan*); a third Board member is aggravated by certain kinds of movies that give out too much information on narcotics. It would not be too harsh or unjustified to conclude that the subjectivities of the Board of Censors in Maryland run rampant through the gamut of decisions and that the overall context of a particular movie is often of little consequence. Nor would it be irrelevant to point out that the effect of these subjectivities was compounded by the fact that the Board did not have to justify legally, at the time, any restrictions it wished to place on movies until appeals were filed (note the answers to Questions 3 and 19). To demonstrate the extent and meaning of these procedures it is only necessary to recall Mr. Gebhart's answers to Questions 22 and 26. Clearly movies that feature nudity cause the agency the most difficulty, yet some of these films get through unscathed while others do not. If in deciding what is offensive any member of the Board uses any criteria, other than the extent to which the male or female body is revealed in a particular segment, the interview failed to disclose this.

## Movie Censorship in Virginia

Of all of the motion picture censorship agencies that were examined during this study none has enjoyed greater stability in terms of statutory regulation than the Virginia film bureau. Movie censorship has remained relatively unchanged in the Old Dominion since 1930; it is, indeed, somewhat startling to observe that Supreme Court decisions of recent years have not led to one single change in Virginia law in this area, nor have they even stimulated bringing a single law suit against board officials which would reach into either the federal courts or the Supreme Court of Virginia.

The applicable state law[321] begins by establishing a Division of Motion Picture Censorship in the State Department of Law. This Division is to consist of three censors with equal powers who are to be appointed by the Attorney General from among the citizens of the Commonwealth. These appointees must be "well qualified by education and experience to act as censors" and shall hold office at the pleasure of the appointing official. While the law provides that one of these censors is to serve as Director, to be chosen by the Division itself, the powers and duties of the group are to be exercised under the supervision and control of the Attorney General.

Section 2-105 of the relevant chapter specifies that the Division is to examine each motion picture that desires the right of exhibition for commercial purposes and is to grant an applicant the appropriate permit unless "such film or any part thereof including sub-titles, spoken dialogue, songs, or words or sounds is obscene, indecent, immoral, inhuman, or is of such a character that its exhibition would tend to corrupt morals or incite to crime." If the Division refuses to grant a license for a movie it must furnish the applicant a written report of the reasons for such refusal and a description of each rejected part of a film not rejected in toto. When only two members of the board are available to screen pictures and there is a disagreement between them the deciding vote is to be cast by the Superintendent of Public Instruction.

The Division is given the prerogative of issuing permits without inspection both for films portraying current events and for movies intended solely for educational, charitable, and religious purposes. It is required to pass automatically any picture of a strictly scientific character intended for use by the learned professions if the owner certifies that such movie will not be exhibited commercially.

It is the responsibility of the Division to assess a fee of two dollars for each one thousand feet of original film inspected and,

[321] *Code of Virginia,* Title 2, Ch. 11 (1950). The first statute passed by the state of Virginia relative to movie censorship can be found in the 1922 *Acts of Assembly,* Ch. 257, p. 434.

furthermore, a fee of one dollar is to be collected for each one thousand feet per duplicate that is licensed. A somewhat novel provision in the statute exacts similar payments for current events movies and a fee of fifty cents per permit for each film of a scientific, educational, charitable, or religious nature regardless of whether these are inspected or not. Compensation for the censors, it should be noted, is to be fixed by law, but the amount is not specifically set out in this particular chapter.

The law provides that in the event a movie or some segment of a movie is found to be unacceptable by the board, the applicant has the right of appeal. If appeal is made the picture is to be promptly reexamined in the presence of the applicant by the entire Division; and, if his requests are denied as a consequence of such rehearing, he may as a matter of right lodge a protest with the circuit court of the City of Richmond.

As was true in both New York and Maryland, no person is to exhibit any advertising matter in connection with any film that is "obscene, indecent, immoral, inhuman, sacrilegious or of such a character that its exhibition would tend to corrupt morals or incite to crime." These standards are a carbon copy of the criteria to be used in deciding if a movie itself is censorable, with the exception that the guideline "sacrilegious" is curiously inserted at this level of decision-making. In view of the fact that the Virginia law has never included this criterion as a gauge for assessing movies its use here is indeed difficult to explain.[322]

Once a year the Division is required to file with the Governor a record of its activities. The report is to be printed and distributed as are the reports of the other departments. Such accounts are readily obtainable and while they give a numerical breakdown of films approved, cut or suppressed per year, they do not enu-

---

[322] Section 21 of the Maryland statute, it will be recalled, bans "sacrilegious, indecent, inhuman or immoral" advertising matter but these standards were also used, up until 1955, as criteria for evaluating movies. It can hardly be doubted that in spite of the fact that states exercise greater care in the standards they employ in judging movies as opposed to banners, posters, etc., that it is also unconstitutional to ban sacrilegious or immoral advertising appeals.

merate particular movies nor do they discuss what portions of pictures were unacceptable.

The final specification of interest is a provision for a fine of between twenty-five and fifty dollars to be paid by anyone who commits a first offense contrary to any of the law's commands. Any subsequent offense is to result in a fine of between fifty and one hundred dollars; but it should be noted that the illegal exhibition of any movie or advertising material on any day constitutes a separate offense. Actually, in view of this feature, the schedule of fines is far heavier than one might normally assume to be the case.

Only one legal controversy has ever reached the Supreme Court of Virginia relative to the work of the Motion Picture Division. This dispute occurred in 1940 when the City of Lynchburg banned the movie *The Birth of a Baby* on grounds of obscenity and indecency after this film had been approved by the board. The Court found, on complaint lodged by an exhibitor, that the Virginia censorship statute had preempted the field of motion picture regulation by establishing a uniform set of standards to be used in determining whether movies to be shown commercially in any part of the state met minimal standards. A municipal corporation, being a creature of the state, thus could not pass regulations contravening this general law.[323]

In April of 1963 the writer obtained an interview with Mrs. Lollie Whitehead, Chairman of the Division of Motion Picture Censorship of Virginia, and Mrs. Russell Wagers, another member of the board.[324] At the conclusion of this interview Mrs. Whitehead and Mrs. Wagers extended an invitation to watch them screen a particular movie, entitled *Sin You Sinners*.[325] They had already seen this film once and had voted to suppress it, but

[323] *Lynchburg* v. *Dominion Theaters*, 175 Va. 35 (1940).

[324] See Appendix IV for an account of this meeting.

[325] Mr. Gebhart mentioned this movie as one that was exhibited in Maryland with alterations. Information as to the identity of the producing company was, unfortunately, not available because the credits were flashed on the screen before it was possible to make note of them, and, furthermore, the board will not supply such data.

were previewing it again upon a request of the producer that they cut out only those parts that were clearly objectionable.

The story-line of *Sin You Sinners* ran as follows:

The movie opens with a woman in her early forties doing a striptease routine in a nightclub. She disrobes almost completely and her figure is frontally displayed for the benefit of all viewers. In the next scenes, this woman returns to her home where she is greeted by a younger man who is evidently living with her. They engage in a protracted love scene highlighted by open-mouth kissing. It is soon made apparent that while this man enjoys living off the salary earned by his "partner in sex" and that he further appreciates sleeping with her, his real affections are toward her twenty-year-old daughter who is also living there. The man is continually propositioning this girl but to no avail. She finds him repulsive, mostly because he is a shiftless leach, and, furthermore, wishes her mother would "reform." At this point the daughter's reactions seem real and it is difficult not to pity her surroundings.

The audience then follows the daughter into a drug store where a conversation between some boys watching her makes it clear that she is considered the "choice morsel" of the neighborhood. One of the youths commissions himself to ensnare her. He strikes up a conversation with her and invites her into a building close by. At first she resists but eventually relents. When the other boys show up she realizes that she has been "set up" and flees. In another scene she is pictured walking on the street and being followed by a man whose designs are clear. She escapes only by moments when a bus pulls up to take her to her destination.

In the next several scenes the man with whom her mother is sleeping makes dramatic overtures to her. He dearly loves her, he says, and wants to run away with her. At first she does not believe him but, again, finally relents. They go to a neighboring city where the audience witnesses the girl submit to all her pent-up emotional drives by participating in sexual intercourse with the man. The technique used by the camera during the scene is to picture the girl's face every few minutes as she becomes more and more excited. In between these segments, the audience watches the mother who, at the same time, is disrobing for her patrons. The result is an intermingling of two separate incidents each building to a sexual climax.

The film now moves into its concluding scenes and one receives the impression that the author has become bored with his product. The man leaves the girl and returns to the mother stating that the mother wears a gold medallion around her neck that possesses mystical powers which chain him to her. He further claims that this charm acts as an aphrodisiac upon the woman and it is this which makes her "act" so seductive that audiences are entranced by her.

The girl follows him back to her mother's apartment. Eventually, after some twists and turns in the plot that are more confusing than anything else, the audience sees the mother murdered by another woman who, it seems, has also been sleeping with David (the man). Somehow the gold medal winds up around the neck of the daughter and the film concludes with the girl performing a wild striptease in front of a mixed gathering with David in the arms of still another girl.

There can be little question that, given its third-rate production values, this was not a film issued by any of the well-known Hollywood studios. It evidently was made at very low cost by one of the "fly-by-night" companies that various censors had on many occasions discussed at some length. While it would be unwise to assume that *Sin You Sinners* is typical of the sort of movie which is put out by these small American firms and which meets with censorship problems, nonetheless it would seem that some remarks concerning the movie's standing under the First Amendment are in order.

First of all, did the movie, taken as a whole, have any artistic merit at all? To answer in the negative seems irresistible. As has been pointed out the movie was very cheaply made. The acting was at times comical and was never better than mediocre. The mother is depicted as a robot whose only motive for existence consists in sexual gratification. Her personality is not grounded in reality. The man is interested only in having sexual relations with whomever he can seduce. There is almost no attempt to delve into his standard of values, to explain why he is what he is. His "love" for the girl when viewed against the closing scenes of the movie is clearly only lust.

It is true that at times the daughter's reactions seem real and she evokes pity. The audience is given the impression during some moments that this girl is crying out for love and understanding, but that there is no one to hear her. But when one takes the ending of the film into account this empathy vanishes entirely. It is replaced with a feeling that the early scenes in the film which show the girl fighting against improper advances were devised to whet the audience's appetite for her submission. The presentation of the intercourse scene as described seems to be consistent with this evaluation. Of course, the business of the gold medallion is not only patently absurd, but is also the type of nonsense one finds in hard-core pornography.[326] Logic cannot explain the daughter's "sex dance" that concludes the picture if it is to be assumed that her emotions are genuine and normal.

If this evaluation is accurate, there can be no question but that a jury could reasonably find that the dominant effect of this movie would, to the average person, be nothing more than an appeal to prurient interest. The story and the sequence of events as they unfold in this movie are so foolish, nonsensical, and illogical that it is hard to reach any conclusion other than that they are window-dressing used to set off a series of sex incidents, all arranged in climactic order, so as to titillate prurient interest to the maximum. It would be enlightening to see if the Supreme Court's interpretation of free speech would be broad enough to include a movie like this one.

How does this evaluation compare with comments made by the censors throughout the viewing of this movie? During the opening sequence which showed the mother's various movements while undressing before the nightclub audience, Mrs. Gregory, one of the board members, remarked that all bumps and grinds of the type being shown are invariably deleted because the board

---

[326] Kronhausen, *op. cit.*, pp. 201-3. More typically, a magic potion is the medium which is used to bring on the ultimate in sex urges. The use of the medallion in such circumstances smacks of witchcraft, tribal ceremonies, etc., which are typically thought of as being characterized by strong emotional fervor.

feels they are obscene. As to one of the several scenes showing
David and the mother in the throes of sexual excitement, she
further stated that the bureau doesn't get too much open-mouth
kissing but that these segments, when they occur, are always cut
out. At the conclusion of the showing the consensus was that
this movie would probably have to be banned because if eliminations were made very little would be left to exhibit. Mrs. Gregory's remarks were in no sense atypical of the censors' general
feelings about *Sin You Sinners* and movies like it. From such
statements it is more than apparent that the Virginia board will,
as a rule, order cuts made of certain kinds of scenes not in
accordance with the context in which such action takes place
but because of the nature of the behavior itself. But, of course,
this is to be expected because the relevant state law permits the
expurgation of obscene segments.

Clearly, it is of greater advantage to watch a group of censors
actually inspect a movie and discuss its contents than it is to ask
questions about how they perform their various tasks. Even if the
opportunity to see *Sin You Sinners* with the board had not been
afforded, however, certain statements elicited during the interview cast much doubt on the nature of the criteria the Virginia
bureau are using with which to evaluate motion pictures. A reading of the written statement presented by Mrs. Whitehead in
response to Question 25 is illustrative of how unclear these guidelines are. The first paragraph of her declaration puts the board
on record as operating under the assumption that its basic task is
to protect young people from scenes and script that would tend to
corrupt their morals. In the third paragraph of this statement of
views, however, the board seems to be saying that its censorship
authority can be justified because it proscribes material that is
offensive to the average man. A reading of this declaration, then,
in no way solves the riddle of whether the bureau is using the
*Hicklin* rule or the *Roth* test to discern the audience that must be
contaminated before film segments are deemed objectionable.
Nor does the fact that the censors showed a lack of familiarity
with the "dominant theme" aspect of *Roth* in emasculating *Sin
You Sinners* necessarily mean that the "average man" portion of
Mr. Justice Brennan's formula is also ignored. The reason for

this is simply that the board, in drafting the aforementioned statement, clearly admitted that it never pays the slightest attention to movies as a whole. And, as has been noted, this latter practice is officially countenanced by state law.

This dilemma is further complicated by two other facts. First, the censors, in a procedure for which they have dubious statutory authority, insist that some movies be labeled for "adults only." It is hard to believe that the board would use the "most susceptible audience" portion of the *Hicklin* rule and, at the same time, classify some movies as off limits for juveniles. Yet, the answer to Question 25 seems to lead in this direction. In replying to Question 20 Mrs. Whitehead stated that the bureau only deletes obscenity which its members can readily pinpoint. All evidence, however, runs to the contrary because the response elicited for Question 25 delineates two kinds of film that are especially dangerous to the community: (1) "scenes and script that would tend to be *suggestive and degrading* to the *morals of* . . . young people," and (2) "script and scenes that would be *offensive* to the ordinary person." These definitions of obscenity cannot stand up under the rigorous *Roth-Alberts* test and, consequently, it is hard to believe that any aspect of this formula has as yet reached Richmond.

Yet, it is also possible that the solution to this problem is simplicity itself. If the board thinks a movie would be deleterious to children it might simply forbid this age-group admittance. On the other hand, as Mrs. Gregory indicated in her comments on *Sin You Sinners*, materials that are thought by the censors to be especially noxious may be merely labeled "obscene" and eliminated. In other words, the board may not use a hypothetical audience at all in gauging what it defines as obscenity.

Throughout the entire interview Mrs. Whitehead and Mrs. Wagers reiterated again and again the point that the board of censors receives maximum cooperation from all people it comes in contact with. Responses given to Questions 5 and 9, moreover, indicate that this means that no one attempts to undercut seriously the board's authority. Newspapermen know there are limits to information they can procure, and appeals are never the serious problem they are in New York or Maryland. It is also clear that pressure group requests are never burdensome. Indeed, Mrs. Whitehead stated in answer to Question 9 that all the other censorship agencies are jealous of this cooperation and Mr. Gebhart's remarks about the Virginia program would seem to bear this out. Why should this be so?

In the first place, the Virginia censors are niggardly in the information they allow to be publicized. It is impossible to find out what movies they ban, cut or restrict to adults, what scenes they cut, and why they make the decisions they do. Hopefully, the foregoing analysis will throw some light on the latter point. Secondly, the board is located in the State Department of Law. As Mr. Gebhart intimated, this means that anyone who desires to challenge the bureau in any of its day-to-day decisions will run right into the Attorney General's office, a formidable foe indeed. It also means that the censors receive maximum aid when it is necessary for them to go to court. In this regard, it is interesting to note that in Question 39 Mrs. Whitehead and Mrs. Wagers made no bones about admitting that the local courts rarely reverse a censorship ruling. In the light of what has happened in Maryland and New York such cooperation is indeed a fortuitous circumstance. No important case has ever come before either the Supreme Court of Virginia or any federal court relative to what these censors are doing. Not only does this mean that only sympathetic local courts have adjudicated controversies involving the board, but it also means that there are no records of judicial decisions involving the bureau because opinions handed down by these tribunals are never printed and circulated. It can be seen, therefore, that while Virginia's statutory procedures for review of censorship decisions may be contrary to the *Freedman* holding, there is scant likelihood that closer judicial scrutiny by her courts will play a major role in altering the substance of agency rulings.

One final question requires discussion at this point regarding movie censorship in Virginia. How well qualified to perform this task are these three women? The answers to Questions 25 and 31 as well as the *Sin You Sinners* episode are probably sufficient to justify the conclusion that these officials are not well versed in First Amendment rights which protect motion pictures. Furthermore, each of these women is over seventy years old and while the impact of advanced age is relative, it is hard to believe that these elderly ladies, cordial and affable though they are, constitute what a censorship bureau ought to be if it is to have sound insight into contemporary community standards. Finally, it must be noted that none of these women possesses work experience that at all qualifies her for the work she does. Indeed, it is evident that long association with the Democratic Party in Virginia was certainly one of the important criteria, if not the most essential, used to determine if these women should be given the jobs they now perform.

## Movie Censorship in Kansas

Motion picture censorship was first written into the laws of Kansas as long ago as 1913.[327] Two years later the Supreme Court of the United States, in a four-paragraph opinion that in reality was nothing more than a per curiam adjunct to its famous holding in the *Mutual Film Corporation* decision involving Ohio movie censorship, found this statute to be well within the scope of state legislative authority.[328] Since that time this law has undergone only the slightest of alterations but, as it is written today, it is the only state film censorship enactment whose basic provisions are divided in the statute books between two distinctly different chapters.[329]

Chapter 74, Article 22, states that the Kansas State Board of Review shall consist of three citizens of Kansas "well qualified by education and experience" to act as censors. Each member of the Board is to serve a three-year term and is evidently eligible for reappointment. The Governor, at his pleasure, may remove anyone from the bureau for incompetence or neglect of duty and, in his discretion, may require the Board to present written reports

[327] *L. 1913*, Ch. 294.

[328] *Mutual Film Corp.* v. *Hodges*, 236 U. S. 248 (1915).

[329] The makeup of the censorship board itself is discussed in *Gen. Stats. of Kansas*, Ch. 74, Article 22 (1949). This section as it is now written dates from 1914 (see *L. 1917*, Ch. 308). The nature of the work load delegated to this agency is described in Ch. 51, Sects. 51-101 through 51-114 and reads as it did in 1913.

to him containing such information as he may desire concerning its activities.

It is also the responsibility of the Governor to designate one of the three censors as Chairman and such person shall not only be administrative head of the Board but shall also be responsible for all moneys paid to the Board. The Chairman is to receive a salary of $2400.00 per annum while the other two censors are to be given $2100.00, but this does not include monies to be given to compensate for traveling expenses incurred in the performance of legal obligations.

The key stipulation contained in the applicable portions of Chapter 51 requires the Board of Review to examine, prior to the granting of a license, any film to be commercially exhibited within the state including all subtitles, dialogue, songs, and advertising matter used in connection with such movies, and to approve only those that are moral and proper. If any movie or any type of advertising matter is found to be "cruel, obscene, indecent or immoral" or tends to corrupt or debase morals then a license is not to be issued. However, these standards are to be waived in the case of newsreels; indeed, no examination or approval is to be required for such movies. Furthermore, the Board may, in its discretion, grant special licenses for films of a purely educational, charitable, or religious purpose without charging any fee. Anyone who exhibits an unlicensed motion picture will be found guilty of a misdemeanor and fined a maximum of twenty-five dollars for a first offense and not less than one hundred dollars nor more than five hundred dollars, or be imprisoned for thirty days, for each succeeding offense. Each day an uncensored film is exhibited is to be deemed a separate offense.

As seems to be common practice in states that employ motion picture censorship, the standards used in judging objectionable advertising matter are far different from those used in measuring objectionable movies. Thus, any person who exhibits such matter that is either not licensed or which is "indecent, profane, scandalous, or which tends to unduly excite or deceive the public" is to be punished by a fine of not more than fifty dollars or by imprisonment of not more than thirty days.

The Board of Review is required to keep a record of all

movies it inspects and is to note on these records whether or not particular films were approved and, if not licensed, to specify why permission to exhibit a given film was not granted. If any person wishes to lodge an appeal against a censorship decision he may have redress in the District Court of Wyandotte County.

The final specification of note contained in this enactment imposes a fee not to exceed two dollars to be paid to the bureau for each one thousand feet of film that is granted the right of exhibition in Kansas. This applies to both an original movie and to a copy. Such fees are to be paid monthly into the state treasury and are to be used to pay the salaries and expenses of Board members. The bureau is given the prerogative, if it wishes to use it, to reduce the examination fee if and when such charges are more than sufficient to pay all of the costs that result from carrying out the censorship program.

In addition to the statutory standards utilized by the Board of Review in evaluating pictures, the censors have adopted the following general rules to guide them in their work:

> (1) Pictures shall be clean and wholesome, and all features that tend to debase morals or influence the mind to improper conduct should be eliminated.
>
> (2) Ridicule of any religious sect or peculiar characteristics of any race of people will not be approved.
>
> (3) Evil suggestion in the dress of comedy characters will be eliminated.
>
> (4) Loose conduct between men and women will be eliminated, and whenever possible, barroom scenes and social drinking.
>
> (5) A display of nude human figures will be eliminated.
>
> (6) Crimes and criminal methods, such as give instruction in crime through suggestion, will be eliminated or abbreviated.
>
> (7) Prolonged and passionate love scenes, when suggestive of immorality will be eliminated.[330]

The Supreme Court of Kansas has heard only a handful of cases relative to the powers of the Kansas State Board of Review and, curiously, three of these were a product of the pre-1920's. The first of these involved a petition by film exhibitors objecting to the fact that income derived from the fees collected by the

[330] *The 1962 International Motion Picture Almanac, op. cit.,* p. 734.

bureau so far exceeded the expenses incurred in enforcing the law that the statute was nothing more than a revenue measure in disguise. If so, then the enactment, it was asserted, must be void because it was an undue interference with the flow of interstate commerce and because it violated the Kansas Constitution's stipulation that a revenue bill be identified as such (Article 11, Section 1). The first of these claims was swept aside on authority of the *Mutual Film Corporation* holding which, of course, had denied the applicability of the commerce clause to state movie censorship. As to the second of these claims, the Court reviewed the receipts and expenses of the bureau and found that while there was a clear difference between the intake and outflow of funds (for example, in the period from July 1916, to January 1917, $8700.00 were received while $3600.00 were spent), the discrepancies were not so great that bad faith on the part of the legislature could be inferred, particularly as overhead costs were not included in the latter.[331]

The other two cases involved censorship decisions. In the first of these the State Supreme Court laid down the rule, which was to retain great popularity in all of the states until the *Burstyn* decision, that it would reverse a Board order only when it could be shown that the censors had acted arbitrarily or fraudulently or had clearly overstepped their statutory limitations.[332] The second of these was somewhat unusual in that it involved a ruling compelling the producer of *The Birth of a Nation* to send this movie back to the Board of Review for further inspection after a license had once been granted. Judging from both the Court's opinion and that of a dissenting justice, much public pressure had been brought to bear against the bureau for allowing a permit to issue. A majority was of the feeling that the Board had the power to recall a movie for further inspection and that the presumption was that in so examining the movie the Board would act in good faith. This latter position was in opposition to the views of one dissenting justice who argued that the Board intended to reject the movie entirely because of public pressures

---

[331] *State ex rel. Brewster* v. *Ross,* 166 P. 505 (1917).

[332] *Photo-Play Corp.* v. *Miller,* 102 Kansas 356 (1918).

and that he knew of no legal principle requiring plaintiff to so acquiesce by returning his product to the censors.[333]

Since these early cases the Supreme Court of Kansas has been asked on only one occasion to review an order emanating from the Board of Review. This was, of course, the famous *Holmby* decision of 1955. In this case, as has been previously noted, the state's highest judicial body overruled a lower court holding to the effect that the bureau could not deny a permit to *The Moon is Blue* because of "sex theme throughout, too frank bedroom dialogue: many sexy words; both dialogue and action have sex as their theme."[334] As has been described, the United States Supreme Court, in a per curiam ruling, reversed this judgment citing only the *Burstyn* holding.[335] *Alberts* v. *California* and the now famous *Don Juan* decision have since made it perfectly clear that a community can censor movies if they are obscene. When the *Holmby* ruling was made, however, it could well have been argued that the Supreme Court meant to nullify altogether the use of this criterion in evaluating films, at least in a prior restraint setting.[336] Even the less radical assumption that the Court had merely struck down the use of obscenity in this context because it had been used in conjunction with less acceptable criteria (immorality, tending to corrupt morals, and indecency) and interpreted in an entirely arbitrary manner to proscribe *The Moon is Blue* should have had repercussions in the legislative and censorship chambers of Kansas. What have been the nature of these anticipated repercussions?

During the course of the 1955 Kansas Legislative Session, the State Senate passed a bill relating to registration of motor vehicles belonging to nonresidents. The House concurred in this action, but not before it had attached an amendment to the proposal which abolished the Kansas State Board of Review and, for that matter, motion picture censorship.[337] It seems logical to

[333] *State ex rel. Brewster* v. *Crawford,* 103 Kansas 76 (1918).
[334] See *Holmby Productions* v. *Vaughn,* 177 Kansas 728 (1955) and the relevant discussion of this decision at footnote 152, *supra.*
[335] *Holmby Productions* v. *Vaughn,* 350 U. S. 870 (1955).
[336] See remarks relevant to footnote 158, *supra.*
[337] Senate Bill No. 222, 1955 Kansas Leg. Sess.

assume that this amendment was prompted by the United States Supreme Court's adverse ruling in *Holmby*. In any event, the Senate approved this addition and the bill was sent on to the Governor, who signed the measure. The upshot of this was that a lawsuit was instituted in the form of a declaratory judgment proceeding to determine if this law violated the stipulation contained in Article 2, Section 16 of the Kansas Constitution which states that "no bill shall contain more than one subject, which shall be clearly expressed in the title. . . ." By unanimous vote the Court found that this statute was unconstitutional because it dealt with two clearly unrelated legislative areas of competence.[338]

It might be assumed that in response to this ruling the Kansas Legislature at its very next session would simply pass a law consistent with Article 2, Section 16 that would once and for all do away with movie censorship. The fact of the matter is that the reprieve granted the Kansas censorship statute by the *Shanahan* ruling has proved to be a long-lasting one. The laws of Kansas have not been altered one iota on this subject since 1955. Furthermore, the Supreme Court of Kansas has not rendered any decision during this time, as other courts have done in other states, to check the power of the Board of Review. No cases relative to movie censorship have been appealed to it since 1955.

With this information in mind, attempts were made either to interview in person, or to send a detailed questionnaire to, Mrs. Kitty McMahon, Chairman of the Kansas film censorship bureau. These attempts were rebuffed. Mrs. McMahon declined to participate in an interview or to answer any questions by mail because "most of them (the answers being solicited) are not available for publication."[339] The only information she was willing to volunteer was that the censors have made it a practice since 1959 to try to abide by the terms of the *Roth* decision in their evaluation of all movies. It seems clear, then, that the Board of Review is probably now doing what New York, Maryland, and Virginia are doing; that is, it is enforcing only that criterion which condemns the obscene and is disregarding other standards spelled out in the Kansas statute.

[338] *State ex rel. Fatzer* v. *Shanahan,* 178 Kansas 400 (1955).
[339] Letter of February 4, 1963, received from Mrs. Kitty McMahon.

In an effort to procure a minimum amount of data as to the situation in Kansas, I wrote a letter to Mr. William M. Ferguson, Attorney General of the State, asking whether he might send out copies of reports filed with the Governor relative to the work of the Board of Review. This letter was written with the knowledge that the Governor is granted the statutory power to ask the Board for any information of this type, that the Board, in fact, does file such reports,[340] and that the Attorney General would have ready access to these. This letter was never answered.

While it is almost impossible to generalize about what movie censors are doing in Kansas at the present time without interviewing those engaged in the actual decision-making process, there is still some significant data available from the findings of others that is worthy of comment. There was a time, for example, when the Kansas Board traditionally frowned on all drinking scenes and not merely those which seemed to condone the consumption of alcoholic beverages. Thus, several sequences were eliminated from the Oscar winning *The Lost Weekend*, even though the movie openly condemned addiction to liquor.[341] However, in 1957, censorship officials in Kansas evaluated themselves as being more liberal than their predecessors.[342] While the fact that no cases have reached the Kansas Supreme Court since this claim was made could, at first glance, be used to help verify this assertion, it must be remembered that the work load in the appellate courts of a state is clearly no indication of the censorship that is countenanced. This was found to be true in Virginia, as noted above. As proof of this so-called liberal attitude, it has been noted that in July of 1957 the Kansas Board of Review passed forty-one new movies, banned only one and altered only one.[343]

[340] Leary and Noall, *op. cit.*, footnotes 27 and 49.

[341] *Ibid.*, p. 334. See the fourth censorship criterion listed in the Board of Review's table of general rules discussed earlier.

[342] *Ibid.*, p. 332 and, especially, footnote 47. See other instances of Kansas' censorship practices cited in Murray Schumach, *The Face on the Cutting Room Floor* (New York: William Morrow and Co., 1964), pp. 200, 202.

[343] *Ibid.*, p. 332.

At that rate, however, Kansas would suppress twelve films a year, undoubtedly more than all three of the other states combined.

It would help to cast light on the censorship policies of the Kansas Board if it were known whether this agency is still using the seven-point table of rules described earlier.[344] These criteria are as confining as any delineated in other state or city censorship statutes and at least as vague. Leaving aside constitutional objections, to be discussed in the concluding chapter, a reading of these informal ground rules seems to pose a number of questions concerning definitions which, of course, are in no sense exhaustive:

(1) What are "clean and wholesome" pictures?
(2) What is "loose conduct between men and women?"
(3) What does the phrase "evil suggestion in the dress of comedy" refer to?
(4) When do love scenes begin to suggest immorality?
(5) When does disagreement with stated religious practices become ridicule?

If these criteria were being rigidly applied in Kansas in 1965, the motion picture industry would soon be forced out of business in that state. Even if construed liberally, however, their scope is nebulous and subject entirely to the whims of the individual censor. Since the bureau claims to be using the *Roth* case standards (for better or worse) to measure the element of obscenity in movies, it is probably safe to assume that these other criteria lie dormant along with all the more formal statutory standards save obscenity. Even so, the fact that the use of these guidelines is of recent vintage added to the refusal on the part of bureau members to publicize even the least controversial of their activities seems to lead irresistibly to the assessment made by those perhaps best in a position to know—other censorship boards. It is the Maryland (Question 26) and Virginia (Question 29) censors, then, who have provided what is probably the most enlightening data that is available on the Kansas situation. They maintain that censorship in Kansas is more confining than that found in any other state.

[344] See comments relative to footnotes 330 and 341, *supra*.

# Chapter IV

# Local Censorship of Motion Pictures

It was once believed that as many as ninety cities and towns were involved in one way or another with the censorship of motion pictures.[345] While there is no doubt that this number has decreased appreciably in the wake of liberalizing Supreme Court holdings such as *Burstyn* v. *Wilson* and *Kingsley Pictures* v. *Regents*, the fact is that no one is really quite sure how many localities now censor films in at least some, if not all, circumstances. One authority, for example, has found that in 1954 there were about sixty of these communities ranging from cities as populous as Boston to towns no larger than Winnetka, Illinois and Chester, South Carolina.[346] A more exhaustive study, launched in 1957, concluded that there were actually less than twenty of these localities,[347] while yet a third compilation indicated that the number is really closer to fifty.[348] Of course, it is too early to tell whether the Court's accepting a limited form of film censorship as set forth in the *Don Juan* and *Freedman* rulings will result in either an expansion or contraction of these local agencies.

It follows from these evident discrepancies that there is much disagreement about whether particular cities and towns are, in fact, involved in movie censorship activities and, if so, what is the nature and extent of this involvement. Boston, for instance, has acquired a reputation as a hot-bed of prior restraint.

[345] Leary and Noall, *op. cit.*, p. 382.
[346] Lasker, *op. cit.*, pp. 587-88.
[347] Leary and Noall, *op. cit.*, p. 382.
[348] *The 1962 International Motion Picture Almanac, op. cit.*, pp. 734-36.

Yet, there is no censorship board at work there, nor has a movie encountered any difficulty from law enforcement officers in recent years.[349] In two law review articles published in 1954 one author found that the California cities of Long Beach, Oakland, Pasadena, Palo Alto, San Diego, and Stockton censored movies,[350] while another insisted that only Pasadena utilized such procedures.[351] Lasker has noted that cities such as Tacoma and Oklahoma City are involved in censorship of motion pictures, but a closer examination reveals that the former community has banned only *The Outlaw* in the past ten years while the latter locality has, over the previous twelve year span, limited itself to deleting a scene from an Ingrid Bergman picture.[352] There is much dispute over the activities of censorship authorities in Houston and the procedures they are using.[353] Nor is there any correlation between the extent of film censorship in a community and the frequency or importance of court actions relative to these operations. Two important state court decisions that have been handed down recently emanated from controversies over censorship in Aurora, Illinois and Portland, Oregon, neither of which community is noted for its systematic prior restraint activities.[354] To sum up, it is apparent that the procedures of municipal censors are widely varied, that very few of these censors preview all of the movies being exhibited in their communities, that they concentrate only on those films that are controversial and that such censors consequently serve mostly on a part-time basis and receive minimal compensation if they receive any at all.[355]

[349] Letter of November 5, 1962, received from Mr. Reuben Goodman, counsel for the Massachusetts Civil Liberties Union.

[350] Lasker, *op. cit.*, pp. 590-91.

[351] Harris, *op. cit.*, p. 125, footnote 28.

[352] Helen B. Shaffer, "Censorship of Movies and TV," *Editorial Research Reports*, April 12, 1961, p. 271.

[353] Cf. Nimmer, *op. cit.*, pp. 640-44 with Leary and Noall, *op. cit.*, p. 330, footnote 34.

[354] See *Aurora* v. *Warner Brothers*, 16 Ill. App. 2d 273 (1958) and *Portland* v. *Welch*, 364 P. 2d 1009 (1961). Considering the limitations of court actions in Virginia as a check on the state board, this generalization should hardly be surprising.

[355] Leary and Noall, *op. cit.*, pp. 329-30.

Are there any cities that do censor movies on a day-to-day basis comparable to the tasks performed by the agencies of Kansas, Virginia, Maryland, and New York? To obtain an answer to this question, inquiries were made to the Motion Picture Association of America on the assumption that it would certainly have more data on prior restraint activities at the local level than anyone else. The "Johnston Office" verified that censorship of movies by cities is typically performed "on a very haphazard basis" with censors confining their duties to those situations where "there is public pressure with respect to a particular picture." However, there are four cities, Chicago, Detroit, Memphis, and Atlanta that not only provide for the pre-screening of all movies to be shown within their jurisdictions by vesting censorship powers in local officials, but also receive systematic, day-to-day enforcement of their particular censorship rules.[356] This chapter is a comparative examination of these rules, their implementation, and the attitudes and qualifications of those in charge of making them work.

### Movie Censorship in Chicago

Pursuant to a state law which permits each city and town to "license, tax, regulate or prohibit . . . theatricals and other exhibitions, shows, and amusements; . . . license, tax and regulate all places for eating or amusement,"[357] Chicago inaugurated, in 1907, the first movie censorship ordinance ever passed in this country. While this measure has been amended on various occasions it was not until the year 1961 that its basic provisions, drafted more than forty years earlier, were drastically revamped.

The ordinance, as it read prior to 1961,[358] began by making it unlawful for any person to exhibit publicly any movie without first having secured a permit from the Superintendent of Police. Anyone who violated this provision was to be fined not less than fifty dollars nor more than one hundred dollars for each offense,

---

[356] Letter of December 3, 1962, received from Barbara Scott.
[357] *Ill. Rev. Stat.*, Ch. 24, Sects. 23-54 and 23-57 (1949).
[358] *Rev. Chic. Code*, Sects. 1952-61 (1931).

but each day's illegal showing of a picture was to constitute a separate violation. Before a license was to be granted, the particular film to be shown was to be previewed by the Superintendent of Police (for practical reasons the Superintendent delegated this power to deputies) who was to levy a fee of three dollars for each one thousand feet of film inspected. The Superintendent was instructed, however, to reject any movie for licensing which "is immoral or obscene, or portrays depravity, criminality or lack of virtue of a class of citizens of any race, color, creed or religion and exposes them to contempt, derision or obloquy, or tends to produce a breach of the peace or riots, or purports to represent any hanging, lynching or burning of a human being." If the Commissioner of Police found against a movie company or distributor, the applicant was free to appeal this ruling to the Mayor whose decision was to be binding.

This ordinance also contained the first age classification scheme ever used to limit the attendance of patrons at motion picture houses. The applicable section stipulated that "in all cases where a permit . . . has been refused . . . because the (movie) tends towards creating a harmful impression on the minds of children, where such tendency as to the minds of adults would not exist if exhibited only to persons of mature age, the Commissioner of Police may grant a special permit limiting the exhibition of such picture . . . to persons over the age of twenty-one years; provided such picture or pictures are not of such character as to tend to create contempt or hatred for any class of law abiding citizens."

This ordinance was first tested in the courts through the landmark decision handed down in the case of *Block* v. *Chicago,* a holding which has acquired fame simply because it was the earliest movie censorship controversy ever adjudicated in the courts.[359] Chicago censors had refused to license films entitled *The James Boys* (Jesse and Frank) and *Night Riders* because they were deemed to be immoral. The exhibitor of these films argued before the Supreme Court of Illinois that the ordinance was discriminatory because it did not apply to the legitimate

[359] 239 Ill. 251 (1909).

theater, that it constituted a delegation of legislative power to the Chief of Police, and that it deprived him of his property without due process.

Each of these arguments was swept aside. The law was not discriminatory because it "is not special and contains no discrimination against persons of the same class or engaged in the same business." Legislative power was not improperly given to others as "it has never been questioned that power may be delegated to officers to determine facts, such as whether animals are diseased. . . ." As to the relevance of the Fourteenth Amendment the Court was forceful in pointing out that plaintiff could have no legitimate property interest in immoral or obscene commodities.[360] It was true, of course, that pictures depicting the lives of the James brothers help to describe experiences that are a part of American history but movies that attempt to document such happenings "necessarily portray exhibitions of crime . . . (and) can represent nothing but malicious mischief, arson and murder. (Both these movies) are immoral, and their exhibition would necessarily be attended with evil effects upon youthful spectators" badly in need of protection against such noxious presentations. Six years later, a federal circuit court, on authority of the recently decided *Mutual Film Corporation* decision, upheld the Chicago ordinance against the allegation, not presented in the *Block* appeal, that the enactment was in violation of both the First Amendment and of its counterpart in the Illinois Constitution.[361]

These decisions established firm precedents giving judicial countenance to Chicago's censorship; indeed, it was not until two years after the *Burstyn* ruling that the courts for the very first time held that the bureau had gone too far in banning a motion picture. In the meantime, all attempts to override adverse

[360] McAnany has argued that between the years 1915 and 1952 courts seemed to assume that because moving pictures were not embraced by the First Amendment censorship officials could subject them to any form of prior restraint. Such action, in his view, ignored the fact that the property right to these communications might impede arbitrary control which would result in the destruction of their value. See his remarks at *op. cit.*, p. 430.

[361] *Mutual Film Corp.* v. *Chicago*, 224 F. 101 (1915).

censorship findings were beaten back.[362] The most notable example of decisions of this kind revolved around the picture *Alibi* which had been banned because it portrayed "immorality, criminality and depravity." The film evidently featured an attempted warehouse robbery, the murder of a policeman, the use of third degree methods by other law enforcement officers in reprisal, and "the clever plan used by the gang to establish an alibi. . . ." The overall tendency of this movie, the Supreme Court of Illinois found, was to increase crime and disrespect for both the courts and the law. Such a production, then, was clearly proscribable as a deleterious influence on the minds of youthful spectators.[363]

The only judgment handed down by the courts during this period contrary to a censorship order had to do with the construction of the age classification section of the ordinance. The Chicago board had found that the movie *The Spy,* though not obscene or immoral or in violation of any other statutory standard if shown to adults only, could not be shown to children because "the horrifying nature of the tortures which are portrayed as inflicted upon the hero . . ." made the film immoral in its effect on younger members of the movie-going audience. This holding was reversed by a federal court. It was the court's belief that the age classification section was applicable to movies that were in violation of the standards set out in the law but which the bureau, in its discretion, might allow adults only to view. The "harmful impression on the minds of children," as mentioned in the enactment, the court understood, must be something that would be caused by some forbidden characteristic of the movie as judged by its effect on the entire public.[364]

The first case relative to the work of Chicago's movie censorship program to come before the courts after the decision in *Burstyn* v. *Wilson* involved *The Miracle.* The city censorship board acting under the Superintendent's authority had found that this film was obscene and immoral and refused to issue the

---

[362] Typical instances were *People ex. rel. Guggenheim* v. *Chicago,* 209 Ill. App. 582 (1918) and *Hutchinson* v. *Garrity,* 218 Ill. App. 161 (1920).
[363] *United Artists Corp.* v. *Thompson,* 339 Ill. 595 (1930).
[364] *Fox Film Corp.* v. *Chicago,* 247 F. 231 (1917), *affirmed* 251 F. 883 (1918).

necessary license. In a carefully drafted opinion,[365] Chief Justice Schaefer, of the Illinois Supreme Court, found that if the Post Office Department could censor obscenity under the Comstock Act, then a city might censor obscene movies provided this criterion was defined with precision. He then made a painstaking review of many court rulings in this area and concluded that a motion picture was obscene if its dominant effect, as judged by the average person, was to arouse sexual desires. As for the word "immoral," this must be considered as being little more than a synonym for "obscene." These definitions, he agreed, were considerably narrower than those assigned by the Court in the *Block* and *Thompson* cases; but in the light of Supreme Court rulings such as *Gelling* and *Commercial Pictures* it was evident to him that the First Amendment's guarantees of free press and speech were inconsistent with these outmoded decisions. Under the *Burstyn* rule, he concluded, it was the duty of the courts to pass directly on censorship orders and not merely to presume in favor of such findings as had heretofore been the judiciary's responsibilities in this area. For these reasons the Court ruled it was necessary to remand the controversy back to the trial court for a finding on the question of obscenity.

At this point, however, appellant sought an appeal to the United States Supreme Court on grounds that the Chicago ordinance was void on its face under the *Burstyn* doctrine. The high Court in a per curiam holding dismissed the appeal "for want of a final judgment" by the Illinois courts with Justices Black, Douglas, and Harlan dissenting without comment.[366] It was evident that the majority did not wish to become embroiled in this episode of *The Miracle*'s travails until the Illinois courts had determined if the movie was indeed obscene. The upshot of the matter was that a state district court did find the picture obscene, but that the Appellate Court for the First District reversed, holding that there was nothing in this film which would arouse the sexual desires of the normal individual.[367]

This dispute between the City of Chicago and the American

[365] *American Civil Liberties Union* v. *Chicago*, 3 Ill. 2d 334 (1954).
[366] *American Civil Liberties Union* v. *Chicago*, 348 U. S. 979 (1955).
[367] *American Civil Liberties Union* v. *Chicago*, 13 Ill. App. 2d 278 (1957).

Civil Liberties Union was only a prelude to the many courtroom battles that have been waged in recent years over the scope and meaning of the applicable ordinance. Indeed, Chicago has been involved in more litigation than Detroit, Memphis, and Atlanta combined and, in this sense, it has been the New York State among the cities that use movie censorship. Unlike New York, however, Chicago has been somewhat more successful though, at first, it did not appear that this would be the case.

In the first of these disputes, the city's censorship tribunal, in 1956, attempted to ban *The Game of Love* on the grounds that it was immoral and obscene. While a federal circuit court affirmed the ruling by unanimous vote,[368] the Supreme Court overthrew this judgment in a per curiam opinion citing only *Alberts* v. *California*.[369] The high Court evidently did not share the censors' belief that this French film was obscene. Two years later, the same Circuit Court, now clearly on its guard, threw out a finding that *Mom and Dad*, a picture dealing with venereal disease and sex instruction, was obscene.[370] In 1959, another court was equally hostile towards a censorship order refusing a license to exhibit *Anatomy of a Murder* because the use of the words "rape" and "contraceptive" rendered the production obscene.[371] Under present community standards, it wrote, the use of such terminology was not likely to arouse the salacity of the man in the street. Finally, in 1960, a federal district court voided a censorship ruling that *Garden of Eden* was obscene.[372] This film, which had also gotten into hot water in New York, was a portrayal of life in a nudist camp, but expressly avoided exposing the private parts of adults. Considering its dominant effect on the average person, the purpose of the movie, the court felt, seemed to be merely an espousal of nudist camp life rather than an appeal to the prurient. To find otherwise would be to render obscene countless works of art showing men and women in the nude.

[368] *Times Film Corp.* v. *Chicago*, 244 F. 2d 432 (1957).
[369] *Times Film Corp.* v. *Chicago*, 355 U. S. 35 (1957). See the detailed discussion of this case relevant to footnote 212, *supra*.
[370] *Capitol Enterprises, Inc.* v. *Chicago*, 260 F. 2d 670 (1958).
[371] *Columbia Pictures Corp.* v. *Chicago*, 184 F. Supp. 817 (1959).
[372] *Excelsior Pictures Corp.* v. *Chicago*, 182 F. Supp. 400 (1960).

The only court judgment that has been rendered in favor of a Chicago censorship order in recent years was, indeed, the most recent of these controversies to reach this level of appeal. In this holding a federal district court found that the bureau was perfectly correct in suppressing *The Lovers.* This movie was "presented in a tantalizing increasing tempo which intensifies the sexual desire to its apex . . ." and was "completely centered around and dominated by sexual play and gratification."[373] This holding, of course, antedated the Supreme Court's *Jacobellis* decision by four years and today cannot be considered to be "good law." It was followed shortly by the high Court's now famous opinion in the *Don Juan* case that Chicago's censorship ordinance was not on its face unconstitutional. That dispute, it will be recalled, centered on the issue of whether a movie had to be submitted to the board for licensing regardless of its contents and, hence, did not involve an adverse censorship determination.[374]

Of all of the courtroom conflicts that have arisen over the meaning of the Chicago law, the one that has had the most practical effect on the city's censorship program was handed down in 1959. It concerned the provision of the ordinance dealing with age classification. The censorship bureau had granted an "adults only" license for the exhibition of *Desire Under the Elms* and the Paramount Distributing Corporation had protested. In a highly provocative opinion,[375] Chief Justice Sullivan of the United States District Court began his analysis of this section of the city ordinance by noting that "like any other censorship statute this one must be approached with a caution dictated by the fact that it is a patent invasion of the right to freedom of speech guaranteed by the First Amendment." Counsel for the city had tried to argue that this portion of the enactment gave censors the option of granting a permit allowing only persons over twenty-one to see a movie if they believed such "tends towards creating a harmful impression on the minds of children." This contention, said the

[373] *Zenith International Film Corp.* v. *Chicago,* 183 F. Supp. 623 (1960).
[374] *Times Film Corp.* v. *Chicago,* 365 U. S. 43 (1961).
[375] *Paramount Film Distributing Corp.* v. *Chicago,* 172 F. Supp. 69 (1959).

Chief Justice, was based on an "evident contradiction" because a thing is either obscene or not obscene. None of the criteria set down in the statute can change with the age of the beholder. More to the point, however, he found that such an interpretation rendered the classification standard hopelessly indefinite. The word "tend" implied that the movie might be suppressible for children even if it merely approached the harmful. Furthermore, how could anyone know when a picture tended to have a harmful effect on a child if the word "child" was to apply to everyone below twenty-one? In short, the term "tend" provided an arbitrary standard to be applied in gauging a movie's impact on an arbitrarily designated age group of people ranging from children of four to college men of twenty. By way of dictum, Chief Justice Sullivan also found that this section violated the First Amendment because, even if clearly drawn, it contravened the rule set down in *Butler* v. *Michigan* in that it prevented a twenty-year-old, married serviceman from seeing a picture that might not be suitable for a girl of twelve. Thus, the use of the age limit of twenty-one years, though applicable in determining who might vote, could not be used to decide who might see certain movies.

It was this decision that led to several key changes in the Chicago ordinance; changes which received formal approval in the last week of 1961.[376] For the first time, formal recognition was given to the fact that the Commissioner of Police had delegated censorship authority to subordinate officers in that a Film Review Section was created in the Chicago police department. This Section is to consist of at least six members who are to pre-screen each movie before it is exhibited. At least three appointees are to sit in during each preview and are to recommend in writing to the Superintendent if a permit is to be issued or denied. However, all newsreels were exempted from inspection, licensing, and fee assessment.

While no alterations were made in the standards used in judging the acceptability of films, with the exception of the deletion of the word "immoral" which had become obsolete in the first *A.C.L.U.* opinion, the entire age classification scheme was

[376] *Mun. Code of Chicago,* Ch. 155 (1939 as amended).

revamped. Children were to be prohibited from attending the presentation of any movie that "considered as a whole, has the dominant effect of substantially arousing sexual desires in any person less than seventeen years of age, or if the picture is indecent, or is contrary to contemporary community standards in the description or representation of nudity or sex." In instances of this kind, an "adults only" permit can be issued which is to limit viewing to anyone over sixteen.

Another important change instituted at that time deals with the appeals procedure. Prior to 1961 protests from censorship orders were lodged with the Mayor and then with the courts. The new amendment creates a Motion Picture Appeals Board, consisting of five members appointed by the Mayor. These persons must be experienced or educated in one or more of the following fields: art, drama, literature, philosophy, sociology, psychology, history, music, science, and related fields. Members are to be compensated at the rate of fifty dollars for each meeting attended when the Board sits as an appeals tribunal to hear grievances lodged against censorship edicts. The person seeking a license is given an opportunity to present oral and written testimony at these hearings in support of the movie he wishes to exhibit. The Board is authorized to present its decision in writing. A ruling must be signed by at least three of its members and, if the Film Review Section's decision is upheld, "the ground or grounds upon which the rejection is based shall be stated with particularity, and the part or the parts of the picture which are considered in violation of this ordinance shall be cited. . . ."

At this writing, Chicago is the only city that has responded in meaningful fashion to the Supreme Court's ruling in *Freedman* v. *Maryland*. Under the terms of an amendment passed by the City Council on March 25, 1965, any exhibitor who has been denied a permit by the Film Review Section has seven days in which to lodge a protest with the Appeals Board. He then is given fifteen days to submit the picture for that tribunal's inspection and within another fifteen days must be afforded an opportunity to defend his position. The Appeals Board is obliged to render its judgment within five days after this hearing and, if the Section's initial order is upheld, the Corporation Counsel has ten days in which to obtain a court order perpetually enjoining the film from commercial presentation.[377]

It is possible, then, that under this procedure seven weeks could elapse from the time a license is denied by the censors until a court is given an opportunity to enter the picture. While it is true that the exhibitor himself would be partially to blame for such an extensive time lag, it is clear that this mechanism is far less efficient than the New York injunctive remedy upheld in *Kingsley Books*. One wonders if this amendment constitutes the type of expeditious appeal system the Court had in mind when it drafted *Freedman* and *Trans-Lux*.

In January of 1963 an interview was obtained with Sergeant Robert E. Murphy, police supervisor of the Film Review Section, and his assistant, Patrolman James O'Neill.[378] Before launching a discussion of this conversation it must be understood that one of the immediately discernible differences between Chicago's censorship program and those of the aforementioned four states lies in the scope of the ordinance under which the city's Film Review Section operates. A movie can be proscribed (and this has been the rule since 1907) if it ". . . portrays depravity, criminality, or lack of virtue of a class of citizens of any race, color, creed or religion and exposes them to contempt, derision or obloquy, or tends to produce a breach of the peace or riots, or purports to represent any hanging, lynching or burning of a human being." As has been clearly demonstrated, none of these guidelines are currently in use at the state level. Why then does Chicago use them?

Sergeant Murphy's response to Question 18, as well as the very nature of these standards, seems to provide the answer. Chicago is a city with a history of racial strife. Thus, one of the first considerations of those who drafted this law probably was to prevent movies from being used as a platform for attacking Negroes and, hence, threatening communal disorder. The statute

[377] "Seek Changes in Censor Ordinance," *Chicago Tribune*, March 19, 1965, Sect. 2, p. 7.

[378] See Appendix V.

even goes so far as to exclude hangings, lynchings and burnings of human beings from films (in 1907 such atrocities against Negroes were hardly uncommon), and it is indicative of the intent of those who wrote these criteria into the law that no attempt was made to deny a permit to the movie *Joan of Arc* when that picture arrived in Chicago.[379] Evidently the sort of burning depicted in that movie did not disturb the city fathers.

To what extent are these standards enforced today? The answer given to Question 18 revealed that the Section certainly cuts out dialogue it feels will overly offend the Negro. Even the word "nigger," a commonplace term of derogation known to most school children, is usually removed. Furthermore, Nimmer has reported that Chicago banned the film *Letters from my Windmill* in 1957 because it "exhibited lack of virtue in a class of citizens." The film "depicted a Catholic priest in an undignified and perhaps somewhat derogatory manner." He concludes, with apparent justification, that this was an instance of censorship on grounds of "sacrilege" even though this was not the reason explicitly indicated.[380] Nor is the Sergeant willing to condone only present inhibitions. He feels (Question 20) that the law should be even more rigid in curtailing "reprehensible comments" about race, religion, or ethnic stock. It is clear then that these statutory standards are yet to be entombed.

On an entirely different level, this interview yielded much insight into the qualifications of those who censor movies in Chicago. While Sergeant Murphy's comments about the women who initially screen films were superficial, it is apparent that they are political appointees whose knowledge of First Amendment rights is very much open to suspicion, from his answers to Ques-

[379] Lasker, *op. cit.*, p. 588.

[380] Nimmer, *op. cit.*, p. 637. The fact that a permit was given to this movie a year later did not necessarily soften the impact of the initial censorship order. A film's potential profits can be cut in half by a temporary suppression order. It should be noted, apropos the overall effect of local censorship decisions, that Chicago appears to be the only city whose elimination rulings can alter the motion picture fare of other communities. This, of course, is because Chicago is a film distribution center so that deletions made by the Film Review Section are consequently effective over several of the midwestern states. See Leary and Noall, *op. cit.*, p. 330, footnote 28.

tion 25 concerning the general nature of what is censored, and if what is true in Maryland and Virginia is indicative.

Without doubt, however, the best indication of how censorship manifests itself in this city comes from understanding the capabilities of its two administrators, especially the man in charge. Sergeant Murphy is a policeman and, hopefully, a good one. But how does his training in the Youth Division equip him to supervise film censorship? His responses to Questions 29 and 30 (he was unable to name one judicial standard that the Section might use as a guideline for its work) show a lack of understanding about how the courts can act as checks on the activities of his bureau. There is also little sympathy in his outlook for the motion picture as an instrument for artistic expression and the dissemination of ideas. Thus, movies are characterized as appealing only to juveniles or to maladjusted adults (Question 25). In his reply to Question 28 he opined that much of the press is preoccupied with the rights of a few to the detriment of majority protection. Yet, his answer to Question 25, which is an attempt to rationalize the policies of the bureau, is entirely contrary to standards that have been set up to protect the rights of the average person. Thus, the Film Review Section cuts out any brutality or swearing it thinks excessive because there may be teenagers or "movers" in the audience. These, of course, are only examples of what is censored. As Sergeant Murphy made perfectly clear, Chicago will delete anything that can possibly incite to some action that could lead to immorality. Such a general statement is "void for vagueness" and a clear violation of everything inherent in free speech. Nor, indeed, does there seem to be any statutory authority for either this sweeping regulation or for the deletion of curse words and brutality. It is obvious that *Queen* v. *Hicklin* is in command in Chicago even though the city has a special age classification provision to segregate children from certain kinds of movies. Judging from Sergeant Murphy's knowledge of court standards (Questions 29 and 30) it is apparent that these tests simply are not understood rather than defied with impunity. As for his belief that the courts have dealt fairly with Chicago's program (Question 31) his answer reveals that his opinion is based entirely on the fact that the judiciary has done little to bother the bureau since he was appointed as its overseer three years ago.

It is not necessary to belabor the fact that Sergeant Murphy knew nothing of the work of the Production Code Administration (Question 33), his rather naive belief that his board only licenses movies and does not censor or ban them (Questions 1 and 6), and the obvious inconsistency of his saying that everyone is happy with the work of the board (Questions 23 and 26) while at the same time noting that the law is not nearly tough enough (Question 24) and ignoring the fact that Chicago's censors have been challenged more often in court by recalcitrant distributors than all other cities combined. It is important, however, to note the relationship between the Sergeant and his assistant. Clearly, Patrolman O'Neill is of lower rank but, at the same time, his longer tenure of service with the board coupled with Sergeant Murphy's lack of expertise makes him more than a mere underling in the organizational setup. In relation to Question 7, for instance, one notes that it was O'Neill who knew that the names of suppressed movies cannot be released. In attempting to justify censorship (Question 25) it was O'Neill again who got the ball rolling in defense of the bureau's activities. And, finally, it was he who supplied an answer to Question 39 relative to court cases and Chicago censorship. In this regard, the Patrolman's status is probably somewhat akin to Mr. Gebhart's role in the Maryland movie censorship scheme; his influence in decision-making is not reflected in his formal position of authority because of his superior's lack of experience and preparation.

It is true that the new Motion Picture Appeals Board has already taken some of the wind out of the Film Review Section's sails. Thus, it had, through the date of the interview, reversed eight of twelve censorship holdings that had come to it including the classification of *Phaedra* as an "adults only" film. Question 9 reveals that the Appeals Board has also toned the Section down by effecting an informal agreement regarding certain movies so that Sergeant Murphy's board is not as tough as it once was. It is equally clear (Question 11) that the Sergeant is hardly enthralled with the status quo in this regard.

Regardless of the impact of this "blue ribbon" appeals

body,[381] certain obvious procedural difficulties were inherent in the functioning of Chicago's movie censorship program prior to its most recent revision. These problems were of great significance even though they had little relation to basic First Amendment issues that have been touched on already and will be discussed further in the concluding remarks. The fact is that the entire program was shrouded in secrecy until the Chicago City Council realized that the *Freedman-Trans-Lux* doctrine necessitated fundamental alteration. The data presented in the interview with Sergeant Murphy and Patrolman O'Neill demonstrate that it was impossible to find out anything about what had been suppressed and why, what had been eliminated and why, how the censors voted, what movies had been restricted to adults, etc. Somehow the whole business was even more odious because it was being administered by the Police Department. While this interview provides much evidence to establish the presumption that these people lack competence in this area there is more to it than that. It may be true that it is commonplace for civil servants, in this case policemen, to be working under the authority of a political figure, but the reverse is hardly the typical state of affairs. Here one could see political appointees censoring movies in an entirely sub rosa fashion (unless appeals came into the courts) and operating *under the direction of a police department official* who, in theory, is supposed to be a symbol of law enforcement functioning in accordance with the established rules of due process. This theoretical estimate of the nature of police responsibility becomes twisted into the absurd when the censors, as tacitly admitted by Sergeant Murphy in his answer to Question 3, demand by a palpably extralegal procedure that cuts be made if a license is to be granted. It is, perhaps, an unfortunate circumstance that the Supreme Court did not attempt to evaluate evidence of this kind, along with other somewhat dubious bureau practices previously cited, when formulating its assessment of the validity of censorship in Chicago.

[381] An attempt was made to elicit by mail further insight into the work of this new tribunal by contacting Dr. Matthew Schoenbaum, one of its members. All overtures, however, were rebuffed without reply.

### Movie Censorship in Detroit

The history of film censorship in Detroit when compared with the preceding account of what has happened in Chicago is indeed a study in contrasts. While the statutory scheme used to control the exhibition of undesirable pictures is complex in Chicago, it is simplicity itself in Detroit. Furthermore, these legal standards have been altered only slightly in recent years when compared with the wholesale shakeup that has so radically overhauled the scope of Chicago's operation. Nor has Detroit's program been at all harrassed by adverse court action. Indeed, it is impossible to find any significant judicial edict in recent years that is relevant to this city's censorship policies.

On September 24, 1907, an ordinance was enacted authorizing the Commissioner of the Police Department to inspect all moving pictures prior to their commercial exhibition within city limits. It was his prerogative to reject any movie that was "indecent or immoral" and the ordinance stipulated that anyone who showed any film contrary to police order was to be punished by either a five hundred dollar fine, a prison term of not more than ninety days, or both. The law also provided that anyone in the business of exhibiting movies had to apply for a license from the Mayor and that the exhibition of a film that had been found to be immoral or indecent by the Commissioner or his agent was to be considered justifiable cause for the revocation of said license.[382]

This unusually uncomplicated statutory foundation for a movie censorship program remained the law of the city until 1962 when it was repealed in toto. This development is deceiving, however, unless it is noted that its replacement, Ordinance #712-F, differs only in the slightest detail from its predecessor.[383] The only difference of note is that under the new ordinance the Commissioner of Police is to examine, or cause to be examined, each film and if, in his judgment, "the motion picture *or any part*

---

[382] Detroit, Michigan, *Comp. Ord.*, Ch. 89 (1954).

[383] This statute can be found in Detroit, Michigan, *Comp. Ord.*, Ch. 89 (1954 as amended).

*thereof* is indecent or immoral, he shall reject that motion picture *or part thereof. . . .*" Thus, the right to cut out segments of movies deemed indecent or immoral is now clearly spelled out.

In December of 1962 I arranged an interview with movie censorship officials in Detroit. Present at this meeting were three members of the Detroit License and Censor Bureau, a subsidiary of the Detroit Police Department. The tenor of the discussion was one of conviviality. Respondents answered all questions directly, pulling no punches about how the Bureau functions as a censorship unit.

Three years later, in November of 1965 to be precise, Detroit authorities were once again approached, this time to gain their approval so that the facts of this interview could be published. Amazingly, an iron curtain had descended over film censorship activities in the Motor City. I was told that the Police Department was under pressure from various sources (these were not defined but evidently were "libertarian" in ideology), that parts of the interview had become outdated, that no public statements on censorship policies might be released unless the Commissioner himself approved, and that permission to publicize the interview would probably not be given unless the entire book was first scrutinized. Having no intention of submitting my manuscript to the well-honed hatchet of Detroit prior restraint, I refused to comply with this request or any others that might be forthcoming, and thus Detroit joined the State of Kansas as the only movie censorship jurisdictions to resist an inspection into their prepublication activities.

Basic facts brought out by the 1962 interview, however, can and will be reported. It is probable that most of these data hold true in 1965 as well but, in any event, they are crucial because they have never before been documented. Detroit's censorship program, unlike Chicago's, not only functions under the auspices of city police officials, but also is enforced solely by these officials. There is no small group of women or appeals tribunal here. Each movie, before it is licensed for exhibition, is seen by a policeman. If he feels that no changes are in order the picture will be approved. Otherwise, he will consult with his superiors. No votes are taken; each problem is resolved on an informal basis with the

Corporation Counsel for the City approving all censorship decisions. If a distributor protests, a second screening will be set up with the upper echelon of the Bureau present. The distributor is not invited to the hearing and there is no formal appeal procedure. Once again, the Corporation Counsel's judgment is determinative and if petitioner is unhappy he will have to go into court to prove his point. As has been noted, almost none do.

What kinds of censorship decisions does the Bureau make? The applicable city ordinance stipulates that movies which are "indecent" or "immoral" need not be licensed. Surprisingly, this grant of power is construed liberally because no film is ever proscribed in this city. In this regard, Detroit stands alone among censorship communities. It is also true, however, that the Bureau is one of only two agencies studied that keep absolutely no records on what movies have been abridged, the scenes or dialogue removed, or the reasons why changes were necessitated. The only way one can find out what kinds of material are thought to be "indecent" or "immoral" (such portions can be expurgated under the 1962 statute) is to ask.

The type of movie that causes the most trouble is the American "quickie nudie" commodity that is produced by various "fly-by-night" companies. All views of breasts and buttocks are removed. Furthermore, words like "bastard" and "bitch" will, more likely than not, be cut out. The word "whore" is acceptable on the art house circuit but not in theaters that cater to general patronage. It could well be argued that the practice of covering one's tracks carefully by keeping no meaningful records tends to encourage a more free-wheeling attitude towards censorship practices than might otherwise result. The fact that commonplace terms like "bastard," "bitch," and "whore" are usually eliminated seems to be a definite indication that this is so.

One of the interesting features of Detroit's new-found reticence centers around the aforementioned statutory standards of indecency and immorality. During the writer's most recent confrontation with members of the department, whose personnel has undergone a drastic reshuffling in the past three years, it was made clear to him that the agency was in no sense a censorship tribunal. "We are the Obscenity Enforcement Bureau," one of their number stated. "We are engaged in irradicating obscenity." This is indeed a curious phenomenon given the fact that the word "obscene" is not even mentioned in the licensing law. Perhaps this new image is a product of the group pressure which the Bureau seems to perceive clearly. Certainly the fact that the Supreme Court has said that obscenity is not protected by the First Amendment and that movies which fall within this category can be previously restrained affords a haven for scurrying censors. As will be seen, Memphis, like Detroit, is also well aware of the fact that obscenity, even though not mentioned in its governing ordinance, represents the soundest legal footing for abridging films. It may well be that the words "indecent" and "immoral" are dead letters in the Motor City.

Another of the really unique features of the Detroit program centers around the limitations it places on young people. There are three art houses that operate within city limits and, as might be expected, each exhibits its share of off-beat productions. The Bureau has an agreement with the owners of these theaters to the effect that they will be given a relatively free hand provided they keep all youngsters under eighteen off their premises when films of this description are being shown. If this agreement is not honored the censors will be somewhat more indiscriminate in their splicing.

The Bureau also tries to restrict certain "hot" items to the art house belt. The price of admission is higher for movies they exhibit—about a dollar and fifty cents—so that a more adult audience is practically assured. Furthermore, it is against the law for commercial movie house owners to limit their audiences to older people; this device, therefore, provides about the only mechanism through which youngsters can be effectively siphoned off. It should not be assumed, however, that Detroit will allow these three theaters carte blanche. The censors eliminated the rape scenes in *Two Women* and *The Virgin Spring* even when these pictures were shown only to adults.[384]

[384] It has been reported that the Bureau will also confine a movie to the art house circuit if its distributor does not agree to make certain deletions. A notable example which received considerable publicity involved *The Sky Above, The Mud Below,* an Academy Award recipient for being the best

It has been seen that the licensing ordinance provides only that "indecent" and "immoral" films may be denied permits by the Commissioner or his agent. By what legal authority, then, does the Bureau persuade exhibitors to keep those under eighteen away from particular movies and to quarantine various pictures from the so-called commercial theater belt? It seems obvious that the validity of these agreements must be predicated on the assumption that the limitations involved somehow exempt motion pictures from total suppression when they otherwise would come within the scope of what may be proscribed. There may well be movies that are indecent or immoral when shown to audiences of all ages, but which shed these stigmas when exhibited only to older people. In any event, the law of the city uses these terms only as absolutes without regard to the age level of the viewer. It is hard to believe, therefore, that these censors have a legal right to hobble films financially that could have a deleterious effect only on the younger set.

It is interesting to note that Detroit has no direct contact with any of the other communities studied. It can be argued that this lack of give-and-take encourages the development of policies that are sui generis. There is much ammunition to support the allegation. Only the Detroit Bureau does not ban movies. Only Memphis (another jurisdiction which has little communication with the outside world of prior restraint) can approach the Motor City's haphazard job of record keeping. Furthermore, only in Detroit do those that license movies also dabble in literature censorship. The License and Censor Bureau is as much a repository for the allegedly objectionable magazine as it is for the allegedly noxious moving picture. Finally, Detroit's policies are often taken up by small neighboring communities that are anxious to keep certain movies from their doors but do not have the budgets needed to maintain a day-to-day censorship program of

---

documentary film of 1962. The controversial scenes depicted "unclad natives" in their natural habitat. In this instance, however, the board found it expeditious to rescind its order when faced with a recalcitrant distributor. A weapon of this kind can be as deadly in its impact as the more overt tools of prior restraint because it can destroy a movie's profit-making potential. See the *Detroit News*, August 3, 1962, p. 3 and Schumach, *op. cit.*, p. 201.

their own. These towns come to the Bureau for help and do not return empty-handed. Whatever justification there may be for motion picture regulation of the kind under analysis would not appear to override the contention that censors have no good reason to accept as binding the opinions of censorship authorities from some other jurisdiction as to what constitutes a misuse of the right of free speech.

To sum up: The most striking feature of the work of the Detroit License and Censor Bureau (or, if you will, the Obscenity Enforcement Bureau) is that it is under the exclusive management of policemen. Regulations require members of the board to have two years of college training or their equivalent. The latter seems to consist of being able to spot materials that are "indecent," "immoral," or "obscene," and, to be sure, one member of the tribunal, at least, does seem to have a cursory knowledge of Supreme Court decisions. But the fact is that these are men, though undoubtedly highly competent in their traditional law enforcement tasks, who worked their way up the police ladder by walking a beat, doing patrol duty, and by serving in accident investigation. It is not surprising, then, that the sophistication needed to enforce Supreme Court guidelines properly is woefully lacking. The evidence is clear that scenes and script are expurgated in an arbitrary manner which defies "the dominant theme taken as a whole" portion of the *Roth* test.

This, unfortunately, is only the beginning. It was pointed out that the law enforcement officers who are in charge of movie censorship in Chicago are also oblivious to First Amendment rights. In the case of both agencies the problem is one of lack of expertise rather than "malicious intent." What rankled most about Chicago's censorship program was that all decisions were sub rosa, that the licensing law was interpreted broadly to allow for cutting films (Detroit's ordinance, at least, makes allowances for this), and that policemen were directing these procedures. Detroit censors are far more culpable. Law enforcement officials cajole art house owners to keep juveniles from certain productions much to their financial loss. Distributors are somehow kept from marketing particular films with commercial theaters much to *their* financial loss. All of this is extralegal. And, finally, no records of previous restraint are available to the public because none exist. Now that the censors are not talking without the Commissioner's approval, one might well wonder what meaningful checks the citizens of Detroit have against arbitrary motion picture censorship.

## Movie Censorship in Memphis

Motion picture censorship in Memphis, Tennessee dates back to the early 1920's. Since 1931 the statutory powers of the board of review have remained constant and the only amendments of any importance to this legal framework have dealt with the number of people who are to serve on this bureau. The applicable ordinance begins by stating that the Board of Censors shall have the power to regulate "all public exhibitions, plays, motion pictures, performances, pantomimes or other representations in the city."[385] This is the only instance in which a city or state movie censorship agency that operates on a permanent basis is given legal control over other media of expression as well. Furthermore, this bureau is specifically empowered to preview whatever movies, plays or exhibitions it thinks deserve to be subject to prior restraint. Any means of communication mentioned above may be prohibted by the bureau if it is of "immoral, lewd or lascivious character" or is "inimical to the public safety, health, morals, or welfare" or is directed toward "denouncing, deriding, or seeking to overthrow the present form of national government." Finally, the censors are vested with the right to close any "theatre, hall, opera house or (other) place . . ." where these productions are presented whenever such performance or screening is exhibited contrary to a lawful order issued by the bureau.

The bureau itself consists of seven members[386] who are

---

[385] Memphis, Tennessee, *Mun. Code*, Vol. I, Ch. 33, Sects. 945–49 (1949).

[386] The original law provided only for a three-man agency. This number was raised to five in 1957 (see *The Memphis Digest*, Vol. I, Ch. 33, Sect. 945, 1957 Supplement) and has recently been upped again to its present number. Interview with the Chairman of the Memphis Board of Film Censors.

selected by the Mayor and approved by the Board of Commissioners. It is also the prerogative of the chief city official to choose the Chairman of the censorship group. These members are to serve for a period of one year "or until their successors shall be appointed and qualify" and are to receive whatever compensation the city's Board of Commissioners provides. All findings of fact and of law as determined by this tribunal are final "and the same shall be subject to review only for illegality or want of jurisdiction."

For more than twenty years this Board of Censors was under the control of the colorful and famous (or infamous) Lloyd Binford who has often been cited as the prototype of arbitrary and capricious censorship action.[387] Binford came to the bureau in 1927 and acceded to the chairmanship the following year. He left this post in the early 1950's, leaving behind a reputation for movie censorship "so severe and so unpredictable that pictures shown without a ripple elsewhere . . ."[388] were often banned or cut without mercy. Thus, *The Southerner* which depicted how poor whites in Texas tried to overcome the adversities of life while living off the soil was banned because "it reflects on the South" even though the film was endorsed by five chapters of the Daughters of the Confederacy. Cecil B. DeMille's *King of Kings* was suppressed because Binford did not care for the producer's interpretation of the Bible; while *Destry Rides Again* and other raucous westerns were proscribed because of "too much shooting." But the chief victim of Binford's sallies was the Negro entertainer. Any song sung by Lena Horne was automatically deleted "because there are plenty of good white singers." *Brewster's Millions* was banned because Jack Benny's Rochester was "too familiar." And, of course, Negro jazz spokesmen such as Louis Armstrong never had a chance. When asked what yardsticks he used to assess movies Binford retorted that the law vested power in the Board to ban what was "inimical to the

[387] For an interesting account of an interview with Mr. Binford see Lester Velie, "You Can't See That Movie: Censorship in Action," *Collier's*, May 6, 1950, pp. 11-13, 66.

[388] *Ibid.*, p. 12.

public safety, health, morals and welfare" of the city and that from then on "it's just our own opinion."[389]

Ultimately, in 1949, United Artists sought to challenge the Binford dynasty by appealing a ban he had imposed on the movie *Curley*. This film was nothing more than a "comedy of the Our Gang type" but it made the mistake of showing Negro children visiting at school with white youngsters. This, said Binford, provided more than enough reason for suppressing the production because "the South does not permit Negroes in white schools nor recognize social equality between the races even in children."[390]

In a long-winded opinion splattered with obiter the Supreme Court of Tennessee ruled against plaintiff's allegation that this ruling must be overthrown. It was true, said Chief Justice Neil, that race or color could not be used as the sole legal basis for censoring a motion picture. It was also true that the guarantee of the First Amendment could only be invoked by someone who had been denied the privilege of speaking; in this case this meant the exhibitor only and not the distributor. But the real infirmity in appellant's argument was the invalidity of his assumption that because he engaged solely in interstate activities he, therefore, did not have to comply with state statutory provisions demanding that foreign (out of state) corporations qualify before they could maintain legal actions of this kind. While the Chief Justice never once alluded specifically to the ground rules contained in the applicable statute, he was firm in his contention that when a distributor contracts with an exhibitor for the use of moving pictures, his transactions clearly constitute intrastate business. Having not complied with statutory regulations governing such transactions, he could not use the courts to advance his intended purpose. The Supreme Court of the United States evidently felt the decision to be on sound enough terrain for it refused certiorari without dissent.[391]

[389] *Ibid.* Velie has reported that while the bureau, in 1950, was supposed to consist of three members one—a housewife—was absent so often that Binford did not even remember her name.

[390] *Ibid.*

[391] *United Artists Corporation* v. *Board of Censors*, 189 Tenn. 397 (1949),

To what extent does Memphis still adhere to the policies and attitudes of the late Lloyd Binford? In April of 1963 I obtained an interview with Mrs. Minter Somerville Hooker, Chairman of the Memphis Board of Film Censors.[392] In analyzing the fruits of this meeting, one must take note of the fact that in its most general terms, censorship in Memphis is highly unusual because of the startling contrasts it exhibits. There can be no doubt that of all the prior restraint mechanisms of control that were examined the Memphis operation was the most poorly organized. This is in no sense, however, a criticism of the Board itself but is obviously a product of the tepid public support movie censorship is afforded. The bureau has no office space and no staff personnel. Nor is compensation provided even in the form of expenses for censorship business. These policies not only undermine the level of performance of the censors (Question 27) but have engendered a feeling of futility and defeatism in the attitudes of the Chairman (Question 39) that is probably widespread among others sitting on the Board. This pessimistic outlook is entirely unique among censors. Even those who represent the city of Chicago, whose decisions have time and again been knocked down through appeals to the judicial process, view their responsibilites from a rosier perspective.

In spite of this relatively slack support from the city fathers, however, there can be no doubt that movie censorship in Memphis is anything but ineffectual. To be sure Lloyd Binford's somewhat arbitrary (but legally permissible) policy of threatening to close down motion picture houses whose owners were somewhat recalcitrant has been shelved, but it is clear that the bureau has at least as many weapons as it needs to enforce its commands. In answer to Question 23 respondent noted that Memphis censors had become somewhat easy-going in their policies (this must have referred to the transitional period between

---

*cert. den.*, 339 U. S. 952 (1950). For further commentary on the *Curley* controversy see Theodore R. Kupferman and Philip J. O'Brien, "Motion Picture Censorship—The Memphis Blues," *Cornell Law Quarterly*, XXXVI (1951), 273-300.

[392] See Appendix VI.

the Binford era and the present day) but that now a reputation for strictness has become firmly established. The evidence supporting this claim is apparent. The fly-by-night nudist films that pester other censorship agencies cause authorities little difficulty in Memphis (Questions 10 and 32). Nor would those in charge of disseminating *The Connection* even bother to attempt to market that film in this area (Question 30). Furthermore, the Board has remained as free of litigation as the policemen of Detroit. Not one case has been launched in the courts in the past five years in protest over an agency holding (Question 29). And, finally, who can say how many films have been kept clear of Memphis because of the "advisory consultations" the Chairman has had with various "movie chain managers" who would like to avoid alienating the Censor Board (Question 8). The fact is that this check constitutes the only instance of a censorship agency's success in inhibiting the dissemination of motion pictures even before they are presented to the bureau for licensing.

The most provocative answers elicited from Mrs. Hooker probably centered around the ways in which the bureau has construed its censorship duties under the applicable city ordinance. Her answer to Question 11 establishes the fact that Memphis authorities often restrict films to adult audiences and have also dabbled in limiting certain productions to those who attend art house exhibitions, even though no such prerogatives are delegated to them by law. In the light of similar practices in Detroit and Virginia these procedures are not surprising. Again it is worth noting that there is nothing in this interview that conveys what special guidelines other than censorship "feel" are used to ascertain what pictures should be shown to adults only and which can be seen by an unrestricted audience.

The responsibilities of the censors become confusing indeed when the answers given to Questions 17, 18, and 21 are carefully examined. Evidently the only criteria now being consistently enforced are "lewd, lascivious and immoral." But the Board knows that only a finding of obscenity can be sustained in court. The result seems to be that rather than ignoring these three words by simply interpreting them all to be synonyms for the same proscribable phenomenon—obscenity—what has been done appar-

ently is to say that something can be obscene for lascivious
reasons, lewd reasons, or reasons of immorality. Why else would
the Chairman say that each of these three terms was difficult to
interpret (Question 17), that they all give the bureau membership trouble (Question 18) and that there is a difference between
indecency (used synonymously with "immoral") and obscenity?
In Question 18 it is stated that the Supreme Court has formulated
no definition for obscenity (Question 29 also enunciates the view
that the courts have postulated no helpful standards), yet Mrs.
Hooker herself seems familiar enough with the *Roth* test (Question 21). The point seems to be that the courts certainly have
not formulated a test which will justify everything that Memphis
would like to suppress, especially when operating under three
guidelines which have been found contrary to the First Amendment—at least by implication—when used in a similar context.
The thicket in which the bureau has become enmeshed becomes
hopelessly bewildering when all of these data are contrasted with
Mrs. Hooker's desire to amend the city ordinance to comply with
Supreme Court rulings previously labeled as amorphous (Question 24) and her belief (Question 22 b) that American movies
are mostly banned or cut because they are too violent or vulgar.
The latter are clearly not constitutional or statutory reasons for
levying censorship orders.

The preceding commentary by no means exhausts censorship decision-making policies that are seemingly inconsistent with
the implications of the Board's statutory underpinning. It would
appear that the most flagrant misuse of prior restraint authority
lies in the bureau's suppression of movies even when there is no
legal basis for such action. A movie that is forbidden entry into
the city through the process of "advisory consultations" previously
mentioned, may or may not be bannable under the statute. However, *The Rebel Breed* and *Smiles of a Summer Night* were denied permits because it was felt that for some reason they might
transgress "the best interests of the community" (Question 8).
Nor are such actions less odious because the potential exhibitors
of these films "agreed" not to show these pictures. The fact is
that no one can know for certain what manner of coercion was
used to "convince" these businessmen that it would be better

for everyone to keep these movies out of the market place. In any event such actions run well beyond the commands of the city ordinance; indeed, the criterion has already been rejected by the Supreme Court as a censorship guideline.[393]

Finally, there are Mrs. Hooker's replies to Questions 3 and 25 to be considered. They suggest that the Board feels that the legitimate theater in Memphis does not need censorship regulation because it caters to "selected audiences" and because it is less accessible to children. The latter question, of course, is significant because it makes perfectly clear that what the Chairman means by "selected audiences" are those that do not as a rule include viewers with "immature minds" regardless of age. Once again, in other words, the "average man" rule as set down by the Supreme Court finds itself in the role of doctrine rather than legal sanction.


## Movie Censorship in Atlanta

Of the four cities that utilize a policy of movie censorship the program instituted in Atlanta is by far the newest and certainly in the greatest state of confusion. By a 1915 act of the Georgia State Legislature,[394] the Charter of the City of Atlanta was amended so as to give the Mayor and the Board of Aldermen power to create a censorship bureau which was to reject prior to public exhibition any "obscene or licentious pictures or other pictures that may affect the peace, health, morals and good order of said city. . . ." Surprisingly, it was not until December 5, 1944, that the city decided to implement this grant of authority by setting up a movie censorship bureau. The implementing ordinance itself underwent wholesale revision, in form and substance, in 1953.[395] The only important difference between the new ordinance and its predecessor was that punishment for violation of

[393] *Gelling* v. *Texas,* 343 U. S. 960 (1952).

[394] *Ga. L.,* 1915, pp. 480, 493.

[395] This statute is located in *The Charter, Related Laws and Code of General Ordinances of Atlanta, Georgia,* Ch. 56, Article IV (1953). The initial enactment is *Ordinance Governing the Exhibit of Motion Pictures in Atlanta,* Sects. 1-12 (1944).

any statutory provision or board ruling under the earlier law was to consist of a fine not to exceed five hundred dollars, labor on the public works for not to exceed thirty days, or both, while the more recent version not only deleted this stipulation but also failed to provide for substitute penalties. The second of these municipal decrees was in turn superceded by a revised version in 1962 following an adverse State Supreme Court ruling as to its constitutionality.

The 1944 city statute began by specifying that all pictures to be exhibited within the city limits must be approved by the duly authorized film censor but that this should not be interpreted to interfere with the private showing of any film for religious, scientific, or educational purposes. It then went on to set up in the Atlanta Public Library the position of moving picture censor. This office was to be filled by competitive examination such as that typically used in selecting employees for the classified service. The designated appointee was to serve in this post during satisfactory service, subject to the provisions of city law applicable to employees who come within the classified section of the civil service.

This motion picture censor was given sole responsibility to license all approved movies for commercial showing but "if the same were obscene, lewd, licentious, profane, or will in his opinion adversely affect the peace, health, morals and good order of the city" he was to order a deletion of such scene, scenes, or dialogue. Upon compliance with said ruling the film under examination could be presented.

In a somewhat novel twist, the ordinance then went on to vest in the Atlanta Public Library Board "all the power and authority" that the City Charter stated might be placed in a board of censors. While this bureau of overseers was to be known officially as the Atlanta Board of Censorship and was specifically given the right to approve all moving pictures to be commercially exhibited, this stipulation, in fact, meant only that the Public Library Board was to have the power to review any decision promulgated by the motion picture censor. Accordingly, any person aggrieved by any action of this censor could appeal to the Board within ten days and any decision reached by this tribunal was to be final unless court action was initiated. In performance of its appellate duties the Public Library Board was to receive from the censor a "detailed monthly report" of his decisions and was further empowered to subpoena and swear witnesses and conduct any investigations necessary to determine any question of fact.

This enactment was challenged early in its history by an unusually diverse bill of particulars. Miss Christine Smith, the first, and only, film censor Atlanta has ever had, banned the movie *Scarlet Street* because she found it "licentious and contrary to the good order of the community by reason of the sordid life it portrayed, the treatment of illicit love, the failure of characters to receive orthodox punishment from the police, and because the picture would tend to weaken a respect for the law."[396] The distributor for this film at once moved for an injunction against this holding on grounds that its valuable property rights of over one million dollars (the cost of producing *Scarlet Street*) would suffer irreparable damage if the picture could not profit from "first run" distribution and because of the bad name censorship in Atlanta would bring to the movie in other communities. It was also alleged that the law violated both the state and federal constitutional protections of free speech, that the Atlanta City Charter had not authorized vesting movie censorship duties in one person, that the ordinance allowed the censor only to order certain deletions and not to suppress entire pictures, and that the Library Board of Review had voted by a tally of four to four on a motion to dismiss distributor's averments and that the motion had thus failed to carry, the bureau's claims to the contrary notwithstanding. The Supreme Court of Georgia brushed aside these arguments by holding that the facts as presented did not constitute a basis for equity jurisdiction. The terms of the ordinance could only be enforced by criminal prosecution, the Court observed; hence an adequate defense at law was available to fend off any arbitrary censorship policies the city might initiate.[397]

[396] *Atlanta* v. *Universal Film Exchanges,* 39 S. E. 2d 882 (1946) at p. 885.
[397] *Atlanta* v. *Universal Film Exchanges,* 39 S. E. 2d 882 (1946).

Four years later, a second serious attempt was made to impose judicial limitations on Atlanta's policy of prior restraint. Miss Smith had suppressed the film *Lost Boundaries* because it dealt with a Negro doctor who for several years had managed to pass for white in a New Hampshire community without detection. This theme, it was felt, would likely have an adverse effect upon the peace and good order of the city. As has been noted previously, her judgment was upheld in both federal district and circuit courts. The Supreme Court, in an inexplicable ruling, eventually denied certiorari even though Justice Douglas had two years earlier apparently opened the door to such appeals with his famous dictum in the *Paramount Pictures* controversy.[398]

Still another application for redress of grievances was turned away by the State Supreme Court in 1961. Mrs. Christine Smith Gilliam, the former Miss Smith, had refused a permit to the controversial *Never on Sunday* unless certain cuts were made. The Board of Censors then went even further and ruled that in no event could the picture be shown because it was obscene in that it "would be harmful to the average child who might view the film and because (it) presented an unacceptable idea."[399] Once again the Court dismissed a complainant distributor's allegations because he had sought equitable relief. This, it was held, could not be granted because the company had voluntarily sought reversal with the Library Board in conformity with the appeals process set out in the ordinance. Consequently a judicial remedy could only issue after a writ of certiorari had been granted. In other words, once plaintiff had begun to make use of an appeals system that was part of the usual legal proceeding in such cases he could not then exercise the option of changing horses in mid-stream by asking for equitable relief.[400]

It was inevitable, of course, that the highest court of the

---

[398] *RD-DR* v. *Smith*, 89 F. Supp. 596 (1950), 183 F. 2d 562 (1950), *cert. den.*, 340 U. S. 853 (1950). These holdings are discussed at greater length in Chapter I, *supra*. For further discussion of the controversy surrounding the censorship of *Lost Boundaries* in Atlanta see Kupferman and O'Brien, *op. cit.*

[399] *Atlanta* v. *Lopert Pictures Corp.*, 122 S. E. 2d 916 (1961) at p. 918.

[400] *Atlanta* v. *Lopert Pictures Corp.*, 122 S. E. 2d 916 (1961).

state would ultimately be forced to dispose of an appeal lodged against movie censorship in Atlanta on substantive grounds. A short time thereafter, the K. Gordon Murray Production Company, a motion picture distributor, appealed a censorship order banning *Room at the Top*[401] and asked the Court once again to grant a petition for equity. On this occasion, however, the Court agreed that a permanent restraining order could be issued for the reason that the remedy provided for in the ordinance was unconstitutional if petitioner's allegations of free speech deprivation were valid. It also pointed out that the terms of the statute permitted a complete remedy at law only for exhibitors; distributors who could show that a censorship order interfered with potential contractual arrangements they could negotiate with certain movie house owners would not so benefit. Clearly, said Chief Justice Duckworth, there was no way for any distributor to coerce an exhibitor to invoke the criminal process so as to enforce the former's rights.

While plaintiff had lodged a variety of complaints against Atlanta's censorship operation the Court confined its remarks to free speech considerations. It noted that the Supreme Court had held in *Burstyn* v. *Wilson* that moving pictures were one aspect of free speech. However, the 1961 *Times Film Corporation* decision had closed the door to the argument that the First Amendment could be used to strike down this means of control. But what of the Georgia State Constitution? Here the Chief Justice found that the key section in need of interpretation was Article I, Section 1, Paragraph 15, which stated that "No law shall ever be passed to curtail, or restrain the liberty of speech, or of the press; any person may speak, write, and publish his sentiments on all subjects, being responsible for the abuse of that liberty." What this meant was that these protected rights could not be invaded "for one second in any conceivable manner" as a means of curtailing abuses of these privileges. Thus, the City Charter and censorship ordinance were void in so far as they required the prescreening of movies protected by this clause as well as those that

[401] The State Supreme Court did not cite the name of the particular film during its remarks but Mrs. Gilliam's answers to Questions 4 and 7, Appendix VII, leave no doubt as to its identity.

were not so protected because they abused the privilege of free speech.[402]

The Board of Aldermen and the Mayor of Atlanta did not waste time in countering this decision declaring the heart of the city's film censorship ordinance unconstitutional. Two months after the opinion was handed down they enacted an ordinance setting up a screen rating system for the guidance of patrons and the public generally. Any movie to be shown for commercial purposes within city limits must first be previewed by a Motion Picture Reviewer who is to be appointed and to serve in office under the same rules as provided by the previous law. It is the duty of this person to place each movie that is reviewed into one of the three categories as listed below:

A. *Approved.* This rating shall be given to a motion picture which does not contain any matter which tends to arouse sexual, lustful or carnal desires or which tends to appeal to prurient interests.

B. *Unsuitable for the Young.* This rating shall be given to a motion picture which, while not objectionable for the average person or for mature adult persons, would nevertheless be objectionable for children, young people or immature people because it contains matter which is offensive to contemporary moral standards in the community or has a theme which would tend to create immorality, corruption or debauchery or would tend to create a harmful impression of proper moral conduct, according to the standards of the community.

C. *Objectionable.* This rating shall be given to an obscene motion picture. The test for obscenity as applied to this ordinance is whether or not, according to contemporary community standards, as applied by the average person, the motion picture contains any scene or scenes which causes the dominant effect of the motion picture to tend to stir the sex impulses or to lead to sexually impure and lustful thoughts or to appeal to prurient interests.

The ordinance makes it illegal for anyone who is exhibiting a film in the latter two classifications to fail to provide satisfactory notice of this fact in a prominent place at the box-office. However, the enactment goes on to make it unlawful for anyone to show an obscene film under any circumstances so that, in effect,

[402] *K. Gordon Murray Productions, Inc.* v. *Floyd,* 217 Ga. 784 (1962).

the affixing of the term "objectionable" to any picture means that the exhibition of such a movie will be followed automatically by arrest. Anyone violating these or other statutory provisions is to be fined a maximum of five hundred dollars, suffer imprisonment for not more than thirty days, or both.

The Library Board of the City of Atlanta is once again given appeal powers over decisions made by the Reviewer and is also vested with all authority it held under the previous enactment. Any person dissatisfied with a ruling issued by the film-rater may appeal to this body which then rescreens the movie and either approves the category into which the picture has been placed or assigns it to another classification.[403]

It did not take the film industry long to initiate court action aimed at staying the enforcement of this statute. Several of the more famous Hollywood firms sought out the necessary injunction on the grounds that the city did not have power under its charter to enact the law and also that the ordinance violated the free speech sections contained in the Georgia and United States Constitutions. After winning a preliminary court order below, however, the Supreme Court of Georgia reversed, finding error in that tribunal's assessment of the controversy.[404]

Speaking for the majority faction of a badly divided court, Mr. Justice Grice began by examining what the lower court had decided. He found the crux of its holding to be that Atlanta had no authority under its charter to pass an ordinance of the kind at issue because the *Murray* decision had rendered contrary to the Georgia Constitution any power the city had possessed to institute a prior restraint against movies. This, in his opinion, was a misreading of that judgment. The *Murray* case, while it had voided the work of a censorship board that might license some films for exhibition while rejecting others, in no way undercut another grant of power set out in the Charter which provided that:

---

[403] It is impossible to provide a citation for this law because it has not, as yet, been included in the Atlanta statutory volumes. This legislation was adopted, however, on June 18, 1962, and approved by the Mayor two days later.

[404] *Atlanta v. Columbia Pictures Corp.*, 130 S. E. 2d 490 (1963).

. . . the Mayor and general council . . . are hereby authorized and empowered and given full authority to regulate by ordinance places where moving pictures are shown . . . and, furthermore, governing the matter of pictures displayed and to prevent the display of obscene or licentious pictures or other pictures that may affect the peace, health, morals and good order of said city.[405]

Thus, Atlanta might still pass laws which make showing obscene movies a crime. And, further, this broad grant of power also included authority to require the pre-screening of movies for the protection of youth. As to respondents' arguments asserting the unconstitutionality of this classification scheme, the lower court had in no way passed on their validity and thus it was not the prerogative of an appellate tribunal to prejudge their merit.

In a dissenting opinion notable for its acrimony rather than its articulation, Chief Justice Duckworth, joined by Mr. Justice Candler, vehemently insisted that the *Murray* holding had cast aside *all* charter provisions that could be used to buttress prior restraints. The classification of films accomplished through pre-screening, he felt, was as much a prior restraint as the overt censorship activities frowned upon earlier. In concluding, he invoked the mantle of obiter by arguing that the majority had compelled "the futile return of the case . . . knowing that after considerable time and expense have been spent, the ordinance will and must ultimately meet the fate it deserves of being declared unconstitutional because it imposes a prior restraint."[406]

In April of 1963 I recorded an interview with Mrs. Christine Smith Gilliam who is now serving in the capacity of Motion Picture Reviewer for the City of Atlanta.[407] An examination of this interview shows at once that movie censorship in Atlanta is taken very seriously. Mrs. Gilliam is a civil servant with an office in city hall. She was chosen with great care and her formal credentials match those of any other official who was interviewed. The records she has kept show her to be an efficient public servant and there can be little question that she is a woman of strong conviction as her straight-to-the-point answers clearly verify.

[405] *Ibid.*, p. 493.
[406] *Ibid.*, p. 495.
[407] See Appendix VII.

With this in mind what has movie censorship in Atlanta been like? Has it been appreciably different from the work of Detroit and Chicago which place so much authority in the hands of local police officials, or the levels of performance reached in Memphis or the state of Virginia where all censorship responsibilities are vested in political appointees? And, finally, are there any critical differences in procedures used under the city's two respective ordinances that need to be enlarged upon in formulating helpful generalities?

Motion picture censorship in Atlanta was grounded upon the guidelines set up in the first ordinance until the basic prior restraint contained in that law was voided in 1962. In her answer to Question 14, Mrs. Gilliam stressed the point that she was well aware of the courts' antipathy toward most of these guidelines so that on most occasions she tried to justify her rulings against movies by saying that they were either "obscene" or "licentious." Leaving aside the question of whether the word "licentious" can be used as a basis for banning or cutting movies (a highly improbable supposition) it is of greater importance to note how films declared to be "obscene" under the old law have been classified under the new one. How is it, for example, that *Never on Sunday* and *Room at the Top* could be banned under the old statute and yet receive a "UY" label under the grading system now utilized (Question 7)? And what of 1960 where every one of the nine movies suppressed has since been classified "UY" (cited earlier in response to the same question)?

The same basic point can be made in examining movies that were cut during this period of time. Mrs. Gilliam, in answering Question 8, was not enlightening about elimination orders she had issued under the old ordinance but her library reports are most informative. In the year 1960, for instance, 29 out of the 267 movies previewed were cut while in 1961, 14 out of 267 pre-screened pictures were forced to accept the deletion of particular portions.[408] What kinds of material were removed by Mrs. Gil-

---

[408] Of the 29 movies slashed in 1960, 21 were foreign-made while in 1961, 12 of the 14 subjected to cutting were made abroad. Hence, it would appear that conclusions reached by respondent in her answer to Question 11 (American films cause most problems) were somewhat inaccurate.

liam? In reply to Question 16 she reported that words like
"bastard" and "by God" were taboo. Kilpatrick has cited other
significant data in his commentary on Atlanta's censorship program. Thus, in *Green Eyed Blonde* a scene showing a Negro girl
being kissed by white girls was removed; in *Passionate Summer*
close-ups of the birth of a kid were deleted; in *Girls on the Loose*
two cuts concerning details of the commission of murder were
required.[409] In short, the "greater flexibility" that she felt existed
under the old law (Question 16) provided the statutory impetus
for cutting out all kinds of material irrespective of the context in
which such scenes or dialogue was presented. Furthermore, as
has been noted, entire pictures were suppressed under the old
ordinance for ostensibly being obscene which are now classified
in such a way as to refute the validity of the initial judgment if
the *Roth* rule had been followed.[410] Indeed, Mrs. Gilliam's answer
to Question 17 is a point-blank admission of the fact that this
doctrine was ignored.

The new ordinance enacted in 1962 ostensibly relieves the
Atlanta movie reviewer of any censorship obligations. She is given
the responsibility of merely labeling films either "approved," "unsuitable for the young" or "objectionable." It is not easy to determine exactly how this legislation is being interpreted because
Mrs. Gilliam keeps no files on why she believes a movie to be
objectionable or unsuitable for the young (Question 13). Indeed, the statute itself nowhere defines the term "young" so that
the reader is left in the dark as to what the age limit is that Mrs.
Gilliam and the Library Board have decided should be the "cut-
off point."

A good place to start in discussing important procedures

[409] Kilpatrick, *op. cit.*, p. 279. This information along with Mrs. Gilliam's
comments in Question 16 help to understand "what specific material was
excluded . . ." as was asked, but not answered, in Question 9.

[410] It should be recalled, furthermore, that *Never on Sunday* was found
to be obscene by the Library Board because it "would be harmful to the
average child . . . and because (it) presented an unacceptable idea." The
latter criterion is clearly unconstitutional under the *Lady Chatterley's Lover*
holding handed down by the Supreme Court in 1959. The former notion,
of course, runs afoul of *Butler* v. *Michigan* (1957).

utilized by Atlanta's team of film reviewers is with the criteria set up by the law itself. Judging by the terms of the ordinance as set out earlier an "approved" picture is one that, at the very least, is free of anything that is morbidly preoccupied with sex. It cannot contain "any matter" which arouses lustful thoughts. One might ask at that point *whose* prurient interests this clause is referring to, but the reply is explicit in the next paragraph. Motion pictures are "unsuitable for the young" if they contain material that would not appeal to the carnal desires of the average person but which is offensive to children, young people, or immature people because it propagates in some way that vast reservoir of behavior that is lumped together by the term "immorality." The important questions posed by the standards found in this section are: (1) is there not a difference between the statutory command that a film can be "approved" if it is free of anything appealing to the lustful interest of the young and this paragraph which sets out the dominant criterion for segregating movies from youngsters to be the presentation of anything that falsely interprets the community concept of morality (a far broader concept), and (2) how are Mrs. Gilliam and the Library Board interpreting all of this.

The third set of standards to be taken into account by the Atlanta movie reviewers is clear enough. A film is to be classified as "objectionable" if it is obscene and obscenity is defined in approximately the same terminology used by Mr. Justice Brennan in *Roth* v. *U. S.* However, the scope of this subsection is somewhat broader in its conception of obscenity than was the Court's most recent description of the term set out in *Jacobellis.* There, it will be recalled, Mr. Justice Brennan noted that obscenity was "utterly without redeeming social importance." Furthermore, there is a slight difference between the statutory definition and *Roth-Alberts* that also deserves comment. This section of the new ordinance defines an obscene picture not as one whose dominant effect is an appeal to the prurient interest of the average person but as one that "contains any scene or scenes which causes the dominant effect of the motion picture to tend to stir the sex impulses. . . ." From the standpoint of First Amendment coverage there may be no difference in the two definitions. However, there can be little doubt that the second of these definitions encourages censorship, because if a movie contains certain scenes that render the dominant theme obscene, the natural recourse is to delete these objectionable scenes. This, indeed, is precisely what Atlanta is now doing. In her response to Question 7, Mrs. Gilliam mentioned four films whose ratings had been changed from "objectionable" to "UY" through the expurgation of certain segments. This business of correctly assessing a film as obscene and then using a scissors to make it acceptable is obviously a very delicate matter requiring the most careful balancing of aesthetic values.[411] Frankly speaking, the history of censorship in Atlanta does not lend itself to an optimistic outlook about how well this task is being performed. Furthermore, there are grave doubts about the legality of the operation as Mrs. Gilliam herself has indicated (Question 3).

In her answer to Question 6 Mrs. Gilliam stated that the banning of moving pictures in Atlanta is no longer permissible. This, of course, is true only in theory. An "objectionable" picture is, by definition, an obscene picture (if the system is properly enforced) and obscene pictures cannot be shown legally in the city. By labeling a movie objectionable *in advance* and by enforcing her own judgment by telling the police about this decision (Question 11) Mrs. Gilliam unquestionably suppresses almost all movies *she* believes obscene. The basic point is that censorship is not dead in Atlanta—pictures are still being altered and are still being suppressed.

The foregoing analysis seems to lead to the irresistible conclusion that in spite of the fact that Atlanta has given civil service status to its movie censor, has chosen her by competitive exam, and has placed appellate jurisdiction in a group of people who, it is to be assumed, are not lacking in intelligence or sensitivity, its program has nonetheless fallen victim to the same excesses as those of less sophisticated communities. Under the old ordinance decisions were made with regularity that could not have been enforced had they reached the United States Supreme Court.

---

[411] For an assessment of the constitutionality of this procedure see Chapter V in "The Hiatus in the Enforcement of the 'Supreme Law,'" *infra.*

The new ordinance, on the other hand, is so sweeping in its changes that censorship is now a secondary power rather than a primary tool. Only in rare cases are pictures now found obscene or are any scenes or dialogue deleted. Still one may wonder precisely how such rulings are made today, whether such duties are performed with legal justification, and how it is that some movies come to be classified in the "UY" group.[412] It should be apparent, then, that regardless of how much time is spent in selecting censors and in devising ways for them to exercise their responsibilities, it will be impossible to achieve conformity with First Amendment freedoms unless certain values are accorded the highest status in the minds of those in charge of such regulatory bureaus. These values have not been preeminent in the unfolding of Atlanta's movie censorship policies.

---

[412] The basic question of the constitutionality of grading ordinances leading to the categorization of movies for the protection of the young will be discussed in the last chapter.

*Chapter V*
# Conclusion

## The Hiatus in the Enforcement of the "Supreme Law"

From the standpoint of descriptive analysis, the basic supposition in this investigation of state and local movie censorship policies is the notion that Supreme Court decisions are of minimal value unless they are given support at the communal level. It is now time to summarize the data that have been presented and to ask the basic question: To what extent are these government agencies violating the "supreme law of the land" as enunciated through high Court interpretations of the First Amendment? This can best be done, it would seem, by a community-by-community examination.

The relevant New York statute demands that a permit be granted for a picture unless such film "or a part thereof is obscene, indecent, immoral, inhuman, sacrilegious, or is of such a character that its exhibition would tend to corrupt morals or incite to crime." From a practical standpoint, however, the state board is using only the term "obscene" as a censorship criterion. Unfortunately, this policy of restraint does not alter the fact that that part of the law which gives New York the power to cut out obscene parts of movies is contrary to the *Roth* doctrine in that such segments cannot be ruled objectionable apart from the context in which they are placed. It is clear that New York and other jurisdictions which attempt to enforce this policy can do so only by refusing to license movies whose custodians will not abide by the censors' "expurgation orders." By withholding the required permit in this manner, these productions, in short, are treated as though they are themselves hard-core pornography or some noxious equivalent. It is impossible to cull any such censorship authority or, indeed, subsequent punishment authority from Supreme Court holdings that have dealt with the regulation of obscenity. Officials serving on the New York tribunal are not only aware of the subtleties of *Roth-Alberts*, but they are also aware of the application of this test to movies, as illustrated by their understanding of the *Times Film* decision of 1957. Yet, they steadfastly refuse to put it into practice.

The situation in Maryland is far different from New York's, because attempts there are clearly made to enforce each of the guidelines specified in the state law. The Maryland enactment begins by saying that the Board of Censors shall approve all pictures that are "moral and proper." It is not necessary to belabor the point that these criteria, in and of themselves, are "void for vagueness" under the Supreme Court's doctrine enunciated in *Winters* v. *New York*. The statute, however, goes on to pinpoint those movies that cannot be so classified. These include films that are "obscene, or such as tend . . . to debase or corrupt morals or incite to crimes." And, furthermore, these terms are also given detailed specification. An obscene movie is regarded in that state as one that "when considered as a whole, its calculated purpose or dominant effect is substantially to arouse sexual desires, and if the probability of this effect is so great as to outweigh whatever other merits the film may possess." As has been noted earlier,[413] this test bears a superficial resemblance to the *Roth-Alberts* definition of obscenity, but the differences between the two are, in reality, considerable. These disparities stem in some measure from the fact that Maryland uses the words "arouse sexual desires" to characterize the type of behavior films must not incite, whereas the Supreme Court talks of arousing "prurient interest." The differences between the two hinge on the fact that if the dominant theme of any work of art is sex it is likely to arouse the libido of the average reader. Yet, at the same time, such books or paintings or movies might not go beyond "customary limits of candor" or, indeed, be either "shameful" or "morbid." The latter criteria, of course, constitute the touchstones of Mr.

---

[413] See comments relevant to footnote 309, *supra*.

Justice Brennan's conception of the prurient. In short, the wording of this provision is not explicit enough to guarantee that only movies that are "patently offensive" will be proscribed as advocated by Justice Harlan in *Manual Enterprises* v. *Day*. Indeed, the whole concept of "weighing" nonobscene aspects of films over and against obscene attributes flies in the face of Brennan's statement so forcefully made in *Jacobellis* that obscenity cannot contain anything of artistic or social import.

The second of these standards involves the debasement or corruption of morals. Any picture guilty of violating these guidelines is one whose "dominant purpose or effect is erotic or pornographic; or if it portrays acts of sexual immorality, lust or lewdness, or if it expressly or impliedly presents such acts as desirable, acceptable or proper patterns of behavior." The last of these criteria is no longer enforced in Maryland as a consequence of the Supreme Court's ruling in *Kingsley Pictures* v. *Regents* that *Lady Chatterley's Lover* could not be banned in New York because it depicted adultery as a proper pattern of behavior. At the same time, no one would doubt that a film whose dominant theme is pornographic is suppressible. Any such movie could not clear the *Roth-Alberts* barrier as it characterizes obscenity.

But what of movies that portray in full detail on the screen sexual intercourse or other acts that are equally taboo such as masturbation, fellatio, etc.? It is obvious that the *Roth* formula does not characterize such pictures as necessarily appealing to prurient interests because it confines itself to dominant theme. This was precisely the problem New York faced when it thought *The Connection* could be proscribed because the word "shit" was used throughout. If *Roth* v. *U. S.* is to be the last word in this matter then no movie can be censored no matter how offensive one of its segments is unless, perhaps, it "infects" the basic message of the presentation.

The final criterion contained in the Maryland statute is "incite to crime." This is described as characterizing any picture "where the theme or manner of its presentation presents the commission of criminal acts or contempt for law as constituting profitable, desirable, acceptable, respectable or commonly accepted behavior, or if it advocates or teaches the use of, or the methods of use of, narcotics or habit-forming drugs." The first part of this section is clearly unconstitutional under *Kingsley Pictures.* The second portion dealing with the use of narcotics has been construed by the Maryland Supreme Court to mean that a film must advocate the behavior indicated in order to fall under its ban. While this judgment saved *The Man With the Golden Arm* from the snip of the censorship scissors it in no way frees the provision from the onus of unconstitutionality as delineated in both *Kingsley Pictures* and *Burstyn* v. *Wilson.* It is simply not permissible under the First Amendment to ban a movie that advocates something when the term "advocate" is defined as meaning "teaching with the purpose of inducing or encouraging."

If it is true that the Maryland censorship law is largely unconstitutional because of the standards it sets out for evaluating movies, the work of the State Board provides an even gloomier picture. Scenes that show "too much nudity" (whatever this is) are constantly being deleted regardless of dominant theme. One of the censors dislikes certain films because children should not see them. This, of course, is "burning the house to roast the pig." Dialogue is eliminated because it is "offensive." It goes without saying that this kind of expurgation is predicated on a foundation that is so amorphous that it contravenes due process of law. And finally, *The Narcotics Story* was slashed to ribbons mostly because the Chairman of the bureau would "rather his son and daughter saw nudist films than know how to use drugs." Certainly such emasculation cannot be justified under the *Burstyn* declaration.

These cutting procedures, of course, at once raise the question of how constitutional it is to expurgate motion pictures per se. New York censors have specific legal authority to remove offensive scenes, but this statutory underpinning is "void on its face" because it violates the dominant theme test of *Roth-Alberts.* Does this mean that all forms of cutting or emasculation are similarly void? The answer must be given in the negative. Censors can, at least theoretically, conform to judicial standards by eliminating portions of obscene pictures so as to render them viewable. The question in every case, then, will be to note whether or not censors are in fact guided by this principle when they resort to expurgation.[414] There can be no doubt that Maryland makes no attempt to follow *Roth-Alberts* in this regard.

What of the situation in Virginia? Here, as in New York, the censors are instructed to ban a movie "or any part thereof . . ." that "is obscene" or violates a number of other criteria. But, like New York, each of these other guidelines is ignored, while the statutory command authorizing the elimination of particular scenes regardless of overall setting is obeyed to the letter. The Virginia bureau adds a flourish of its own, however, by classifying some movies as being for "adults only" even though the law is silent regarding this practice. While the question of whether an age categorization system for motion pictures is consistent with the First Amendment requires extensive exploration, it is hard to believe that the Supreme Court would countenance such regulation unless minimal statutory standards are provided. This system of control is further complicated by the fact that the *Roth* test seems to be thoroughly disregarded in Virginia. The result is that motion pictures are suppressed or expurgated either because of the scope of the defunct *Hicklin* rule and its preoccupation with "immature minds," or because the censors simply believe the particular material to be objectionable. Neither test is rigorous enough to guarantee the complete protection of free speech for movies in Virginia.

The state of affairs in Kansas, as might be expected, is cloudy, given the fact that it is almost impossible to determine what movie censors are actually doing in this state. No motion picture is to be exhibited, reads the applicable state law, if it is "cruel, obscene, indecent or immoral" or tends to corrupt morals. Indications are that the Kansas Board of Review is only applying the criterion of obscenity, and while there is evidence that bureau members are aware of the Supreme Court's decision in *Roth* v. *U. S.*, there is no proof that the terms of this judgment are being observed.

In fact, there is considerable circumstantial evidence to the

[414] This procedure would seem to be equally defensible even under the *Jacobellis* definition of obscenity. While cutting movies cannot make them of "redeeming social importance," it can at least suppress what is "patently offensive."

effect that Kansas' brand of prior restraint is exceedingly harsh. First of all, the bureau has been guided in the not-too-distant past (it can probably be assumed that these rules are no longer enforced) by a set of informal policies that have had no equal in their overt unconstitutionality. Thus, pictures were to be "clean and wholesome" and were not to "influence the mind to improper conduct"; "ridicule of any religious sect" was taboo; the depiction of all criminal methods that would serve as models for further action could not be shown. These standards fly in the face of the protection given to the dissemination of moving pictures by the *Burstyn* case. Free speech cannot be limited to that which would depict man as an asexual, unthinking robot.[415] The recency of known use of these rules by the Kansas Board, added to the fact that all censorship activities there are sub rosa, along with the claims of other censors that this state is the strictest of all in regulating movies, hardly paints an optimistic picture regarding the application of Supreme Court holdings by authorized censorship officials.

To what extent do the censorship laws and practices of cities conform to Supreme Court judgments regarding the rights of the motion picture medium? Are they more or less apt to obey such holdings than are the four states whose work has been summarized thus far?

Chicago's film censorship statute requires the suppression of any picture that "is obscene, or portrays depravity, criminality or lack of virtue of a class of citizens of any race, color, creed or religion and exposes them to contempt, derision or obloquy, or tends to produce a breach of the peace or riots, or purports to represent any hanging, lynching or burning of a human being." Leaving aside the question of obscenity, the Supreme Court has never passed on the constitutionality of any of the above guidelines in a censorship setting. However, in 1952, the Supreme Court did find an Illinois subsequent punishment statute valid which forbade the dissemination of material which "exposed the citizens of any race, color, creed or religion to contempt, derision

[415] The complete list of these commands can be found in Chapter III, in "Movie Censorship in Kansas," *supra*.

or obloquy, or which is productive of breach of the peace or riots." Petitioner had distributed pamphlets calling for "one million self-respecting white people to unite to prevent the white race from being mongrelized by the Negro." In defense of the law, a majority of the Justices were of the opinion that if a state could punish expressions of "the lewd and obscene, the profane, the libelous and the insulting or 'fighting' words" when aimed at individuals (as had been decided in the *Cantwell* and *Chaplinsky*[416] holdings), then it also had the power to make certain that groups could be protected against "libel" by such noxious attacks.[417] Nevertheless it is one thing to uphold a subsequent punishment law predicated on these criteria and quite another to approve a prior censorship ordinance of the same ilk. This, at least, is suggested by *Near* v. *Minnesota*, and it is not easy to forget Justice Clark's warning in the *Burstyn* decision: "It is not the business of government in our nation to suppress real or imagined attacks upon a particular religious doctrine, whether they appear in publications, speeches, or motion pictures."[418] In any event it is difficult to conceive of the Supreme Court's placing its stamp of approval on the commonly used practice of deleting from movies "certain words" like "nigger" that might offend the Negro. Nor is it possible that scenes in moving pictures that depict hangings or the burning of human beings can be cut out arbitrarily, consistent with free speech guarantees.

The enforcement of this unique collection of standards, however, is only a prelude to the scope of Chicago's censorship activ-

[416] *Chaplinsky* v. *New Hampshire*, 315 U. S. 568 (1942).

[417] *Beauharnais* v. *Illinois*, 343 U. S. 250 (1952).

[418] These comments, of course, are equally applicable to that part of the ordinance which proscribes movies that "portray depravity, criminality or lack of virtue of a class of citizens. . . ." It is not likely that movies which "tend to produce a breach of the peace or riots" can be censored as is the practice in Chicago. While the issue has not been litigated none of the Justices has indicated, by way of dictum, the constitutionality of either of these standards. It would appear to be impossible to construct " a narrowly drawn statute" which would isolate movies of this sort unless the words "tend to produce" were construed to mean "incite." However, censorship predicated on these terms would be consistent with Chief Justice Hughes's analysis of the question in *Near* v. *Minnesota*.

ity. In implementing the ordinance the Film Review Section watches out for the lewd (especially nudity that is "just thrown in"), excessive brutality and swearing, and anything else that would incite to immoral conduct. All of this is done because the censors feel they must protect both children and senile older people from their own fallibilities. Of course, it is patently unconstitutional under the *Commercial Pictures* doctrine to suppress anything because it may corrupt morals. Furthermore, both of the basic rules of *Roth-Alberts* are flouted when nudity is emasculated as a matter of course because of its effect on those who are too young or too old. It would also appear evident that it is impermissible under the First Amendment to delete brutality that is "offensive" to the censors regardless of context, and, also, to eliminate profanity that is "excessive." These policies are clear examples of arbitrarily applying the standards of social deportment to an artistic milieu. Such criteria become especially violative of free speech privileges when gauged against the sensibilities of the immature mind. And, of course, it is highly dubious that words like "excessive" and "offensive" are precise enough to satisfy due process.

In addition to these censorial shortcomings Chicago's Film Review Section is also given the right to designate movies that minors under the age of seventeen cannot view. Under the applicable statute the audience in attendance can be so limited for any film that "considered as a whole, has the dominant effect of substantially arousing sexual desires in any person less than seventeen years of age, or if the picture is indecent, or is contrary to contemporary community standards in the description or representation of nudity or sex." The Supreme Court has passed only tangentially on the question of age classifications in relation to speech and press. In *Butler* v. *Michigan* Mr. Justice Frankfurter noted that Michigan could have tried appellant under a state law specifically aimed at protecting children against obscene matter. On the other hand, the infirmity of the state law being enforced against the defendant (making it illegal to publish or sell anything tending to the corruption of the morals of youth) was that it was "not reasonably restricted to the evil with which it is said to deal."[419] The weight of scholarly analysis leans heavily in favor of the notion that these remarks constitute approval of age classification schemes as a permissible kind of legislation regulating the sale of printed matter.[420] Permissible limitations on the use of this kind of power that would be predicated on First Amendment considerations have never been determined.

The Detroit censorship ordinance is succinct, indeed. A movie is to be rejected if it is "indecent or immoral" and, further, any part of a film that is indecent or immoral in and of itself is to be eliminated. While the Supreme Court has long ago voided the use of the word "immoral" as a basis for prior restraint, it has never passed on the nature and acceptability of indecency as a regulatory criterion. It might be argued, on the one hand, that the term reasonably apprises the public of the conduct that is forbidden, as in the case of ordinances that regulate indecent exposure, and that the courts would therefore uphold its use given the broad scope of a community's police power. The contention, however, is not persuasive. Indecent exposure is one thing, but what is an indecent speech or an indecent movie? An analogous controversy centered around the constitutionality of the statutory standard "immorality." In the *Commercial Pictures* case the New York courts thought it a permissible guideline within a censorship context because the phrase "moral turpitude" was a legitimate criterion for employment that a public agency might utilize. The Supreme Court reversed per curiam. In short, to say that behavior is immoral or indecent is one thing; to say that speech is immoral or indecent is something else. And, of course, the Court will countenance a *prior restraint* on speech only under exceptional circumstances (*Near v. Minnesota*).

Even if these standards could be properly invoked, however, indecent or immoral segments can no more be cut out of movies without regard to the dominant theme of the presentation than obscene segments can be deleted in the manner continually employed in New York and Virginia. It seems clear that this vital

---

[419] 352 U. S. 380 at p. 383.
[420] See, for example, Kilpatrick, *op. cit.*, pp. 127–28; Nimmer, *op. cit.*, p. 656; Leary and Noall, *op. cit.*, p. 341, footnote 109.

element of *Roth-Alberts* is necessarily applicable to *any* censorship criterion if it is to be found valid. As has been mentioned, there is a strong indication that Detroit is now construing the terms "immoral" and "indecent" to mean "obscene." From the standpoint of constitutional law, however, the difference is not vital because the Bureau delivers the coup de grace to *Roth-Alberts* by admitting that it deletes nudity, rape scenes, and profanity irrespective of the context of the movie itself.

Over and above these usual censorship rules, Detroit also tries to limit the exhibition of certain "off-beat" movies to so-called art houses. The Supreme Court has yet to hear a controversy involving this procedure; but it would seem that if age classification schemes in general are constitutional, so likewise would the limitation of exhibition of some films to certain movie houses that cater only to adults. In Detroit, for example, it is impossible to keep children out of "commercial" theaters. Censors therefore let art houses show relatively unexpurgated film fare if patrons under eighteen years are disallowed. The constitutional problem with this scheme, however, is that Detroit, like Virginia, has no statutory criteria for determining when a picture is to be denied juvenile consumption. Consequently such decisions, when overzealous, cannot help but abridge free speech considerations. Nor should it be forgotten that even these art houses are subject to the other somewhat dubious constitutional standards and practices hereinbefore stipulated.

It follows from this that the Supreme Court would probably void any attempt to limit the presentation of films to certain movie houses unless this procedure could be justified as a rational implementation of constitutional censorship. Otherwise the greatest source of financial remuneration for these productions could be stifled in a manner that would make it unprofitable for anyone to make a picture contrary to stated government regulations. Of course, limitations of this kind could be so stringent as to render the film's access to the hypothetical "market place" nugatory. As to Detroit's policy of "punishing" movies that will not submit to cutting by restricting these films to particular cinema houses, this tactic would probably stand or fall on the constitutionality of the censorship operation itself. If the deletions were ordered contrary to First Amendment rights (as many undoubtedly are in Detroit) then any prohibition based on a refusal to obey these commands would also seem to be unconstitutional.

The Memphis ordinance makes it possible to proscribe films that are of "immoral, lewd or lascivious character" or are "inimical to the public safety, health, morals, or welfare" or are believed culpable of "denouncing, deriding, or seeking to overthrow the present form of national government." While the last of these three sets of standards is no longer enforced, the City Board counterbalances this self-restraint by telling exhibitors in special instances that it would be "for the best interests of the community" if certain pictures were not shown. This policy, as has been touched on earlier, is contrary to the principle set out in *Gelling* v. *Texas* (the *Pinky* case).

There is, of course, no more common justification given for the passage of local laws than that they are designed to promote the public safety, morals, etc., of a community. Certainly the behavior patterns of the citizen can usually be constricted for these reasons. But can a movie be censored on such grounds? Again, the doctrine of *Near* and *Burstyn* that prior restraints are legitimate only in the most exceptional cases (even for movies) would seem to be controlling.

The statutory guidelines most typically used to restrict movies in this city are the terms "lewd, lascivious and immoral." While the Supreme Court has not had occasion to construe the first two of these in a censorship controversy and has rejected the use of the third per se, it is highly likely that if afforded the opportunity to examine this overall phrase it would probably find it to be synonymous with obscenity. This, at least, was precisely what Mr. Justice Harlan held when interpreting similar standards contained in the Comstock Act. Such criteria, he stated, had reference to materials that were "patently offensive" and, of course, offensiveness of this kind is the prototype of the obscene.[421] To the de-

---

[421] For present purposes it can be safely assumed that any movie that is "patently offensive" is also obscene under the *Roth-Alberts* formula and vice versa because, as Harlan pointed out in the *Manual Enterprises* decision, it is only in the rare circumstance when materials are being distributed that appeal to the prurient interest of deviant groups that the two concepts

gree that Memphis is now construing these words so that they have reference to obscenity it is seemingly conforming to free speech guarantees.

In practice, however, these censorship authorities do not interpret these three guidelines to mean the same thing. Each is merely considered to be a separate aspect of a greater whole. The result is that all are probably "void for vagueness" because the Board has never given them any meaningful description. The confusion becomes rampant because movies are also banned or cut if they are indecent—an extremely suspect term from the constitutional standpoint. Furthermore, indecency is considered synonymous with the immoral, a *clearly* unconstitutional standard. Throw in the fact that "vulgarity" is another censorship criterion (and the use of a word like that in the present context is surely "indefiniteness" on its face) and the result is a potpourri of censorship guidelines which make a laughing stock of the Supreme Court's careful evaluation of free speech liberties.

It logically follows from the use of these amorphous criteria that censorship decisions themselves will be highly arbitrary. It should not be surprising, for example, to learn that both scenes and dialogue are invariably cut out regardless of context. Furthermore, the values of the immature viewer constitute the basic preoccupation of the bureau; over and above its rejection of *Roth-Alberts,* the Board also forbids persons under eighteen from seeing certain pictures. In this regard, it appears to violate First Amendment rights just as Virginia and Detroit do because there are no statutory standards used to guide the censors in applying this limitation.

Two other matters deserve comment. First, as has already been cited, censorship authorities in this community exercise a powerful informal check on movie exhibitors that rivals their licensing prerogatives. This is accomplished by attempting to persuade middlemen who rent pictures to movie house owners not to market certain films because they are objectionable. It seems

---

are not congruent. Given the fact that film censors invariably seem to overstep the limitations of *Roth-Alberts* it seems obvious that the first movies to "feel the axe" are those that are "offensive on their face."

evident that this type of prior restraint, exercised in a behind-the-scenes manner by officials acting under color of law, violates the teaching set down by the Supreme Court in *Bantam Books, Inc.* v. *Sullivan.*

Secondly, in a manner that is sui generis only to Memphis, the bureau seems to presume against the legitimacy of movies that do not carry Hollywood's seal of approval (Question 32). This, of course, cannot be construed to mean that P.C.A. clearance is mandatory, otherwise practically no foreign picture would ever come to Memphis whereas some, in fact, do. It does mean, however, that a sizeable percentage of American movies other than those produced by the large companies plus many films made abroad may not receive even a preliminary hearing. Indeed, the case of *The Connection* illustrates the point graphically. Reliance on Hollywood's grading system which, by definition, is applicable to only a limited number of the world's motion picture companies amounts, in effect, to an unconstitutional delegation of administrative authority to a private agency. The First Amendment does not permit the use of power designed to "filter out" abuses of First Amendment rights to be in part surrendered by the body politic to any nongovernmental tribunal.

The work of movie censors in Atlanta can be clearly divided into two periods. Under the old ordinance, which was repealed in 1962, a picture could be denied a license if it was "obscene, lewd, licentious, profane or will . . . adversely affect the peace, health, morals, and good order of the city." However, a movie could be "saved" if objectionable scenes or dialogue were removed. As a matter of practice, however, the terms "obscene" and "licentious" were used on almost all occasions to justify bannings and elimination orders.[422] It is difficult to believe that the Supreme Court would approve the use of "licentious" as a censorship guideline unless it was construed to be synonymous with the obscene. At the very least, its contours are as vague as "that which corrupts morals."

While the statutes used by New York, Virginia, and Detroit

---

[422] The suppression of *The Birth of a Nation* so as to protect the good order of the city was undoubtedly a violation of the *Burstyn* doctrine. See the previous discussion in this chapter.

are void on their face in that they allow for the cutting of objectionable scenes without regard to the validity of the work as a whole, the Atlanta law was of a different species because its scope was limited to offensive scenes that corrupted the total product. It hardly mattered, however, because Atlanta censors freely admit that the *Roth-Alberts* test was ignored from 1957 until 1962. Allegedly "obscene segments" such as the use of words like "bastard" and "whore" and, of course, "nudity scenes" were commonly deleted. As seems to follow inevitably from these circumstances, the procedures invoked were justified because they protected "the immature regardless of age."

Where do things stand under the new ordinance? This enactment, as has been described, instructs the Reviewer (formerly the Censor) to label a picture "approved," "unsuitable for the young" or "objectionable." The most provocative procedure now being utilized in effectuating these new provisions is the Reviewer's blue-penciling certain scenes in "objectionable" films so as to relegate them to the "UY" category. The theory of this operation may well be within constitutional bounds because the definition given to characterize an "objectionable" movie is closely akin to *Roth-Alberts*. If a censor can delete obnoxious portions to salvage at least part of a production, he would seem to be doing nothing more than making the obscene nonobscene. Unfortunately, there have been no court cases arising out of the use of this technique, and it is impossible to know the extent to which this theory governs what Atlanta is doing in this regard.

While the prior classification of motion pictures for exhibition according to age groups of viewers is probably constitutional, the letter and enforcement of Atlanta's ordinance may create special problems. For one thing, the ordinance does not specify the age of the so-called "young" who are being warned that particular movies are unsuitable for them. The Reviewer may affix a "UY" rating to any picture which "while not objectionable for the average person or for mature adult persons, would nevertheless be objectionable for children, young people or immature people because. . . ." How old are children? Are "young people" older than children or are the two one and the same? And, what about "immature people?" Unless these three categories are interpreted to mean the same age group this section is clearly contrary to due process. Otherwise, one could readily argue that many adults are immature. What is objectionable for an immature man is not a rational or precise criterion for limiting what a child may see. But suppose the three phrases are synonymous? To what age do they commonly refer? It is obvious that what might "corrupt" a fifteen-year-old might have no meaning at all for a child of eight. In other words, by not fixing any precise or even approximate age limit the statute gives rise to a "void for vagueness" question.[423]

As has been mentioned earlier, a second prominent difficulty that seems inherent in the guidelines set up by the new Atlanta ordinance is that it defines an "approved" movie as one that must not contain prurient sequences, while the section that specifies those pictures that must be classified as "UY" includes all films that exhibit "matter which is offensive to contemporary moral standards in the community or has a theme which would tend to create immorality, corruption or debauchery or would tend to create a harmful impression of proper moral conduct, according to the standards of the community." These conflicting criteria raise the following dilemma: If the reviewer holds to the first criterion he will inevitably give an "approved" rating to movies that deal critically with community standards of morality other than those of sexual relevance, while if he applies the second, he clearly flies in the face of the straight-to-the-point meaning of the first section which forbids "youth" from seeing only the prurient.

---

[423] If the courts were to find the words "young" and "immature" controlling in this clause they might then construe the statute as calling for the cut-off point to be the onset of puberty. However, this construction would seem to run against the "legislative intent" of the entire program because a movie is to be rated "approved" if it does not contain any matter that appeals to prurient interest. This specification, plus Atlanta's demonstrable preoccupation with film material dealing with sex, seems to indicate that, basically, the city was trying to devise this portion of the law so as to make sure that youths whose minds could not understand such materials would not be exposed to them. These people, of course, are teen-agers and not third graders.

Again, the lack of clarity and precision in the standards set up by the ordinance might endanger its status if a claim of "void for vagueness" is pressed.

How is Atlanta coping with these dual problems? It is impossible to tell. The Reviewer keeps no records on why she decides to grade films as she does, so it is impossible to see how she is interpreting the terms of these sections of the enactment. Indeed, who can say how carefully she is following the *Roth* test in deciding that a movie is "objectionable?"[424] Nor have there, as yet, been any court cases germane to these procedures which could cast light on these inquiries. Clearly, some are needed.

One more issue must be considered in connection with the hiatus between Supreme Court holdings and state and local movie censorship regulations. This involves the fees assessed in New York, Maryland, Virginia, Kansas, and Chicago before the inspection of any movie will commence. In *Murdock* v. *Pennsylvania*, the high Court forcefully struck down a nondiscriminatory license tax to be paid by all vendors when this ordinance was used to exact a fee from Jehovah's Witnesses selling religious pamphlets. How can one square this decision[425] with levies charged *only to movie companies?* Why should movies, no matter how immune they might be to assault under the censorship laws, be forced to pay a charge for the privilege of dissemination while the legitimate theater, newspapers, etc., remain free from such exactions?[426] The problem is an extremely serious one. While it may be a rather trivial task for Metro-Goldwyn-

---

[424] Mrs. Gilliam did find *The Connection* obscene under the ambit of the new law contrary to the New York court opinion stating otherwise. Of course, this judgment carries no legal weight in Georgia.

[425] But see *Cox* v. *New Hampshire*, 312 U. S. 569 (1941), for a contrary ruling.

[426] A similar problem occurs when cities and towns insist that moviehouse owners pay license taxes as a prerequisite to exhibiting moving pictures for profit. Thus, an Illinois law sanctioning local taxation of this kind has been upheld (see *Metropolis* v. *Gibbons*, 334 Ill. 431, 1929), while on authority of the *Murdock* doctrine, the Illinois courts have held that Jehovah's Witnesses cannot be forced to pay a license fee prior to selling the Watchtower for profit (see *Blue Island* v. *Kozul*, 379 Ill. 511, 1942). Nor is it possible any longer to countenance state laws that give local communities the right to prohibit the showing of motion pictures within their jurisdiction.

Mayer to write out the necessary checks, such fees (or taxes) are certainly a formidable barrier for any smaller company either here or abroad to clear. If the *Murdock* rule has any substance as a protection against the use of the taxing power previously to restrain free speech, then this "fee system" on the use of this form of communication must likewise be void.[427]

To sum up: Each city and each state using a systematic program of movie censorship here surveyed operates under a legal framework that is in some measure at the least, violative of due process and at the most, in conflict with *Burstyn* v. *Wilson* and its free speech corollaries. In 1961 the Supreme Court ruled, in the second *Times Film* controversy, that administrative licensing of motion pictures by censorship boards was not unconstitutional on its face. As has been noted, the consensus among legal scholars is that this decision countenances the suppression of obscene movies by prior restraint. And, it must be remembered, the recent *Freedman* ruling waters down the impact of prior restraint only from the standpoint of procedural guarantees. The problem is that none of the censorship agencies investigated seem to appreciate the true limits of obscenity and, consequently, are continually overzealous in the materials they place under this rubric. Other than the *Don Juan* holding the significant decisions that the Supreme Court has handed down in recent years which have had a direct impact on the content of statutory standards which censorship bureaus may utilize have been: (1) the *Burstyn* ruling, which ostensibly emancipated movies from the second-class citizenship accorded to "entertainment" in the market place of ideas, and, (2) the *Roth* decision which attempted to construct reasonable guidelines for gauging obscenity that printed matter, and presumably movies, have an obligation not to transgress. In interpreting these decisions, censorship officials have flouted their scope and meaning with impunity.

---

This is no more consistent with free speech rights than is a state law prohibiting the sale or distribution of newspapers within its borders. See comments, *supra*, relative to footnote 27.

[427] In several instances there is little or no relationship between the intake of funds and monies needed to subsidize censorship. See Leary and Noall, *op. cit.*, p. 335, especially footnote 67.

### Should Motion Picture Censorship be Abolished?

The merits and demerits of censorship for the film industry have been bandied about by many. On the one hand, the opinion has been advanced that it provides a measure of security to the exhibitor because he knows that a licensed picture has been approved by duly constituted authority. Furthermore, the status of a particular film need not be determined by the helter-skelter method of repetitive local prosecution; one lawsuit following an adverse ruling by a censorship body will suffice. On the other hand, it has been argued that the censor is a somewhat abnormal person who is "morbidly interested in seeking out material to be kept from the sight of his fellow citizens."[428] There is little empirical data to validate this last allegation, nor is there anything in this study that would lend encouragement to its proponents. Those who view movie censorship with distaste have also contended that regulations of this ilk are essentially weapons of state control used to instill an ideological conformity into the sociopolitical community. In this sense censorship confines man's intellectual horizons and can corrupt his fundamental liberty to search out his salvation in his own way.[429]

The most impassioned defense of motion picture censorship one might care to encounter was a by-product of Mr. Justice Michael Musmanno's dissent in the *Hallmark Pictures* (Pennsylvania) case. It is worth careful study:

> How will the (subsequent) punishment of the exhibitor heal the lacerating wounds made in the delicate sensations of children and sensitive adults who witness a picture of lewdness, depravity and immorality. Damage is done at the very first exhibition of the film. There are theaters in Pittsburgh and Philadelphia which accom-

---

[428] Leary and Noall, *op. cit.*, pp. 337-38.

[429] Haney has argued in a provocative, though oversimplified, manner that the natural law philosophy of Leo Strauss and Walter Berns offers no defense against the excesses of censorship because it is overly committed to the premise that the task of government is to make men virtuous. He advocates the Jeffersonian notion of limited government as the best defense against such dangers. Robert W. Haney, *Comstockery in America* (Boston: Beacon Press, 1960), pp. 61-65.

modate 4,000 patrons for one show. If a picture should last but one day, many thousands nevertheless have seen it by the time it is withdrawn from circulation. That is why reason dictates that control over immoral films must be found in prevention and not in subsequent punishment. . . .

There is a very fallacious notion afloat on the waves of idle thought that in a free society, the least control makes for the biggest happiness. The slightest reflection will demonstrate that there would be considerable misery, not to say plagues and pestilences, if government did not hold an analytical and punitive eye on producers of medicine, drugs, foods and beverages. . . . A good citizen not only does not object but is happy for the fact that someone far more skilled than he determines whether the can of peaches he opens . . . is free of deleterious ingredients. A worthy member of society, who is just as much concerned about mental purity as he is over bodily cleanliness, is grateful that the government which protects him from contact with physical contagion will also save him from association with moral trash and garbage. . . . The virtue in rejection does not lie alone in the discarding of what is improper but in the maintenance of a standard of decency and morality which assured each year the manufacture of less and less undesirable films. But with the elimination of censorship, the light in the lamps of standardized corruptness dims, and as a consequence, there will not be lacking producers who will be guided only by the beacon of profit which can hardly be depended upon to keep the course of the ship of production traveling within pure waters.[430]

The sentiments expressed by Justice Musmanno cannot be squared with the Supreme Court's holdings in *Near v. Minnesota, Burstyn v. Wilson* and all of the companion decisions that have been handed down which carefully circumscribe the area of mass media dissemination that may be regulated by censorship. But over and above these judgments and, indeed, over and above the supposition that censorship is invidious because it goes hand-in-hand with the politics of the authoritarian state, the most evident difficulty with this articulate statement of views is that it ignores what movie censorship is all about. In short, it talks of

---

[430] *Hallmark Productions v. Carroll*, 384 Pa. 348, 121 A. 2d 584 (1956) at pp. 594-95.

these practices only in the abstract. The basic problem with motion picture censorship is that wherever it is put into practice it flouts the supreme law of the land day after day and year after year.

There are, of course, those who will argue that the tool is sound, but that it has not been placed into the proper hands. Yet, this survey of communities presently utilizing movie censorship shows that Atlanta vests these responsibilities in a civil servant and public library trustees, Detroit uses police officers and Virginia favors political appointees. The Supreme Court itself, however, has displayed a willingness to countenance motion picture censorship if judges participate in the process. It will be recalled that in his *Freedman* opinion Mr. Justice Brennan suggested that an injunctive remedy of the type that was held constitutional in the *Kingsley Books* holding be utilized to ascertain the obscenity of motion pictures.[431] The problem with Brennan's recommendation was that he then went on to imply that communities could constitutionally subject films to prior restraints other than the *Kingsley Books* prototype; and that one alternative control system might consist of the censorship tribunal hedged about by judicial checks. It must be remembered, however, that there is nothing in *Freedman* that guarantees the enforcement of its broadly stated ground rules (recall Chicago's permissive legislative response) any more than there is anything in *Burstyn* or *Roth-Alberts* that guaranteed their unconditional acceptance. But to repeat, even if given implementation at the grass-roots level, what is there in this doctrine that exempts the clearly nonobscene movie from censorship molestation in the form of fees to be paid and harshly restrictive censorship board and court orders that may be promulgated?[432] To put it bluntly, the tragedy of *Freedman* v. *Maryland* is that the Supreme Court missed its chance to provide the same protections for works of art that have

[431] A review of the literature appears to indicate that this proposal was first advocated in my "State and Local Motion Picture Censorship and Constitutional Liberties with Special Emphasis on the Communal Acceptance of Supreme Court Decision-Making," doctoral dissertation, University of Michigan, 1964, pp. 356-58.

[432] See pp. 120–21, for a more detailed examination of these points.

been placed on film that it has allotted to masterpieces that lie between the covers of books. The existence of censorship boards such as those described herein makes all the difference; nor can one easily forget the warnings by Chief Justice Hughes in *Near* and Mr. Justice Roberts in *Cantwell* v. *Connecticut* that unjustifiable censorship is no more appetizing when enforced by the judiciary than when implemented by others.[433] It is herewith submitted that the illegal policies practiced by each and every censorship bureau analyzed are a product of the fundamental premise implicit in the system, i.e. that one need only set up a board of control at the state or local level and one can be assured that only "unobjectionable" movies will reach the citizenry.

It does not follow, of course, that only subsequent punishment laws need be used to combat really obnoxious movies. Thus far, only obscene pictures have been found by the Supreme Court to be so deleterious to the community that they may be subjected to prior restraint. Would it not be feasible for a state to demand that motion pictures be subject to the same in rem procedures that the Court has stipulated may be used to restrain obscene literature? Surprisingly enough, the state of Florida, with its haphazard censorship scheme, provides an interesting precedent for this kind of community control. The applicable statute allows a state attorney to obtain an injunction in a state circuit court enjoining the pending exhibition of a movie that would violate the terms set out in the law; however, a defendent is entitled to a trial of the issues within one day after joinder.[434] This procedure, when used to inhibit the free flow of movies believed to be obscene, is nothing but the *Kingsley Books* restraint applied to film fare.

At the proposed hearing, the court is to receive evidence from both the distributor or the producer, on the one hand, and the state, on the other hand, as to the predominant appeal of the motion picture considered as a whole, the artistic, scientific, or

---

[433] See the discussion of these two decisions in Chapter I, in "Constitutional Limitations on Prior Restraints on Speech," *supra.*

[434] The Florida statutory mechanism is analyzed in Chapter III, in "Movie Censorship in Louisiana and Florida," *supra.*

educational values of the production, the intent of those who have created the film, and its effect on the average person. If no answer is filed in defense of the picture the court might simply view the movie and render a judgment predicated on *Roth-Alberts*.

The advantages of this kind of scheme are impressive. As opposed to the typical movie censorship operation, it guarantees an immediate open hearing hedged about by the rules of procedural due process, a complete record of all testimony, both oral and written, and a judge's decision based on an evaluation of First Amendment freedoms in complex fact situations. Even more essential, however, it provides maximum free play for the "presumption of innocence" postulate because only pictures that are suspect will be restrained. As opposed to the workings of the penal law, it takes virtually all power away from police officials who are totally unequipped to act with expertise on the constitutional issues at stake in this area. And, of course, it affords a large measure of protection to the exhibitor who is equally unequipped to determine what appeals to the prurient interest of the average man, but who must pay a heavy fine or face imprisonment if he should show an obscene movie contrary to a subsequent punishment enactment. It must be noted, however, that this recommended procedure is a prior restraint on speech and because the Supreme Court has only approved of this kind of regulation to combat obscenity, it could not be used to inhibit the free flow of other kinds of motion pictures thought to be offensive.

Actually, this hypothetical scheme has two definite advantages over the New York law affirmed in *Kingsley Books*. Under the terms of that statute any local law enforcement official could seek an injunction against the sale of a particular publication thought to be obscene and the eventual ruling in that case would be binding upon all other book merchants throughout the state. As Mr. Justice Douglas pointed out, this procedure might enable prosecuting officials to select carefully a locality with the most rigid judge or the most conservative juries to obtain a favorable judgment. This drawback is avoided here because only state attorneys can file for an injunction and, even then, only in a state circuit court. Secondly, logic dictates that this mechanism has greater utility in screening out obscene movies than obscene literature; there are simply far fewer movies and movie houses than there are books, photographs, post cards, and those that sell them.

It is true that the proposed mechanism does strike at the film before it has circulated publicly, and so there is no chance to weigh communal opinion. But this objection is largely theoretical because under the workings of the penal law suspected obscene productions typically are seized after one or two showings so that in most cases public reaction is of minimal importance. It might well be feasible to counterbalance even this minor flaw by inviting the public to attend showings of each film as it is introduced into evidence before the court. It should be noted that there is no infirmity arising out of the fact that a judge and not a jury will make findings of obscenity because the Supreme Court appears to have accepted Mr. Justice Harlan's contention that this task is inherently a part of the judge's domain.

While recommendations of this type may have appeal for students of American constitutional law who view current movie censorship practices with alarm, it would be naive to think that they would dispel the onus of censorship that hangs, albatross-like, around the neck of the motion picture industry. The reason for this is that movies have "gone adult," so to speak; one can see the most intimate of sex acts and hear the vilest of profanity on the screen in 1966 whereas twenty years ago no one would have dared to film such sensationalism. While most intelligent people realize that these developments are part of a long term and long overdue maturation process for the cinema (assuming that obscene pictures can be filtered out), there are many who honestly believe that something must be done to keep such film fare away from children and teen-agers who are unequipped to deal with this kind of content. Surely when "implications of cunnilingus," the exposure of private parts, and the frequent use of the word "shit" are screened before audiences of all ages basic regulatory reforms are justifiable.

The mildest of these proposals for control calls for Hollywood to classify each of its productions voluntarily so that parents can readily see if a movie is fit for their youngsters.[435] Support for this approach has come from various groups—the Protestant Motion Picture Council, the National Congress of Parents and Teachers, the Film Estimate Board of National Organizations (the "Green Sheet") and the American Jewish Committee. The typical means of control, perhaps, is that advocated by the Roman Catholic Episcopal Committee for Motion Pictures, Radio, and Television. This group simply asks that producers label their pictures "suitable for children" if in their judgment films deserve this rating.[436]

A more ambitious proposal is espoused by those, such as journalist John Crosby, who believe that the voluntary system used in England might be tried in the United States.[437] Under this regulatory scheme, the British Board of Film Censors, a nongovernmental body financed by the cinema itself, categorizes movies as "U" (suitable for general exhibition); "A" (more suitable for adult audiences—children under sixteen not admitted unless accompanied by a parent or guardian); and "X" (suitable for adults only).[438] Legal effect is given to these findings by local

[435]However, the so-called Kefauver Subcommittee which in 1955 investigated the relationship between movies and juvenile delinquency, felt that most antisocial behavior caused by moving pictures could be eradicated if Hollywood's voluntary censorship code was updated, its enforcing arm (the P.C.A.) was staffed, in part, by professional people from the behavioral sciences, and producers obeyed suggestions advanced by this agency. *Motion Pictures and Juvenile Delinquency,* Report of the Committee on the Judiciary Containing an Interim Report of the Subcommittee to Investigate Juvenile Delinquency, S. Rep. No. 2055, 84th Congress, 2d Session, 1956, pp. 66-68, 70-71. This proposal has received little support from either the movie industry or interested private groups.

[436] See the remarks of Representative Kyl of Iowa in the *U. S. Congressional Record–House,* Feb. 14, 1963, p. 2139. For the text of H. Res. 255 introduced by Mr. Kyl calling upon the moving picture industry to "put its house in order" or face federal censorship, see *ibid.,* p. 2140.

[437] John Crosby, "Movies Are Too Dirty," *Saturday Evening Post,* Nov. 10, 1962, pp. 8, 11.

[438] Dr. Hugh M. Flick, former chairman of the New York film censorship board, favors this method of regulation but would go one step further and add a "C" category—recommended for children. See Alpert, *op. cit.,* p. 53.

authorities who have the option of inserting or not inserting the appropriate conditions into licenses granted to each production.

While recommendations on this order are propounded with great zeal, there are innumerable obstacles that stand in the way of their ever being successfully employed in this country. For one thing, the Motion Picture Association of America has fought against any kind of age classification mechanism since these were first seriously considered.[439] Secondly, Hollywood's ratings would not cover either foreign movies or those put out by independent American companies and it is precisely these presentations which cause most of the controversies as the work of state and local censorship bureaus indicates. Finally, what guidelines would the industry use to police its films? Would these criteria be acceptable to the groups that clamor the loudest for age classification? In other words, just because Hollywood says that movies are "suitble for children" or "for adults only" does this mean that interested parties will agree? Certainly the industry's highly flexible interpretation of its own code does not afford a basis for optimism that this would occur.[440]

If self-imposed age classification is mere naivete, can one expect state-controlled agencies to satisfy the demands of the many groups which insist that youngsters be quarantined from movies that can be taken in perspective only by adults? What kind of scheme could accomplish this task when weighed against the many criticisms that have been leveled at the validity of age categorization? The notion that young people ought to be protected against noxious speech and press is as old as Plato's *Republic*. His conception of the role of censorship tailored to accomplish this end ran as follows:

> Shall we just carelessly allow children to hear any casual tales which may be devised by casual persons, and to receive into their minds ideas for the most part the very opposite of those which we should wish them to have when they are grown up? . . .

[439] Typical critical remarks about such notions can be found in Joe Hyams, "What Should We Do About the Crisis in Movie Morals?" *This Week Magazine*, Feb. 26, 1961, pp. 8-10.

[440] For an analysis of how Hollywood has perverted its own voluntary censorship regulations see, for example, Carmen, *op. cit.*, Chapter III.

Then the first thing will be to establish a censorship of the writers of fiction, and let the censors receive any tale of fiction which is good, and reject the bad; and we will desire mothers and nurses to tell their children the authorized ones only. Let them fashion the mind with such tales, even more fondly than they mold the body with their hands: but most of those which are now in use must be discarded.[441]

It is, of course, impossible to discuss in a meaningful way the utility of age classification programs for motion pictures without first dealing with the question of their constitutionality. The Supreme Court, by way of dictum, appears to have placed its stamp of approval on such statutes in *Butler* v. *Michigan* as was noted earlier. But this judgment is by no means the only available piece of evidence in support of this view. In the 1944 case of *Prince* v. *Massachusetts*[442] the Court was asked to void the conviction of a Jehovah's Witness for encouraging his daughter to sell religious magazines contrary to a state child labor law. In answer to the parent's contention that his prerogatives under the First Amendment plus his right to bring up his child as he desired were controlling, a majority of eight replied that the community's control over the activities of minors is broader than over corresponding activities of adults: "The state has a wide range of power for limiting parental freedom and authority in things affecting the child's welfare; and this includes, to some extent, matters of conscience and religious conviction." Given this assumption, it is probable that the Supreme Court will not insist that movies whose market is to be limited to an adult audience consist only of those that present a "clear and present danger" of antisocial conduct when viewed by juveniles. It will only be necessary to balance the interest of the state in protecting minors with the rights of film producers and exhibitors under the First Amendment.[443]

---

[441] Plato, "The Republic," *Dialogues of Plato* (New York: Pocket Books, 1950), Bk. II, pp. 254-55.

[442] 321 U. S. 158 (1944).

[443] Note, "For Adults Only . . . ," *op. cit.*, p. 145, footnote 29. Cf. *Dennis* v. *U. S.*, 341 U. S. 494 (1951) with *Schenk* v. *U. S.*, 249 U. S. 47 (1919).

In attempting to bring these factors into balance a community would first have to draw up a set of standards to be used in categorizing motion pictures. It will not do simply to hang an "adults only" tag on certain films and let it go at that. While it is likely that to shield minors from objectionable movies the Supreme Court will more readily adjust free speech guarantees to accommodate the standards used than this would be done in movie censorship programs designed to protect adults, it will insist that these standards designate areas of speech which might reasonably have a deleterious impact on youth. Implicit in this requirement is the fact that these criteria stand for subject matter that is apprehendable in the light of common understanding and practice. In short, due process dictates that these guidelines be definite enough to warn the producer as well as the so-called classifier or grader of what is involved.

In the light of these remarks, how do the age classification standards used in Chicago and Atlanta measure up?[444] Do they seem to be susceptible to criticism in this regard or are they deserving of emulation? To begin with the old Chicago ordinance, one can hardly fault the finding of the federal district court that a statute which allowed minors to be prohibited from viewing productions that "tend toward creating a harmful impression on the minds of children . . ." was "hopelessly indefinite." After all, if ever a criterion failed to keep a censor from being "set adrift upon a boundless sea" then this one surely did.

The new Chicago enactment allows the Film Review Section to keep children who are sixteen and under away from any movie that "considered as a whole, has the dominant effect of substantially arousing sexual desires in any person less than seventeen years of age, or . . . is indecent, or is contrary to contemporary community standards in the description or representation of nudity or sex." The first of these standards presents a problem because it is difficult to tell what sort of movie the most maladjusted child will think is prurient. In other words, the adjective "any" in this stipulation might jeopardize its constitutional stand-

---

[444] Dallas, Texas and Portland, Oregon also use grading systems for motion pictures but these are not implemented by day-to-day enforcement. *Ibid.*, p. 143, footnote 16 and Nimmer, *op. cit.*, p. 656.

ing. The law goes on to provide that minors under seventeen shall not be allowed to see "indecent" pictures. Again, this term is very hard to define, but its usage is so prevalent in the criminal law that the courts might let it go by. In sharpening its meaning it is probable that judges would take note of the fact that this standard is used here in an unqualified sense, thus indicating that it was meant to refer to that which is indecent to the average adult mind. Finally, it would appear that the third statutory specification is consistent with the First Amendment in this context because it relies on "contemporary community standards," one of the touchstones of *Roth-Alberts*.

By way of contrast, the new Atlanta ordinance has innumerable pit falls not the least of which is the blatant discrepancy, already elaborated upon, between movies to be rated "approved" and those to be classified as "UY." Over and above this flaw, however, is the nature of the second of these guidelines. A movie is to be graded "unsuitable for the young" if it "contains matter which is offensive to contemporary moral standards in the community or has a theme which would tend to create immorality, corruption or debauchery or would tend to create a harmful impression of proper moral conduct, according to the standards of the community." Without slipping into the abyss of moral relativism it should be clear that reasonable men would have a tortuous time indeed trying to construe this terminology in anything other than a subjective manner.

It would seem, however, that that part of the Atlanta law which says that a picture shall be marked "approved" if it "does not contain any matter which tends to arouse sexual, lustful or carnal desires or which tends to appeal to prurient interests" opens the door to a meaningful discussion of age classification standards that are narrowly drawn enough so as not to offend free speech privileges and precise enough so as to be free of due process objections. The key phrase here is "prurient interest" which the Supreme Court has defined to mean "a shameful or morbid interest in nudity, sex, or excretion." Any movie whose dominant appeal is directed at such instincts and which "goes beyond customary limits of candor" in describing or characterizing these matters can usually be constitutionally censored. Furthermore, pictures of this kind must be patently offensive as, indeed, they invariably are when produced for commercial exploitation. The problem is that the *Roth-Alberts* test developed by the Supreme Court defines obscenity only in terms of dominant theme; it provides no answer for those who object to their children seeing snatches of film that overtly appeal to the prurient. Indeed, judging by the information gleaned from interviewing censorship officials much of the material they expurgate is surely patently offensive. It would appear that a general rule of thumb emerges from these facts that can be used to circumscribe what a minimal program of age classification must accomplish: The basic purpose of such a program should be to shield the underaged from microscopic examples of what the Supreme Court has said adults may be protected against in its macroscopic state through the use of previous restraint. In other words, what is needed are state age classification ordinances which will insulate youngsters from movies containing *any scene or dialogue* whose dominant theme appeals to the prurient interest and which is patently offensive. This, of course, is nothing more than a restatement of the *Queen v. Hicklin* standard. The controlling factor will not be the overall motif of the production but will rather be particular scenes or episodes, per se. This, however, is the *Hicklin* rule being used where it can do some good, i.e. regulating the films children, not adults, are to see.

But more will be needed if due process is to be satisfied. To whose mind will the appeal of the objectionable scenes have to be prurient? One highly sophisticated school of thought holds to the belief that obscenity has been largely defined in terms of its appeal, and so "it is therefore logical to determine a film's obscenity according to its appeal to children—an actual rather than an abstract audience."[445] This argument, however, opens Pandora's box all over again. How can you talk about the prurient interest of the "average youngster" when this age group runs from five years old to twelve, sixteen or twenty years old? Furthermore, if you apply this criterion to "any child" you jeopardize the high school

---

[445] Note, "For Adults Only . . . ," *op. cit.*, p. 145.

student's needs in order to save the grammar school child. All of this can be avoided. Why not simply use *Roth-Alberts* here? Thus, no movie would be shown to youngsters that contains any scene that appeals to the prurient interest *of the average person*. The result will be that the group being protected will not see exposed breasts, private parts, "bumps and grinds," "open mouth" kissing, words like "shit" and "fuck," and so forth. It should go without saying that such segments are patently offensive on their face.

This leads to another question that merits careful study and that is the maximum age of the group that is to be protected. In the *Paramount Film* holding the court found that Chicago's old grading statute was void partially because it lumped all minors (those under twenty-one years) into one category. Given the fact that so many young people, especially women, marry before they reach this age, that thousands of men who serve in the armed forces would thus fail to qualify, and that "the lower the age, the less the restriction on free speech and the stronger the argument for the constitutionality . . ." of the law, it would seem more feasible that the upper limit be seventeen years. Of course, the cut-off point will be somewhat arbitrary no matter what, but given the fact that precedents such as drivers' licenses, compulsory education, and selective service have already been established on a wide scale this line of demarcation would appear to be as justifiable as any.[446]

Of course, there are those who point to the fact that more than 200,000 students between the ages of fourteen and seventeen are enrolled in college and that there are 227,000 married women under the age of eighteen in this country.[447] More generally, critics of the seventeen-year age limit find any cut-off point to be "completely arbitrary and unrealistic because chronological age is a hopelessly unreliable index to the intellectual, emotional, and social maturity of a person."[448] It does not follow, however, that because some teen-agers are bright enough to be in college or

[446] *Ibid.*, p. 144 and especially footnote 23.

[447] *Memorandum on Motion Picture Classification,* issued by the Motion Picture Association of America, Jan. 19, 1960, pp. 6-7.

[448] Bosley Crowther, "Movies and Censorship," *Public Affairs Pamphlet* No. 332 (1962), p. 22.

hasty enough to marry, the state should therefore abrogate all the police power it possesses to see to it that young people who are just beginning to find their way in the world are not exposed to the obscene. No one would deny that this will penalize members of this group who are precocious. But highly intelligent and sensitive adults are equally ignored by countless laws geared to suit the behavior of the average man. If restrictive legislation was possible only when catered to the tastes of the exceptional, governmental action designed to protect the public morals, health, and welfare would be impossible.

Several other commonly used arguments that are put forward by the opposition warrant comment. Some of these involve deeply complex matters deserving of careful consideration. A primary point of controversy centers around the type of movie that should be kept away from viewers under the specified age. Advocates of this kind of supervision ask such questions as: Why not filter out all derogatory comments about particular races and creeds such as are contained in words like "nigger," "kike," "chink," etc.? Why not censor movies that might incite youngsters to crime, or which feature an excess of violence? Such notions are espoused by many responsible groups,[449] and, perhaps, have considerable merit.

The recommendation elaborated upon above, however, is an attempt to isolate the most offensive material that is now reaching younger people and to deal with it first. This minimal program of age classification is based on an objective guideline emanating from the Supreme Court; it enables the under-aged to be protected from viewing small doses of what is considered so distasteful and inflammatory that censorship boards are allowed to keep large doses of it away from the normal adult. It seems appropriate that a grading system for movies first try to deal with this problem area successfully before launching into the far more dubious en-

---

[449] The New York State Council of Churches, a Protestant group, is worried because the mass media often "portrays brutality and crime as desirable and acceptable" while a group of Roman Catholic prelates feels that children are seeing pictures that advocate prostitution and seduction as well as others that present "improper and dangerous standards." See citation listed under footnote 436, *supra*.

deavor of trying to filter out what is "too violent" or what "incites to criminal behavior." This first step, moreover, is not without its pragmatic value for the film industry itself because it will help to quiet those who are the most vociferous in their opposition to adult movies. These people appear to be most concerned about the fact that portrayal of intimate sexual conduct should not be made available to the youth of the nation.[450]

This question also can take a reverse form. Thus, those fearful of controls of this sort often wonder whose experience or what criteria will determine if a film can be exhibited to all. Again, the objective guidelines that the courts have found to be the essence of obscenity provide a clear point of demarcation. If the Supreme Court has determined that special censorship measures aimed at such noxious matter are within constitutional limits, then surely this unique class of suppressible conduct can be treated by legislators as a thing apart to be expurgated from movies shown to the young. There is nothing in this standard which invites an opening of the floodgates that might drown all provocative cinema in a sea of age classification.

A second fundamental issue occasioned by demands for grading systems is purely economic in nature. Geoffrey Shurlock, the Director of the Production Code Administration, has stated that the biggest difficulty with such proposals is financial because the loss of adolescent patronage would bankrupt the Hollywood producer.[451] Proceeding from this assumption the argument is then advanced that movies will be commensurately "watered down" by producers so as to bring them within the confines of what is permissible for juvenile exposure. The result, it is contended, would be indirect censorship of adult fare. This train of thought ignores the possibility that this hazard will be averted through the increased box-office appeal of pictures produced for the sole enjoyment of adults.[452] Inglis has contended, for instance, that a major

[450] Typical of this are the responses elicited from the various censors interviewed. See also Crowther, *op. cit.*, p. 23.

[451] Leary and Noall, *op. cit.*, p. 342, footnote 112. According to 1953 statistics, one-third of the movie-going audience was under eighteen years. Note, "For Adults Only . . . ," *op. cit.*, p. 149, footnote 57.

[452] *Ibid.*, p. 149, footnote 58.

cause of "stereotyped and empty films" is that they are made for an undifferentiated, mass audience. Age categorization would make it possible for artists in the cinema to create really notable movies without worrying about the immature.[453] Furthermore, the minimal standard advocated here would require only that movies which are available to everyone not violate the common canons of good taste that are flouted by the obscene. There is no reason why Hollywood cannot explore adult themes within these confines and thereby avoid the limitations of "no young people allowed" ratings. Indeed, it is less than remotely conceivable that this sort of response by movie makers would exclude from cinematic entertainment only those adults who seek out such offensive, demented materials. It will be no great financial loss to the movie industry if this class of customers returns to the burlesque houses.

Aside from the question of where one would draw the line in establishing criteria for a grading recommendation, the most commonly voiced objection to governmental control programs of this kind comes from critics who wonder what harm allegedly offensive films can and do have on juveniles. The American Civil Liberties Union believes that age classification is justifiable only if "the effect of the material, proved beyond a reasonable doubt, . . . would directly cause criminal behavior."[454] The premise of this assertion is that free speech considerations are undermined unless this nexus can be validated. The fact is, experts are widely split on the possible effects that obscenity can have on the immature person (and the adult as well). Little empirical data has been unearthed which proves the allegations either of those who say there is a direct relationship or of those who insist that none exists.[455] But why should it be necessary to predicate legislation of the kind at issue on irrefutable evidence of social injury? Why

[453] Ruth A. Inglis, *Freedom of the Movies* (Chicago: The University of Chicago Press, 1947), p. 201.

[454] *Freedom Through Dissent*, 42nd Annual Report of the American Civil Liberties Union (New York: Oceana Publications, 1962), pp. 2-3.

[455] For statements of those who feel that a relationship is evident see Kilpatrick, *op. cit.*, pp. 235-37. A forceful argument to the contrary is presented in Paul W. Tappan, *Juvenile Delinquency* (New York: McGraw-Hill, 1949).

should possible dangers be ignored simply because the behavioral sciences have not yet discovered how to graph human action with the precision of the laboratory scientist? An exact science of human behavior may well be beyond man's best efforts.[456] The best that can be done, given the present state of social psychology, "is to apply common sense to known social ills and to weigh the testimony of experts."[457] This, indeed, is the very touchstone of Supreme Court opinions handed down in *Roth* and *Alberts*. There is no other way to balance individual liberties with communal responsibilities in the context at hand.

One final issue must be settled. How is this system of age classification to be implemented? As has been documented, censorship boards have to a considerable degree hamstrung the enforcement of Supreme Court decisions. The argument is persuasive that these agencies would probably find prurient sequences in countless situations where none exist if they were left with the responsibility of making the final decisions on this point. A passionate kiss is rarely patently offensive in and of itself; sex and obscenity are not synonymous.

It can be argued, however, that the limited censorship of movies approved in *Freedman* v. *Maryland* might be utilized within this context. Thus, a licensing tribunal would have to go to court before the affixing of an "adults only" label could be finalized. In other words, the alleged obscenity of particular film segments or dialogue would have to be proven in a judicial setting. The difficulty with this proposal is that all of the old problems inherent in the movie censorship practices of today would come to the fore. Each picture, regardless of its content, would have to undergo pre-screening. The services rendered by the board of review would have to be financed, thus stimulating the state to set up the usual fee system. The prospective hiatus between Supreme Court doctrine and administrative decision-making would again, perhaps, require the scrutiny of the social scientist so that its depths could be successfully gauged.

As a substitute recommendation, it is submitted that a sound

[456] Note, "For Adults Only . . . ," *op. cit.*, p. 147.
[457] Kilpatrick, *op. cit.*, p. 235.

rating system can best be enforced through the use of the in rem proceeding that has been hereinbefore advocated as the proper means for implementing *Roth-Alberts*. It is true that it will be considerably more difficult to anticipate, prior to a first showing, a movie that contains only one obscene segment as opposed to a picture that is obscene in toto. As a matter of practice, however, it is possible that temporary restraining orders will under certain circumstances not be sought out against allegedly obscene movies until initial presentations reveal their complete contents. Surely representatives of state attorneys (policemen or movie reviewers) can also make use of similar opportunities to initiate age classification proceedings; but only a judge would have the power to classify movies whether on a temporary or permanent basis. Should a producer or distributor wish to eliminate all obscene sequences so as to exhibit his movie to an audience of all ages, the court could issue the necessary order. It seems eminently clear that this process, like the mechanism upheld in *Kingsley Books* itself, comprises the best elements of both prior restraint and subsequent punishment. Certainly it is clear that the burden of proof will rest on the state during each and every stage of its unfolding and that the rights of totally nonobscene productions will therefore be afforded maximum protection.

To sum up: The First Amendment guarantees free speech to each member of the American political community. But this privilege can be the bane of an adult citizenry if it is misused, abused, or corrupted. In short, free speech is impossible without ground rules. One of these consists of society's right to be free from the revulsions of obscenity. With respect to the motion picture and its role in the community, this means that adults may be kept from seeing films whose dominant appeal relates to the prurient instincts of the average person. For the child, this should mean immunization from everything that is obscene regardless of other competing values that a movie might enhance. Control over matter reaching the minds of youngsters can and should be more stringent than control over matter to which adults may be exposed, because a free society buttressed by a First Amendment presupposes an enlightened, mature, average man who more times than not can work out his destiny better than others can do it for him.[458] Methods of control for both these elements of society must be balanced and regulated by guarantees of due process such as are afforded in the courts. It is herewith offered as a considered judgment that, under a system of regulation set out above, the motion picture should be allowed to take its place as a first-class medium for cultivation of artistic and intellectual values; and it should never be condemned to the purgatory of censorship domination.

[458] Zechariah Chafee, one of the stoutest defenders of the value of First Amendment rights, has advocated a program of age classification. Inglis, *op. cit.*, p. 176. See also Chafee, *op. cit.*, p. 543.

# Appendix I

*The Questionnaire*[459]

Q. 1. *How many people serve with you on the censorship board?*

Q. 2. *Do you preview each full-length movie and each short subject before it is shown in ————?*

Q. 3. *(If answered no). How does the board decide which films ought to be previewed?*

Q. 4. *(If Question 2 was answered no). Over a year's time what percentage of films shown in ———— would the board normally preview?*

Q. 5. *When the board finds that a film is objectionable does it make recommendations to the exhibitor or producer as to what changes ought to be made?*

Q. 6. *(If answered yes). Are the recommendations of the board usually followed?*

Q. 7. *(If Question 5 was answered yes). What does the board do if the recommendations are not followed?*

Q. 8. *Does the board practice a policy of banning movies when it thinks such action is necessary?*

Q. 9. *(If answered no). Why not?*

Q. 10. *(If Question 8 was answered yes). How many films have been banned in ———— in the past five years and do you recall the names of these films?*

Q. 11. (a) *How many films shown in ———— in the past three years have been altered or cut in some way before they were exhibited?*

(b) *What are the names of these films and how many times were each of them cut?*

Q. 12. *(If detailed records are kept). Could you tell me what specific material was excluded with each particular cut?*

---

[459] Professor Warren Miller of the Survey Research Center, University of Michigan was especially helpful in his suggestions relative to the framing of several of these questions and the order in which they might be most feasibly presented.

Q. 13. *(If no detailed records are kept or if Question 12 was answered no). In general, what kinds of alterations or cuts have you found it necessary to make during this time? Could you mention some specific examples that come to mind?*

Q. 14. *Have you placed other kinds of restrictions on movies during this time? For example, have you restricted some films to certain kinds of movie houses, or have you placed a minimum age requirement on those viewing some films?*

Q. 15. *(If answered yes).*
  (a) *How many films have required such action in the past three years?*
  (b) *What are the names of these films and how were each of them restricted?*

Q. 16. *(If no records are kept on banned and/or altered films). Which type of film would you say you have been forced to ban most often—foreign films or American films? Which type of film do you think you have had to alter or restrict most often prior to exhibition—American films or foreign films?*

Q. 17. *When there is a question of whether a movie is to be restricted in any way or not, are formal votes taken to decide on what the board ought to do?*

Q. 18. *(If answered yes). How many votes are needed to ban or to alter a movie?*

Q. 19. *(If Question 17 was answered yes). Do you keep a record of such votes?*

Q. 20. *(If answered yes). When you have voted to restrict films in some way during the past three years could you tell me how many members of the board voted for and how many voted against each such restriction?*

Q. 21. *(Ask this question unless detailed information is elicited through Question 20). Is there generally much disagreement among members of the board when it comes to restricting films? Do you recall any instances of this and what the disagreements were about?*

Q. 22. *Which of the standards in the statute, if any, do you find difficult to interpret?*

Q. 23. *Is there much disagreement among members of the board as to how these standards should be interpreted?*

Q. 24. *Which of these standards, if any, are ambiguous to the board as to meaning?*

Q. 25. *(If there are ambiguous standards). What are the usual differences of opinion as to the meaning of these ambiguous standards?*

Q. 26. *Does the board keep records of why it banned, altered, or restricted certain films?*

Q. 27. *(If answered yes). Over the past three-year period, could you give me the specific reasons why the board voted to ban, alter, or restrict the films it did? What particular standards were involved in each case?*

Q. 28. *(If Question 26 was answered no). Which of these standards do you feel films probably tend to violate most often?*

Q. 29. *(If Question 26 was answered no).*
(a) *Would you say that objectionable American films tend to violate the same standards as foreign films or do they seem to violate different standards?*
(b) *Which standards do each seem to violate most often?*

Q. 30. *Do you feel the board is too strict or not strict enough in judging the suitability of films? Why?*

Q. 31. *Should the standards the board is now using be amended and, if so, in what ways?*

Q. 32. *Some people wonder how important movie censorship is. Do you feel a community needs film censorship? Why?*

Q. 33. *Do you feel a film censorship program that uses a system of prior restraint is better than one that would punish the exhibitor of an objectionable movie after he has once shown it to the public?*[460]

Q. 34. *Can you think of any other changes in the way your film censorship program is devised that might be helpful? I am thinking now in terms of the way members of the board are selected, their terms of office, the system of appeals, etc.*

Q. 35. *Does the board keep in touch with the censorship policies and decisions of other cities and states? If so, which ones?*

Q. 36. *(If answered yes). How is such communication helpful to the board? Do you base your decisions at all on the findings of other boards or, to your knowledge, do any other boards consider first what you do before they make a decision?*

Q. 37. *Are there any standards adopted by the courts that you feel are helpful to you in your work? Which ones are these?*

Q. 38. *Are there any standards adopted by the courts which you feel make it more difficult for you to do your job? Which ones are these?*

Q. 39. *Do you think the courts as a whole are doing a good job in this area? Why?*

[460] This inquiry along with Questions 50, 59, and 60 was not incorporated into the questionnaire until after interviews had been held with censorship officials in Detroit and Chicago.

Q. 40. *Do you base your decisions at all on whether or not a movie was given or denied a seal of approval by the film industry itself?*

Q. 41. *Do you feel the film industry's P.C.A.[461] is stricter or less strict than it ought to be?*

Q. 42. *Do you base your decisions at all on ratings issued by any private groups? What groups are these?*

Q. 43. *Do you ever come in contact at any stage in your work with representatives of any private groups? What groups do they represent?*

Q. 44. *(If answered yes). Do you find any of these groups particularly helpful in your work? Why?*

Q. 45. *(If Question 43 was answered yes). Do you find any of these groups particularly troublesome in your work? Why?*

Q. 46. *How would a person go about appealing the board's decision to restrict a film?*

Q. 47. *Have any film executives or movie-house owners challenged any of your decisions in the past 5 years? Which decisions and what films were involved?*

Q. 48. *(If answered yes). As a result of such disagreements have any appeals been made and by whom? What was the final decision of the board of appeals?*

Q. 49. *(If Question 47 was answered yes). Have any court cases resulted from such disagreements? If so, can you recall the motion pictures involved and the final decision of the courts?*

Q. 50. *Could you tell me if your board falls under some civil service system?*

Q. 51. *Have you had any schooling other than high school?*

Q. 52. *(If answered yes). What other schooling have you had?*

Q. 53. *(If attended college). Do you have a college degree?*

Q. 54. *Along with your work as a censor do you have another job? What is that?*

Q. 55. *(If answered yes). Which of your jobs constitutes your basic source of income?*

Q. 56. *(If Question 54 was answered yes). Regarding the job that gives you the better salary, what did you do before you held this job? How long ago was that?*

Q. 57. *(If Question 54 was answered no). What did you do before you held your present position? How long ago was that?*

Q. 58. *Could you tell me in general terms what your yearly salary is? Would you say you earn: (1) less than $4000, (2) between $4000*

[461] The Production Code Administration is charged with the responsibility of enforcing Hollywood's voluntary censorship rules.

*and $6000, (3) between $6000 and $8000, (4) more than $8000?*

Q. 59.  *In order to obtain a position on the censorship board was it necessary for you to pass some kind of examination?*

Q. 60.  *(If answered yes). Could you briefly describe this examination? For instance, was it oral or written and, in general, what subject matter did it deal with?*

# Appendix II

*Interview with Mr. Louis Pesce*[462]

**Q. 1.** *How many people serve with you on the censorship board?*

At the decision-making level there are four reviewers, the Assistant Director and myself. We all serve at the "first level." The Board of Regents comes into the picture when there are appeals. Initially, at least two of the reviewers will pre-screen a film. If there is some problem everyone will take a look at the movie. Only then do the Assistant Director and I become involved. Discussion at this stage will be very informal, but the final decision will likely be influenced by the views of the two officers in charge.

**Q. 2.** *Do you preview each full-length movie and each short subject before it is shown in New York?*

We see everything that is to be exhibited commercially.

**Q. 3.** *I see that under the New York ordinance your board may, if it wishes, issue a permit for the showing of newsreels without prior inspection or the paying of a fee. To what extent do you allow newsreels an exemption under this law?*

Newsreels are not subject to prior examination and fee. We don't bother to preview any movie that is not to be shown commercially though the law is vague here. This is how we construe the statute. We can't see that there is any problem with such films.

**Q. 4.** *When the board finds that a film is objectionable does it make recommendations to the exhibitor or producer as to what changes ought to be made?*

---

[462] Unless indicated as such, respondent's answers are not direct quotes; however, the answers attributed to him have been taken directly from the writer's notes almost *verbatim* except where rephrasing was needed for grammatical reasons. This technique was also used in editing and writing up each of the five subsequent interviews.

When we feel that a scene contravenes the statute we order
them to make the necessary changes. We know that this could
not be done with books but the New York law "constrains us
to do this."

Q. 5. *Are the recommendations of the board usually followed?*

Yes, though there are a few appeals. When protests are filed
there are rescreenings as is provided by the law. An informal
meeting will then follow and exhibitors are allowed to present
evidence in their behalf.

Q. 6. *What does the board do if the recommendations are not followed?*

We won't issue a license.

Q. 7. *Does the board practice a policy of banning movies when it
thinks such action is necessary?*

The law demands it.

Q. 8. *How many films have been banned in New York in the past five
years and do you recall the names of these films?*

In the past ten years, from 1952 through 1962, we licensed
12,246 movies including short subjects. Twenty-one films were
rejected entirely while 480 were licensed only after deletions
were made. We do not disclose information as to cuts made or
movies banned unless we have the permission of the applicant
or he himself has made the action public by, for example, taking
the case to court. If he lodges an appeal with the Board of
Regents, which is his statutory right, such action will be duly
noted in its monthly reports as will the final judgment that was
rendered. This, however, will not be made public without the
approval of the applicant.

It is our belief that since an applicant does not voluntarily
submit his films for examination, but must do so as a legal
requirement, the State has a responsibility to protect his property
rights inhering in the "marketability" of his film. Consequently
actions taken to comply with the requirements of the law, such
as deletions or editorial changes, must remain confidential, since
this information could be exploited by competing distributors, or
exhibitors, to the economic disadvantage of the applicant. Of
course we have no hesitancy in discussing such information if
we have his permission, or if he himself has already made the
matter public.

So far as specific movies are concerned there was *Lady Chatterley's Lover*. I ordered cuts in this one but the Regents wanted the whole thing banned. Then there was *The Connection*. This was an American film dealing with narcotics. They used the word "shit" throughout the dialogue. I thought that the basic question was whether or not some words were obscene in and of themselves. The courts overruled my judgment. They found that "shit" was not obscene per se. This movie was eventually shown. But if the use of this word in this context is not a "shameful preoccupation" as Justice Brennan uses the phrase then what about the word "fuck?" Would the use of this word be cleared as well?

Q. 9. (b) *What are the names of some of the movies that were cut and how many times were each of them altered?*[463]

We cut *Les Liaisons Dangereuse* because there was too much nudity in amorous situations. This was a borderline case. Also, we ordered two brief views of the rape scene in *The Virgin Spring* taken out because they were too explicit. These views depicted a shepherd in coital position with the victim's bare legs being pulled around his body by a second shepherd. Then there was *The Lovers*. We cut thirty-five seconds of this. It became very erotic toward the end—there was an implication of cunnilingus which we could not allow and too much nudity especially of the breasts. The distributor agreed to cut some of this. A compromise was made.

So far as books are concerned the rule is clear; you begin with the work as a whole and the intent of the entire piece. It is not clear that the *Roth* standard, as far as this rule is concerned, is to be applied to movies.

Another important dispute was with *Garden of Eden* —a nudist film. A state court applied the *Roth* decision here and overruled us. The court's ruling, however, contained a dictum to the effect that the board could only censor a movie on grounds of obscenity. We have been following this dictum.

Q. 10. *Have you placed other kinds of restrictions on movies during this time? For example, have you restricted some films to cer-*

---

[463] Part (a) of this question (#11 on the original questionnaire) was deleted because respondent had already covered the point in his reply to Question 8.

*tain kinds of movie houses, or have you placed a minimum age requirement on those viewing some films?*

The answer is "no" for both. We have no authority to do these things. I would like a minimum age limit for certain films. Ephraim London, the attorney who has represented many exhibitors and distributors in court cases, agrees with me on this. I would like to see censorship applied only to movies shown to children unaccompanied by adults.

Q. 11. *Which type of film would you say you have been forced to ban most often—foreign films or American films? Which type of film do you think you have had to alter or restrict most often prior to exhibition—American films or foreign films?*

The movies we cut are, as a rule, either foreign-made or else produced by small "fly-by-night" American companies. We ban more American movies of this type than foreign films. These are typically "girlie films" produced by small American outfits.

Q. 12. *I see that under the New York ordinance a license to exhibit a film can be revoked if an obscene or indecent poster or banner or other advertising matter is displayed in connection with such a film. Does your board play any role in enforcing this law and, if so, what action does it take?*

The board has five inspectors who make the rounds of movie houses to check on this. Also, we get reports from police officials when they come upon unusually exploitive advertising. On the whole, exhibitors are pretty careful about such things.

Q. 13. *When there is a question of whether a movie is to be restricted or not, are formal votes taken to decide on what the board ought to do?*

We don't have a formal procedure. We are flexible about this. "We change each other's minds" through give and take discussion. However, I can overrule the majority opinion. The Assistant Director's views also are especially important. Incidentally, it is his job to supervise the work of the inspectors, to set up a schedule for the review of each movie, and to coordinate the preliminary discussions by the review section.

Q. 14. *Is there generally much disagreement among members of the board when it comes to restricting films? Do you recall any instances of this and what the disagreements were about?*

Not much, but we've had our disagreements. After all, this is a very subjective business and some cases are borderline. You must have a lot of reviewers to check on the subjectivities of each board member. You keep on comparing each controversial movie with past precedents. For example, where you have an erotic moment you must decide how much nudity is allowable. Where to make such cuts is the big problem and can cause conflict.

Q. 15. *Which of the standards in the statute, if any, do you find difficult to interpret?*

The only standard we are applying is the criterion of obscenity, but it is one thing to read Justice Brennan's definition with its "dominant theme," "prurient interest" and "contemporary community standards" and quite another thing to apply it. Take so-called "nudist films" like *Garden of Eden.* I think they constitute a "morbid preoccupation with nudity." The contemporary community standard so far as public nudity is concerned is self-evident. We'd arrest someone who was nude in public. Yet, the courts overrule us on movies like this. They have made their so-called "objective" definition very hard to interpret.

Q. 16. *Is there much disagreement among members of the board as to how these standards should be interpreted?*

Not too much disagreement. Let me say, as an aside, that when we cut movies we are, in effect, going against the *Roth* "whole book" rule. But that decision involved books. Of course, the Supreme Court's *Game of Love* decision was along the same line as *Roth* but it was a per curiam holding. There was not enough of an explanation on the Court's part as to whether the "whole book" rule should also apply to films; where they have had a specific opportunity to settle this issue the courts have not committed themselves one way or another.

Q. 17. *Does the board keep records of why it banned, altered, or restricted certain movies?*[464]

We keep a file on every film. We always tell the exhibitor why he must cut. The only reason we use now is for being obscene.

[464] It will be noted that at this point Question 24 was omitted. The reason for this was simply that all necessary information had already been obtained relative to this inquiry. To ask questions that have lost their utility through previous discussion with a respondent can slow the interview to a walk and cause interviewee's interest to lag. This technique was used during other interviews as well, but will always be marked by appropriate footnoting. Other items that were omitted during this discussion were Questions 27, 29 (b), 47, and 48, all for the same reason.

Q. 18. (a) *Would you say that objectionable American films tend to violate the same standards as foreign films or do they seem to violate different standards?*

American movies are too violent. There is too much so-called "horror" material. The scenes in American movies that deal with sex don't have the "nudity problem" that gets foreign films into trouble. In short, domestic movies are sometimes too violent while foreign items tend to go beyond certain limits in their handling of erotic material.

Q. 19. *Do you feel the board is too strict or not strict enough in judging the suitability of films?*

Actually, I think we're doing a good job. We are very flexible in our views. We usually take the middle road so that critics on both sides gang up on us, but this criticism shows that we are seeing both sides.

But, in another sense, you have to answer a question like that in terms of the state law because this is what we are applying. The law is not strict enough. We should be more concerned with the children of the nation. There is too much violence and the romanticizing of juvenile crime. This is more dangerous to kids than obscenity because children have less access to the latter. The Saturday afternoon "horror shows" are awful. They are too sadistic. We should not allow children to see these movies unless accompanied by an adult. After all, if parents want their children to see such movies, then they should be actively involved in their supervision while they are being exposed to them.

Q. 20. *Should the standards the board is now using be amended and, if so, in what ways?*

As I say, the law should insist that unaccompanied children be excluded from certain movies. I personally don't think that adult movie fare should be subject to prior restraint because mature people should be given freedom of choice. There are freedom of speech considerations to look out for at this level.

Q. 21. *Some people wonder how important movie censorship is. Do you feel a community needs film censorship? Why?*

I think movie censorship along the lines I have indicated is a good thing. Movies have an amazing effect on people. They are a "quasi-public" medium unlike books that one can read in one's own home. The M.P.A.A. seems to agree with this because it makes so much of the impact of motion pictures in the preamble to the Code it espouses.

**Q. 22.** *Do you feel a film censorship program that uses a system of prior restraint is better than one that would punish the exhibitor of an objectionable movie after he has once shown it to the public?*

I think prior restraint has some definite benefits. There is a certain stability under this scheme because the exhibitor knows where he stands. He has clear sailing once he is given a permit by our board. Look at what local juries can find obscene. I will say, however, that it is difficult for the public to check on what prior restraint agencies are sometimes doing. But under the scheme I advocate there would be no problem, since restrictions would only apply to the unaccompanied minor.

**Q. 23.** *Can you think of any other changes in the way your film censorship program is devised that might be helpful? I am thinking now in terms of the way members of the board are selected, their terms of office, the system of appeals, etc.*

No improvements are needed.

**Q. 24.** *Does the board keep in touch with the censorship policies and decisions of other cities and states? If so, which ones?*

Yes. Regular exchange of information with all the state boards. Some with city boards.

**Q. 25.** *How is such communication helpful to the board? Do you base your decisions at all on the findings of other boards or, to your knowledge, do any other boards consider first what you do before they make a decision?*

We're not affected by what they do. They can't influence us because we get most movies before they do. We're affected by our own state courts and whether or not they've reversed or sustained what we do. We do like to know what these boards have to say, however.

**Q. 26.** *Are there any standards adopted by the courts that you feel are helpful to you in your work? Which ones are these?*

The Supreme Court's definition of obscenity is helpful in spite of problems of application and the ways in which other courts think it ought to be used because it does supply direction.

Q. 27. *Are there any standards adopted by the courts that you feel make it more difficult for you to do your job? Which ones are these?*

What can you say? If they feel that a standard is unconstitutional there's nothing you can do. But, so far as enforcing the statute is concerned, if you can't use terms like "inhuman" and "incite to crime" it is impossible under present decisions to protect the public from certain films that seem to be bannable under these criteria. We can't touch movies like *The Horrors of the Black Museum, The Birds,* or *Psycho.* Then kids view these films and start taking horror for granted. This is a bad attitude for them to have.

Q. 28. *Do you think the courts as a whole are doing a good job in this area? Why?*

Their job, like ours, is very difficult. You must balance freedom of speech with the exploitation of sex, etc. The majority of judges do a good job. We need more carefully drafted laws that the courts will approve.

Q. 29. *Do you base your decisions at all on whether or not a movie was given or denied a seal of approval by the film industry itself?*

No.

Q. 30. *Do you feel the film industry's P.C.A. is stricter or less strict than it ought to be?*

They don't apply their own code. They should be stricter considering what it says. As written, it is too strict. It should have a classification scheme by age as Geoffrey Shurlock once recommended.

Q. 31. *Do you base your decisions at all on ratings issued by any private groups? What groups are these?*

No, but we like to know what they're thinking.

Q. 32. *Do you ever come in contact at any stage in your work with representatives of any private groups? What groups do they represent?*

Sometimes. A committee of religious leaders representing all major faiths in New York held a symposium on movies and censorship. We tried to cooperate as much as possible. We also come in contact with the Legion of Decency, the A.C.L.U. and M.P.A.A. These groups bring no pressure to bear on us.

Q. 33. *Do you find any of these groups particularly helpful in your work? Why?*

We ought to know what the community is thinking. There are many different points of view.

Q. 34. *Do you find any of these groups particularly troublesome in your work? Why?*

No. They put no pressure on us.

Q. 35. *How would a person go about appealing the board's decision to restrict a film?*

They have a legal right to take their case to the Board of Regents. What happens is that this Board acts on the recommendations of a subcommittee of three. This smaller group holds an informal hearing, sees the movie, and takes evidence presented by both sides. However, the final judgment is given by the fourteen-member Board of Regents.

Q. 36. *Have any film executives or movie house owners challenged any of your decisions in the past five years? Which decisions and what films were involved?*

There have been several and on many occasions the Board of Regents has gone along with our judgment. For example, there was *Garden of Eden, The Connection, La Ronde, Lady Chatterley's Lover,* and *Teenage Menace,* a narcotics movie. These particular cases went into the courts as well. *Teenage Menace* was a case where the courts reversed us. We had denied that movie a license because we thought it would encourage the use of narcotics even though the film was a preachment against the use of dope. Since 1954 we have not applied the "incite to crime" provision of the statute because court dicta imply we can't use it. Except for the obscenity limitation we have given up on the other parts of the law as well. I might add that *The Virgin Spring* decision made by us was sustained by the Regents but did not get into the courts.[465]

[465] As Mr. Pesce has indicated, appeals from film distributors and exhibitors that are brought to the Board of Regents become a matter of public record if the licensee has tendered his approval or has publicized the matter himself. These appeals and the Board's rulings in these cases may be found in the State Department of Education Reports of the State of New York. In the period between April 28, 1961 and May 24, 1963, the Regents passed on appeals involving the films *Karamaja, The Connection, Twilight Girls, The Virgin Spring,* and *Not Tonight, Henry.* Letter of May

Q. 37. *Could you tell me if your board falls under the state civil service system?*

We are under civil service and have been since 1927.

Q. 38. *In order to obtain a position on the censorship board was it necessary for you to pass some kind of examination?*

There is an open competitive exam given.

Q. 39. *Could you briefly describe this examination? For instance, was it oral or written and, in general, what subject matter did it deal with?*

There was a written part which tested general knowledge such as literature and the arts. There was also an oral segment that tested ability in a foreign language. It is mandatory that the reviewers and Director be fluent in at least one foreign language. I, myself, speak Spanish and Italian.

Q. 40. *Have you had any schooling other than high school?*

Yes. I went to college and received a B.A. I also had some graduate work in the fields of social work and public administration.

Q. 41. *Along with your work as a censor do you have another job? What is that?*

I used to teach at night for awhile. No longer, however.

Q. 42. *What did you do before you held your present position? How long ago was that?*

My last job was with the Board of Education as attendance officer. I left in 1952. Before that I was a probation officer in children's court.

Q. 43. *Could you tell me in general terms what your yearly salary is? Would you say you earn: (1) less than $4,000, (2) between $4,000 and $6,000, (3) between $6,000 and $8,000, (4) more than $8,000?*

$14,000.

---

24, 1963, received from Charles A. Brind, Counsel for the State Education Department. Mr. Brind, however, did not disclose the decisions that the Board had reached in these matters (though it is obvious that the censorship bureau was upheld in *The Connection* and *The Virgin Spring* disputes). How many other appeals were heard over and above these is anyone's guess.

# Appendix III

*Interview with Mr. Elwood L. Gebhart*

Q. 1. *How many people serve on the censorship Board?*

The Board has three members. They are Norman C. Mason, Chairman, Mrs. Louis E. Shecter, Vice-Chairman, and Mrs. Mary Avara, Secretary.

Q. 2. *Do you preview each full-length movie and each short subject before it is shown in Maryland?*

The Board sees everything including previews of coming attractions.

Q. 3. *When the Board finds that a film is objectionable does it make recommendations to the exhibitor or producer as to what changes ought to be made?*

Yes. We'll issue an elimination order. The distributor will make the cuts himself, but we check up to be sure he does this. If our ruling is appealed the Attorney General of the State will advise the bureau whether it has a legal leg to stand on.

Q. 4. *Are the recommendations of the Board usually followed?*

Usually. At times, especially recently, there has been some vociferous opposition. There was a Bardot film called *Please, Not Now*. Chicago and New York passed this film but "we don't care much what they do." We cut this scene of some man kissing Bardot and running his hand up her side. This was a close case. Most resistance comes from foreign film makers. There was a movie called *The Immoral Mr. Teas*. We banned that one. It was nothing but an attempt to arouse sexual desires. The Baltimore City Court went along with us there. It was made by some "fly-by-night" little company. They cause most of the difficulty.

Q. 5. *What does the Board do if the recommendations are not followed?*

The film won't get a license. The distributor will probably go to court at that point. I might add that Virginia is a lot stricter on these things than we are.

Q. 6. *How many films have you banned in Maryland in the past five years and do you recall the names of these films?*

Not counting this year no more than ten. This year (1963) we've banned seven already. We've had a big influx of films where everyone runs around nude. Here are the names of some of them: *Gentlemen Prefer Nature Girls, Have Figure-Will Travel, The Immoral West, Scanty Panties,* and *Shangri La.* Sometimes it's hard to tell if these movies are American or foreign made. Some are made in California and others, that we know of, in Florida. Actually, the companies that produce them don't last that long. Films that stress sex, dope taking, or nudism are our problem children.

Q. 7. (a) *How many films shown in Maryland in the past three years have been altered or cut in some way before they were exhibited?*

In 1960 there were 34, in 1961 there were 27 and in 1962 there were 50.

(b) *What are the names of these films and how many times were each of them cut?*

Here are some titles. For 1963 there were the following: *Hot Bed of Sin, The Passionate Demons, Soho Striptease, Wild Girls of the Naked West, Sin You Sinners, Nature Girl's Frolic* and *Revenge of the Virgins.* For 1962 there were: *She Should'a Said No, Zero de Conduite,* "there was genital exposure in that one," *Place of Shame, Peep Shows of Paris,* a burlesque film, and *Eve and the Handy Man.* "A nude girl struts around in that last one." These are all typical. I don't know the running time of these cuts, but we know the number of eliminations in each movie. I would say the average is from two to five cuts. We also rejected entirely a movie called *Nudes, Nudists, and Nudism.*

Q. 8. *Could you tell me what specific material was excluded with each particular cut?*

We cut out all genital exposure. You don't get too much of this but lately more than usual. We also slash breast exposures and we get plenty of this. Here are more examples: 1. we made five cuts in *Peep Shows of Paris,* all of "obscene pelvic movements" while women were lying on the floor, 2. in *Passionate Demons* we cut some dialogue like "pissing and swinging" and "Mister, your glass is getting dusty." We cut a scene from that film as well. It showed a man running his hand up a woman's leg while she rests her leg on his. We also have had to cut out nude advertisements that have nothing to do with a movie. We did pass a film called *The Sky Above, The Mud Below.* There were genital exposures in this one but it was a true picture of life showing natives in their natural environment. I think all the boards approved it.

Q. 9. *Have you placed other kinds of restrictions on movies during this time? For example, have you restricted some films to certain kinds of movie houses, or have you placed a minimum age requirement on those viewing some films?*

No, but we wish we had a law giving us the right to classify by age.

Q. 10. *I notice that your state has a special ordinance punishing exhibitors who show certain kinds of films to minors. Do you think that it would be better if the power to classify movies for minors was placed in the hands of your board? Why?*

Yes. This law makes each policeman a censor because it is up to him to enforce its provisions. Under such a system there are no uniform standards. Many policemen aren't even high school graduates. If he is a religious Catholic he'll crack down on something others who aren't as strict wouldn't worry about. Anyone who adheres to the Legion of Decency code would probably tend to be too strict.

Furthermore, this law has never been tested in the courts which is unfortunate. If we had this power and used it unwisely you can be sure some distributor would challenge us. But as things are now who will bring cases to the courts' attention? Certainly it won't be housewives whose children are being exposed to questionable movies. They don't have the time.

Q. 11. *Which type of film would you say you have been forced to ban most often—foreign films or American films? Which type of film do you think you have had to alter or restrict most often prior to exhibition—American films or foreign films?*[466]

---

[466] While this question was not intended for instances where records of movies suppressed or altered were obtainable, it was used in this case

I think we ban more foreign products. Most American movies have a seal of approval from the M.P.A.A. so that they are rarely totally offensive. So far as alterations are concerned foreign films head the list too, but American movies that stress nudism make it very close. As I say, sometimes it's difficult to determine where some of these movies are made.

Q. 12. *I see that under the Maryland ordinance relating to film censorship a license to exhibit a film can be revoked if an obscene or indecent poster or banner or other advertising matter is displayed in connection with such a film. Does the Board play any role in enforcing this law and, if so, what action does it take?*

We try to control this matter but it's very difficult so we're not as strict as we could be. If the advertisements don't represent accurately what's in the film we'll try to crack down. A typical example would be nude pictures when the movie has nothing to do with people in the nude.

Q. 13. *When there is a question of whether a movie is to be restricted or not, are formal votes taken to decide on what the Board ought to do?*

Yes.

Q. 14. *How many votes are needed to ban or to alter a movie?*

A majority.

Q. 15. *Do you keep a record of such votes?*

They're in the minutes that are kept of each meeting.

Q. 16. *When you have voted to restrict films in the past three years could you tell me how many members of the Board voted for and how many voted against each restriction?*

No, but usually the votes are unanimous or two to one with Mrs. Avara dissenting. She is stricter than the others.

Q. 17. *Is there generally much disagreement among members of the Board when it comes to restricting films? Do you recall any instances of this and what the disagreements were about?*

We had a "burlesque film" that came in here a few days ago. The movie was a series of "bumps and grinds" but the girls

---

because respondent's answers to previous questions had blurred the distinction (perhaps unnecessarily) between foreign and domestic pictures and it was felt that he might take a position one way or another if queried directly on the point.

never took their bikinis off. Mrs. Avara wanted to ban it, but the film went through. Usually, I should add, when a controversial picture is involved two members of the Board will probably inspect it a second time even if, at first, only one sees it and approves which would be the procedure with most movies. If they don't agree then all the members will view it.

The first movie Mrs. Avara saw as a censor was an Orson Welles picture called *The Crooked Glass*. She objected to parts of that movie having to do with Welles sleeping with a woman while her child was in the same room. She thinks all nudity should be cut out.

There was *Les Liaisons Dangereuse*. Mrs. Shecter objected but was overruled. There was no nudity involved but she didn't like the film being shown because a lot of children go to movies and they should be protected from films that stress adultery, sex perversion, etc. This is her general view regarding certain avant-garde productions.

Mr. Mason is worried about movies that deal with narcotics. He'd rather his son and daughter saw nudist films than know how to use drugs. A film came to us called *The Narcotics Story*. Mason was as mad as could be. The "narcotics people in Washington" have an office here. We had them send a representative over and invited the Maryland police to do the same. Some private group—"I can't remember which one"—also sent somebody. All shots showing how the dope was injected, the smoking of it and how to prepare it were chopped off. You can see that a lot of people were consulted before slashes were made.

Here are other examples. We cut the rape scene in *The Virgin Spring* where the legs of the woman are pried apart. Men were standing around on the screen watching this. But we didn't cut the rape scene in *Two Women* because it wasn't too overt. They just showed facial expressions. Then we had an unusual movie called *Pagan Hell Cat* that came to us recently. We cut a rape scene in that one, too. There was too much struggling. Also, it showed his body over hers. We cut the whole business. But the funny thing about this film was that all the "sexy stuff" was narrated. We made eight eliminations in all and got rid of all the offensive dialogue. The woman says, "They may have entered my body but not my soul." We cut that. Mrs. Shecter saw this one first and ordered the changes but Mrs. Avara wanted even more. I might add that I do get the chance to see all these films before they are banned or cut so I know the kinds of things that don't get through.

To conclude, what we need is an age classification scheme. This would help us more than anything, all of us agree.

Q. 18. *Which of the standards in the statute, if any, do you find difficult to interpret?*

This is a little hard for me to answer because I am not a Board member, but I know the bureau has a hard time with the statutory definition of obscenity. If the dominant purpose of a film is to arouse desires how can it have any artistic merit at all? Furthermore, how do you define "moral and proper?" There is no precision here. Most of my ideas along this line come from talking to Board members and the Attorney General. Part of my job is to sit in on meetings, see objectionable movies, and take messages for the censors when they are out.

Q. 19. *Does the Board keep records of why it banned, altered or restricted certain films?*[467]

At the end of each report on an objectionable movie I just say "Section 6" otherwise "we might be wrong." We don't have a lawyer on the Board or we could be more specific. We only get specific when appeals are filed and an opinion is obtained from the Attorney General.

Q. 20. *Which of these standards do you feel films probably tend to violate most often?*[468]

Too difficult to say.

[467] Questions 23, 24, and 25 were omitted because respondent was not a member of the Board and, once again, because of information he had already supplied concerning the respective points of view of the three censors. Questions 45 through 48 were also disregarded during this discussion not only because the Maryland statute is self-explanatory regarding the appeal system to be used but also because respondent had already supplied an inordinate amount of data regarding the Board's decisions which was highly significant given the fact that the bureau serves as its own appeals tribunal.

[468] Item 27 was omitted because of the nature of interviewee's reply to the previous question. Part (b) of Question 29 was also passed over because of respondent's answers to Items 38 and 29 (a). Question 32 was omitted because the interviewee was not a member of the Board and because he had already addressed himself to the advantages of censorship in several of his previous answers.

Q. 21. (a) *Would you say that objectionable American films tend to violate the same standards as foreign films or do they seem to violate different standards?*

I can't really say, but foreign films do have different problems. They don't make nudist films where everyone stands around posing. Their use of nudism arises out of love-making situations.

Q. 22. *Do you feel the Board is too strict or not strict enough in judging the suitability of films? Why?*

I think we should be a little stricter. We've never had a nudist film tested in the courts. We should stand up to these people and have a court case on this junk. Let's find out where we stand with these producers.

Q. 23. *Should the standards the Board is now using be amended and, if so, in what ways?*

All the standards should be revised. They are obsolete. Some of the criteria are too vague. We need more teeth in the statute to confiscate a movie if deletions are restored by the distributor contrary to the Board's rulings. We've had some trouble with this.

Q. 24. *Do you feel a film censorship program that uses a system of prior restraint is better than one that would punish the exhibitor of an objectionable movie after he has once shown it to the public?*

It is better to have a board. You have centralized control. Under the other system everyone is a censor.

Q. 25. *Can you think of any other changes in the way your film censorship program is devised that might be helpful? I am thinking now in terms of the way members of the Board are selected, their terms of office, the system of appeals, etc.*

"I better not go into this because I'm not a bureau member." But we do need a lawyer on the Board. All three of the censors would agree on this. Virginia's bureau is under the jurisdiction of the Department of Law and this helps them terrifically especially in dealing with people who might otherwise break their rules. The point is that we need day-to-day legal counsel. We would then be on much surer footing in the many censorship decisions we are called upon to make.

Some members of the legislature have recommended that

three clergymen representing all three major faiths be added to the Board. This wouldn't be a good idea. We have trouble enough getting the three members of the bureau here at the same time to review movies. It would be terribly difficult getting all these people together. The situation would be too confusing.

Q. 26. *Does the Board keep in touch with the censorship policies and decisions of other cities and states? If so, which ones?*

Yes. We get reports from Kansas and New York. Kansas is very strict. It is more stringent than Virginia which is plenty tough. We also get *Film Daily, The New York Times* movie reviews, the "Green Sheet" and reports published by the Legion of Decency. From these trade magazines we learned that Chicago had banned *The Sky Above, The Mud Below,* but that the new Appeals Board they created reversed without reservation. Kansas also banned this film but reversed itself upon reconsideration. Virginia and New York as well as ourselves let the film through.

We have a special card catalogue with a file card on each movie. Each card specifies whether any censorship board restricted the particular picture in any way. We are pretty close to New York but don't agree with them all the time. Our laws are similar but sometimes we cut what they let go.

We should have never licensed any movies dealing with nudism just as Virginia refused to do. We set a precedent on this question a few years ago and I think it has made us too lenient.

Q. 27. *How is such communication helpful to the Board? Do you base your decisions at all on the findings of other boards or, to your knowledge, do any other boards consider first what you do before they make a decision?*

Once every four months we might call up Pesce in New York to find out why he cut something. They get movies first as a general rule. We disagreed on *The Lovers.* We went further than they did. We cut a bathroom scene. We might also call to ask why he left something pass that disturbs us.

Q. 28. *Are there any standards adopted by the courts that you feel are helpful to you in your work? Which ones are these?*

I don't know what they've done that could be called helpful though the Times Film Company lost the *Don Juan* case, "thank God."

Q. 29. *Are there any standards adopted by the courts which you feel make it more difficult for you to do your job? Which ones are these?*

I don't know. I'm not a lawyer.

Q. 30. *Do you think the courts as a whole are doing a good job in this area? Why?*

This is hard to answer. The courts talk about freedom of speech all the time. Their interpretation of what this is is backing us to the wall and will bring on federal censorship.

Q. 31. *Do you base your decisions at all on whether or not a movie was given or denied a seal of approval by the film industry itself?*

No. We have records on this but what they say is of little importance.

Q. 32. *Do you feel the film industry's P.C.A. is stricter or less strict than it ought to be?*

Don't know.

Q. 33. *Do you base your decisions at all on ratings issued by any private groups? What groups are these?*

No. The Legion of Decency doesn't help us much but we look at their point of view. They are too strict though they have relaxed a little. They wanted *Two Women* to be shown to adults. I remember some student from Johns Hopkins wrote in and asked us why we had passed *Two Women*. That movie and *La Dolce Vita* stirred up some letter writing. The "Green Sheet" also is of little help. We rarely look at it.

Q. 34. *Do you ever come in contact at any stage in your work with representatives of any private groups? What groups do they represent?*

No.

Q. 35. *Could you tell me if your board falls under the state civil service system?*

No, but as a rule one of the three censors is from Baltimore while the other two are from the counties. They are not permanent employees either; they serve set terms. I come under civil service.

Q. 36. *In order to obtain a position on the censorship board was it necessary for the three members to pass some kind of examination? What about yourself?*

I had to take a merit system test, but the three censors do not have to.

Q. 37. *Could you briefly describe this examination. For instance, was it oral or written and, in general, what subject matter did it deal with?*

My exam was both oral and written but mostly written. They tested on accountancy matters and office management.

I don't think I've mentioned either Mrs. Holland or Mr. Vaughan yet. They are our initial reviewers and are under the merit system. They have to know film law. Part of their exam is on this. They see everything first and if they think there's a problem they pass it on for the bureau's disposal.

When I first came they would file written reports on each decision they made; in other words, whether to let a movie go through or to refer it to the Board. I stopped that practice because it was just duplication. After all, these two aren't even mentioned in the statute. Of course, their jobs are very important and so their qualifications must be of a high order. Mrs. Holland, for example, served on the Board for six years before she took up her present function. While these two will take no chances and will refer all suspicious movies to the Board, their jobs cannot be underrated because anything they don't catch goes right on to the public.

Q. 38. *Could you tell me the extent of your education and that of the three censors and the two reviewers?*[469]

I have a degree in accounting. Mrs. Shecter is a college graduate. Mr. Mason, Mr. Vaughan and Mrs. Holland are high school graduates. Mrs. Avara is not a high school graduate.

Q. 39. *Do the censors, the two reviewers or yourself have other jobs? What would these be?*

The two reviewers and myself are full-time. The three censors

[469] It was evident from the information obtained through the previous question that each of the remaining items needed "on the spot rephrasing" so that as much information as possible could be gathered about Mrs. Holland and Mr. Vaughan. Thus, the rewording of each succeeding question can be justified, hopefully, on this ground and, also, because respondent was not a bureau member and it seemed important to gather background material on both the Board and the interviewee. See the appropriate comments offered in this regard in Chapter III, in "Movie Censorship in Maryland," *supra*.

all do other things so that their membership on the Board is not their sole means of support. We should have full-time membership for these people because you have to break them in too often. Mr. Mason is in the hardware and coal business. He comes from the Governor's home town. Mrs. Shecter sculpts and has sold some of her productions. Mrs. Avara is a bondswoman.

Q. 40. *How long have you, the two reviewers and the three censors served in your present capacities?*

Mrs. Shecter—three years; Mr. Mason—four years; Mrs. Avara —four years; Mrs. Holland—fifteen years; Mr. Vaughan—six months; myself—six years.

Q. 41. *Could you tell me in general terms what the yearly salaries of the censors are? Would you say they earn: (1) less than $4,000, (2) between $4,000 and $6,000, (3) between $6,000 and $8,000, (4) more than $8,000?*

The three Board members have a salary of $3,000. Of course, I don't know anything about their incomes over and above this amount.

# Appendix IV

*Interview with Mrs. Lollie Whitehead and*
*Mrs. Russell Wagers*[470]

Q. 1. *How many people serve with you on the censorship board?*
Three members.

Q. 2. *Do you preview each full-length movie and each short subject before it is shown in Virginia?*
We see everything.

Q. 3. *I see that under the Virginia ordinance your board may, if it wishes, issue a permit for the showing of newsreels without prior inspection. To what extent do you allow newsreels an exemption under this law?*
We gave up inspecting them ten years ago. We did this voluntarily. We also do not charge them a fee and this has cost us $10,000 in revenue.

Q. 4. *When the board finds that a film is objectionable does it make recommendations to the exhibitor or producer as to what changes ought to be made?*
Yes.

Q. 5. *Are the recommendations of the board usually followed?*
There are many appeals, but generally we receive wonderful cooperation from theater managers and private groups that are interested in these matters. We think, frankly, that we are the most liberal board there is.

Q. 6. *What does the board do if the recommendations are not followed?*
We reject the film.

[470] Mrs. Whitehead, as Chairman, undertook to reply to most of the questions so that unless there is a notation to the contrary it should be assumed that she is the respondent.

Q. 7. *Does the board practice a policy of banning movies when it thinks such action is necessary?*

Yes.

Q. 8. *How many films have been banned in Virginia in the past five years and do you recall the names of these films?*

Over the last five years we have banned seventeen movies. We cannot divulge their names, however.

Q. 9. (a) *How many films shown in Virginia in the past three years have been altered or cut in some way before they were exhibited?*

Forty-three movies.

(b) *What are the names of these films and how many times were each of them cut?*

We can't give out that information. We get wonderful cooperation from the newspapers on this; they don't ask us for such information. All other boards are envious of the high level of cooperation that we get from the community. We will give out the total number of cuts per year, however. In the past three years we deleted 452 scenes and pieces of dialogue. You might be interested in knowing that from 1922 up until June of 1962 we examined 50,980 movies. Of these, we banned ninety-three and approved with eliminations 2,313.

Q. 10. *Could you tell me what specific material was excluded with each particular cut?*

We won't give this information to anyone.

Q. 11. *Have you placed other kinds of restrictions on movies during this time? For example, have you restricted some films to certain kinds of movie houses, or have you placed a minimum age requirement on those viewing some films?*

We sometimes ask theater owners to put "adults only" on their billboards for certain films even thought the law does not give us the authority to do so in explicit terms. In our opinion, this is an inherent responsibility we are charged with as movie censors.

Q. 12. (a) *How many films have required such action in the past three years?*

Can't give out such information.

Q. 13. *Which type of film would you say you have been forced to ban most often—foreign films or American films? Which type of film do you think you have had to alter or restrict most often prior to exhibition—American films or foreign films?*

So far as bannings are concerned it's hard to tell but there is probably no great difference. I don't think there is much difference in movies altered either.

Mrs. Wagers: I think we cut more foreign movies.

Q. 14. *I see that under the Virginia ordinance relating to film censorship a license to exhibit a film can be revoked if an obscene or indecent poster or banner or other advertising matter is displayed in connection with such a film. Does your board play any role in enforcing this law and, if so, what action does it take?*

Mrs. Wagers: We have had to revoke licenses in such cases on the rarest of occasions. Again, we are given maximum cooperation. Exhibitors are asked to change their ads and they do so. We usually ask that copies of posters and banners be brought in here to be checked if an especially provocative film is involved.

Q. 15. *When there is a question of whether a movie is to be restricted or not, are formal votes taken to decide on what the board ought to do?*

Yes.

Q. 16. *How many votes are needed to ban or to alter a movie?*

A majority.

Q. 17. *Do you keep a record of such votes?*

We keep a record of all votes plus files on every movie we've passed on, what we've cut, etc. We have a record of every decision we've ever made.

Q. 18. *When you have voted to restrict films in the past three years could you tell me how many members of the board voted for and how many voted against each restriction?*

We can't make this public.

Q. 19. *Is there generally much disagreement among members of the board when it comes to restricting films? Do you recall any instances of this and what the disagreements were about?*

We agree and disagree quite a bit on some occasions, but we

are always able to find a common ground for resolving these problems.

**Q. 20.** *Which of the standards in the statute, if any, do you find difficult to interpret?*

We only enforce the standard that prohibits obscenity. The rest has become obsolete. We take a liberal view of this but we think we can readily identify what is obscene.[471]

**Q. 21.** *Does the board keep records of why it banned, altered or restricted certain films?*

Yes.

**Q. 22.** *Could you give me the specific reasons why the board voted to ban, alter, or restrict the films it did over the past three year period?*

This is not open to inspection.

**Q. 23.** *Do you feel the board is too strict or not strict enough in judging the suitability of films? Why?*

If we abided by our personal views we would be stricter. We try to follow the law as set down in court cases especially those decided by the Supreme Court.

**Q. 24.** *Should the standards the board is now using be amended and, if so, in what ways?*

This is hard to answer, but it is the Supreme Court's task to tell us what the law of the land is. The best we can do is to follow their opinions and verdicts. You see, all three of us were married to men who were concerned with the law—judges and lawyers—so that we have the greatest respect for courts and what they do.

**Q. 25.** *Some people wonder how important movie censorship is. Do you feel a community needs film censorship? Why?*

In answer to this question, Mrs. Whitehead drew from her files a printed statement evidently prepared for occasions such as this. It read as follows:

The Board is governed in its administration of the Motion Picture Censorship Law by the belief that it is established for the purpose of protecting the theater patrons, especially those

[471] Questions 23 and 24 on the original questionnaire were passed over because they had, in effect, already been answered.

who are not of mature age, from scenes and script that would tend to be suggestive and degrading to the morals of the young people who constitute a large portion of the theater audience. Each film is considered in light of its effect upon society.

The Board has adopted the policy of attempting to be realistic and not unmindful of the habits and thinking of the people of this period of time. The Board recognizes the fact that generally the Victorian ideas with respect to proper social conduct are not the same now as they were once.

Whether or not censorship is necessary in Virginia is a question that can only be determined by the legislature. Efforts have been made since the establishment of this Board to repeal the law under which the Board operates but without measure of success. It is obvious, therefore, that the sentiment in Virginia among the lawmakers and their constituents is that some form of control is necessary in this field. While it is true that under federal court decisions the powers of the State Boards are limited; nevertheless, this Board has found that some films that are presented for licensing contain script and scenes that would be offensive to the ordinary person. For example, some films which are censored by this Board contain scenes portraying situations of intimacy that are seldom exposed to public view. We have been able to eliminate scripts and scenes of this nature frequently, and we feel that so long as we are able to accomplish this result censorship is still necessary in Virginia.

Q. 26. *Do you feel a film censorship program that uses a system of prior restraint is better than one that would punish the exhibitor of an objectionable movie after he has shown it to the public?*

Prior restraint is the better method.

Q. 27. *Can you think of any other changes in the way your film censorship program is devised that might be helpful? I am thinking now in terms of the way members of the board are selected, their terms of office, the system of appeals, etc.*

We always had two women and one man until nine years ago, but the system has worked just as well this way. We rotate the chairmanship each year. This is a good policy because it keeps everyone on their toes.

Q. 28. *Does the board keep in touch with the censorship policies and decisions of other cities and states? If so, which ones?*

We keep in touch with some but we don't send reports to them or vice versa. We can't tell you which ones we are in contact with most frequently.

Q. 29. *How is such communication helpful to the board? Do you base your decisions at all on the findings of other boards or, to your knowledge, do any other boards consider first what you do before they make a decision?*

They don't influence us but we get a better insight by knowing their points of view. "The movie censors in Canada are czars, almost." Kansas is the strictest of American boards.

Q. 30. *Are there any standards adopted by the courts that you feel are helpful to you in your work? Which ones are these?*

Nothing much really. Very difficult to answer.

Q. 31. *Are there any standards adopted by the courts which you feel make it more difficult for you to do your job? Which ones are these?*

We don't want to criticize the courts but in facing facts there is no doubt that they have emasculated our law and this has made things much tougher.

Q. 32. *Do you think the courts as a whole are doing a good job in this area? Why?*

The Supreme Court has gone too far. It has lowered standards too much. For example, both of us agree that not letting us censor movies that incite to crime was a bad mistake on the Court's part.

Q. 33. *Do you base your decisions at all on whether or not a movie was given or denied a seal of approval by the film industry itself?*

No. We don't care.

Q. 34. *Do you feel the film industry's P.C.A. is stricter or less strict than it ought to be?*

On this question, Mrs. Whitehead deferred to Mrs. Wagers claiming she didn't know anything about this.

Mrs. Wagers: I don't really know the Code well enough to say, but on the whole the film industry is too liberal.

Q. 35. *Do you base your decisions at all on ratings issued by any private groups? What groups are these?*

No, but we do talk to some groups for reasons of maintaining good public relations.

Q. 36. *Do you ever come in contact at any stage in your work with representatives of any private groups? What groups do they represent?*

Yes. The P.T.A., Catholic Women and the Federation of Women's Clubs of Virginia. We especially come in contact with the latter group. We are never contacted by the A.C.L.U.

Q. 37. *Do you find any of these groups particularly helpful in your work? Why?*

We like their cooperation.

Q. 38. *Do you find any of these groups particularly troublesome in your work? Why?*

No. We get wonderful cooperation.

Q. 39. *Have any court cases resulted from disagreements you have had with exhibitors? If so, can you recall the motion pictures involved and the final decision of the courts?*[472]

We go into court sometimes. We are always sustained. We can't tell you how often we go to court but it is more often than you might think, and always at the lower level.

Q. 40. *Could you tell me if your Board falls under the state civil service system?*

No, with the exception of our paid help such as secretaries, clerks, etc.

Q. 41. *In order to obtain a position on the censorship board was it necessary for you to pass some kind of examination?*

No, but our experience was evaluated. We are political appointees but it is understood that public service is a prerequisite.

Q. 42. *Have you had any schooling other than high school?*

Mrs. Whitehead: A college degree and some graduate work. Mrs. Wagers: Some college work.

---

[472] Questions 45, 46, and 47 were deleted because, as was the case in Maryland, the board acts as its own appeals tribunal so that any protest that is lodged prior to a court suit is merely a part of the board's overall censorship operation.

Q. 43. *Along with your work as a censor do you have another job?*
*What is that?*

No.

Q. 44. *What did you do before you held your present position? How
long ago was that?*

We each came to the board thirteen years ago. Mrs. Margaret
Gregory, the third member, came in 1954. I worked as Director
of the Virginia Art Projects Committee from 1939 to 1942
and I served as Vice-Chairman of the Democratic State Central Committee from 1934 to 1939. Mrs. Gregory is a graduate
of the Amsterdam, Holland Conservatory of Music and served,
prior to 1954, as Head of the Voice Department at Wesley
College and at Virginia College in Roanoke.

Mrs. Wagers: I worked in Lynchburg with servicemen from
Camp Pickett planning entertainment on weekends, etc., prior
to my appointment. I was also a member of the Democratic
State Central Committee.

Q. 45. *Could you tell me in general terms what your yearly salary is?*
*Would you say you earn: (1) less than $4000, (2) between
$4000 and $6000, (3) between $6000 and $8000, (4) more than
$8000?*

Between $6000 and $8000.

# Appendix V

*Interview with Sergeant Robert E. Murphy and
Patrolman James O'Neill*[473]

Q. 1. *How many people serve with you on the censorship board?*

It is my job to oversee the work of the Film Review Section. Patrolman O'Neill is my assistant. The actual previewing is done by a six-member board. Under the new law you will see that the term "censor" is never used. Our job is to license movies, not to censor them. The membership of the board consists of six women appointed by the Mayor. One of these women has been sick recently so that from a practical standpoint there are five censors. The fact that there are no men on the bureau plus the fact that all are widows has led the press to make derogatory comments about "policemen's widows" being in charge of movie censorship. Actually, I think we have a well-rounded bureau. Here is a rundown on the membership all of whom, incidentally, are college people:

(1) Mrs. Joyce—an active committee woman. She is involved in all kinds of city and church functions.

(2) Mrs. Frymire—her husband was an Alderman and she has two sons who are Ph.D.'s.

(3) Mrs. McGill—she is a Negress. Her husband was a school teacher in the South and she is well informed in the area of human relations.

(4) Mrs. Petrone—her husband was also an Alderman.

(5) Mrs. Kare—her husband was a restauranteur.

You can see that this "policemen's widow" business is all nonsense.

Q. 2. *Do you preview each full-length movie and each short subject before it is shown in Chicago?*

---

[473] This interview has been certified as accurate by Melvin Mawrence, Director, Public Information Division, Chicago Police Department. Unless otherwise indicated Sergeant Murphy acted as respondent.

Everything is looked at.

Q. 3. *When the board finds that a film is objectionable does it make recommendations to the exhibitor or producer as to what changes ought to be made?*

We will call the distributor and tell him certain cuts must be made. If not, we will reject the movie. He will either accept the cuts, appeal, or we will issue a rejection order. All eliminations that we insist on are noted on library cards. We have a file on each movie going back to 1914. These also show the reasons why cuts were needed. However, the board does not make these cuts anymore. This is now done "as a matter of honor" by the people themselves, but we do have six inspectors who check up. It is true that the law does not prescribe a means for cutting movies but we feel that this task is inherent in our enforcement duties.

Q. 4. *Are the recommendations of the board usually followed?*

The big companies like M.G.M. and Warner Brothers rarely argue because their reputations are involved. The smaller independents and foreign producers want as much money as they can get so they cause more trouble.

Q. 5. *What does the board do if the recommendations are not followed?*

We call the Corporation Counsel. He will contact the Appeals Board and a rescreening will be set up. Then the courts will usually get into the picture if necessary.

Q. 6. *Does the board practice a policy of banning movies when it thinks such action is necessary?*

We don't have a right to ban movies. We just follow the procedures in the law and won't issue a permit under certain conditions. We will arrest anyone within our jurisdiction who shows a film without a license.

Q. 7. *How many films have been banned in Chicago in the past five years and do you recall the names of these films?*

I would say that about five or six movies have been rejected in the past five years. This is a hard question to answer in full because there was a period where we had no authority to classify movies due to an adverse court decision.

Patrolman O'Neill: We cannot tell you what films were involved.

Q. 8. (a) *How many films shown in Chicago in the past three years have been altered or cut in some way before they were exhibited?*

I would say about ten a year, but this is hard to answer in an offhand manner.

(b) *What are the names of thee films and how many times were each of them cut?*

We can't divulge this information.

Q. 9. *In general, what kinds of alterations or cuts have you found it necessary to make during this time? Could you mention some specific examples that come to mind?*

We cut any nudity that is just thrown in to attract patrons: bare bosoms, buttocks, and any gyrations in dancing scenes unless these are pertinent. For instance, we didn't touch the gyrations in *Gypsy.*

Along this line, Mr. Mulroy, the Chairman of the Appeals Board, got together with the censors so as to avoid conflicts in policies and to avoid a rash of appeals. A common agreement was reached and the censors are not as tough in certain areas as they once were.

Q. 10. *Have you placed other kinds of restrictions on movies during this time? For example, have you restricted some films to certain kinds of movie houses, or have you placed a minimum age requirement on those viewing some films?*

We can't restrict movies to certain kinds of theaters, but we do have an age classification law.

Q. 11. (a) *How many films have required such action in the past three years?*

In 1962 we issued forty-nine adult permits, but we didn't get the program into full swing until May. I would say that sixty a year is an accurate guess.

(b) *What are the names of these films?*

I can't answer this. The story of our age classification law and its history began when the courts knocked out the statute we had been using. Suddenly, we got a flurry of foreign movies. Fortunately Mayor Daly is highly competent and he pushed through a new bill. Usually, "adults only" movies make money in "the loop" but not in the commercial houses, and the censors realize that pictures that play to a more mature audience do not have to be screened as carefully as others. Since the new law we have had only one appeal on age classification. This was when M.G.M. protested about the movie *Phaedra*. The Appeals Board overruled the censors. I told the Corporation Counsel that this decision was "a reflection on the intelligence" of the censors and, in effect, questioned the Section's ability to make "moral evaluations." I told him that while the censors have heated arguments and don't always vote the same way, they almost always agree on the application of the "adults only" section. I lodged a query with him as to the soundness of this decision.

Q. 12. *Which type of film would you say you have been forced to ban most often—foreign films or American films? Which type of film do you think you have had to alter or restrict most often prior to exhibition—American films or foreign films?*

Well, we pay more attention to foreign movies as a rule, because people abroad do certain things that aren't approved of here. It is our own community standards that must be the deciding factor. The problem is that Hollywood is now imitating the foreign producers. While foreign pictures are our greatest challenge I would say that actually we ban a higher percentage of these American "nudist movies." So far as alterations are concerned I think we cut out more scenes from foreign films.

Q. 13. *When there is a question of whether a movie is to be restricted or not, are formal votes taken to decide on what the board ought to do?*

They decide among themselves using whatever procedure they think is best. When a movie is rejected they submit written reports describing their action.

Q. 14. *How many votes are needed to ban or to alter a movie?*

Majority rules.

Q. 15. *Do you keep a record of such votes?*

Each one keeps a private tally and we have such data on the cards we keep for each film.

Q. 16. *When you have voted to restrict films in the past three years could you tell me how many members of the board voted for and how many voted against each restriction?*

We can't tell anybody about these things. It might have a damaging effect on the board if this information was circulated.

Q. 17. *Is there generally much disagreement among members of the board when it comes to restricting films? Do you recall any instances of this and what the disagreements were about?*

There is quite a bit, but we can't tell what these were about. Generally, it boils down to individual interpretations of what the community standards are. You try to strike a balance between the various standards in high-class and low-class neighborhoods.

Q. 18. *Which of these standards in the statute, if any, do you find difficult to interpret?*

Whether you allow certain dialogue in a movie or not is a tough nut to crack. We have racial problems in Chicago and we have to watch out for certain words. For example, what about "nigger?" At first, we felt it would be all right to say this on the screen. Mrs. McGill agreed in our judgment. We have since changed our minds and will allow it to be used only if it is referred to as being in the title of a book or under similar circumstances.

Q. 19. *Is there much disagreement among members of the board as to how these standards should be interpreted?*

There is agreement on fundamentals. "There should be differences of opinion" in specifics. If everyone agrees then why have more than one member? Take Atlanta. It has a one-woman censorship board. This is no good. If she gets out of bed on the wrong side, then what? If you have five people, at least three figure to be on the ball. We can't disclose, however, what decisions were three to two, etc.

Q. 20. *Which of these standards, if any, are ambiguous to the board as to meaning?*

The ordinance should be clearer in making it illegal for a movie to contain reprehensible comments about race, color, or creed.

Q. 21. *Does the board keep records of why it banned, altered, or restricted certain movies?*

Yes. The censors provide me with these in their written reports.

Q. 22. *Could you give me the specific reasons why the board voted to ban, alter or restrict the films it did over the last three years?*

These matters are not only not given out to the average citizen but also no lawyer can obtain them either. You would need a subpoena, or else it would have to be brought out in the courtroom.

So far as standards are concerned, we have trouble with movies that are lewd, prurient, or "sex arousing." It's not just a matter of what is in the movie but its implications that concern us.

Q. 23. *Do you feel the board is too strict or not strict enough in judging the suitability of films? Why?*

Things are running just the way they should. I can see that there is a real "consistency of pattern" in what the censors object to from the monthly and annual reports they file with me. These people weigh all factors on a "justice scale" just as they should. Their points of view must not be "flighty."

Patrolman O'Neill: We would receive complaints if the censors weren't doing a good job, but neither the distributors nor the public seem to be aroused.

Q. 24. *Should the standards the board is now using be amended and, if so, in what ways?*

As a rule, the censorship boards around the country are too lenient mostly because they pass these nudist films.

Q. 25. *Some people wonder how important movie censorship is. Do you feel a community needs film censorship? Why?*

This is a very hard question to answer.

Patrolman O'Neill: Censorship for motion pictures is a "must." Our greatest service is as an aid to the parent because censorship starts in the home with parents restricting children from doing certain things and reading certain things. But parents need us because they can't check to see what's in all the films. So our most important task is keeping our younger citizens away from certain movies.

Sergeant Murphy: Who do movies appeal to? It's either the minors who are in their teens or frustrated older people. Believe me, there are some adults who are worse than kids and, of these, men are more dangerous than women. There are men who we call "movers." They have undergone a "change of life" and it's been more drastic than with women. They go to movies for their kicks and they get all "hopped up."

All the churches agree that we need censorship because "one booklet or movie can undo what doting parents have accomplished in ten years regardless of what the press thinks." Movies can be terribly corrupting and can subvert all moral standards. Because of this we watch out for much more than the lewd. We watch for excessive brutality or swearing. We watch for anything that could possibly incite to some action that would further any immoral end.

I look at censorship as a filtering process like purifying water through a good sanitation system. First, you have the censors, then the Appeals Board, then the courts. Eventually you flush out the garbage. "I think Chicago has a fine sewage system, too."

Q. 26. *Can you think of any other changes in the way your film censorship program is devised that might be helpful? I am thinking now in terms of the way members of the board are selected, their terms of office, the system of appeals, etc.*

No, we are doing a good job. The community is happy and the distributors are happy. We have a "God fearing Mayor" and "five good little women." We don't over-moralize either. The Legion of Decency, for example, provides moral guidance. Our job is to provide legal guidance in a mature fashion. Of course, we make mistakes. You take *La Dolce Vita*. We should have cut out some parts of this or limited it to an adults only audience.

Q. 27. *Does the board keep in touch with the censorship policies and decisions of other cities and states? If so, which ones?*

We keep abreast of what's going on in Detroit and New York mostly through magazines, distributors, and lawyers. This is especially true of Detroit. But such contacts don't prejudice us. We're independent.

Q. 28. *How is such communication helpful to the board? Do you base your decisions at all on the findings of other boards or, to your knowledge, do any other boards consider first what you do before they make a decision?*

Their opinions are reassuring when they agree with us. We like to know if they're doing what we are doing. We have had some contact with Kitty McMahon in Kansas. She wanted to know what we did about some film. We don't know much about other cities except Detroit.

The press sometimes condemns censorship. It has been

known to operate in an ivory tower. Newspapers often think only of freedom of speech considerations. One must remember that audio-visual techniques are the most provocative means of communication and, therefore, must be carefully watched.

Patrolman O'Neill: Some newspapers and magazines bite the hand that feeds them. There are newspapers that make money from movie advertising and then fight censorship. Yet it is censorship that has made it possible to show films that don't arouse the public against movie people.

**Q. 29.** *Are there any standards adopted by the courts that you feel are helpful to you in your work? Which ones are these?*

We don't come in contact with the courts. Only the Appeals Board does. The Supreme Court interprets the law of each state to see if a movie has violated it or not.

**Q. 30.** *Are there any standards adopted by the courts which you feel make it more difficult for you to do your job? Which ones are these?*

Courts don't lay down guidelines for us. There are three branches of government and it is our Council that writes the law. That's what counts. Of course, we can't violate the law to enforce the law.

**Q. 31.** *Do you think the courts as a whole are doing a good job in this area? Why?*

A tough question to answer. The courts are pretty fair. Either a picture is unsuitable or not as the judge decides. But then I might have my own opinions about whether these decisions were good or bad. Since the new ordinance was drafted we have had almost no court action which shows what a good job the Council did in writing it.

**Q. 32.** *Do you base your decisions at all on whether or not a movie was given or denied a seal of approval by the film industry itself?*

This doesn't carry any weight.

**Q. 33.** *Do you feel the film industry's P.C.A. is stricter or less strict than it ought to be?*

I'm not sure I understand this but I'd say that "they're never too strict."

**Q. 34.** *Do you base your decisions at all on ratings issued by any private groups? What groups are these?*

We follow the dictates of our own conscience and are not influenced by anyone. The observations of private groups are interesting *after* a decision is made.

Q. 35. *Do you ever come in contact at any stage in your work with representatives of any private groups? What groups do they represent?*

Very rarely in person and not very often even by mail. The "Citizens for Better Government" has been in touch with us. Also, a church group, but I can't recall the name. Mostly we hear from people outside the city who call to see what our Section is doing and how it works. These are noncensorship areas out of our jurisdiction and these people would like censorship to spread to these drive-ins that operate outside of Chicago where offensive movies are frequently shown. I agree that this would be a good thing. We also are familar with ratings issued by the Legion of Decency.

Q. 36. *Do you find any of these groups particularly helpful in your work? Why?*

You get an idea of public reaction to your decisions by talking with these people.

Q. 37. *Do you find any of these groups particularly troublesome in your work? Why?*

No.

Q. 38. *How would a person go about appealing the board's decision to restrict a film?*

There is a five-member Appeals Board appointed by the Mayor that reviews all our decisions. The City Council approves the Mayor's choices. This Board chooses its own chairman. Before this, a distributor had to go through the Mayor and then into the courts. This relieves the Mayor and the courts of a lot of work in censoring movies although the courts usually went along with us in the past anyway. Since the 1961 ordinance was passed twelve appeals have been lodged with this new agency. The censors were overruled in eight of these cases. These usually involved "nudist productions of the so-called documentary variety" like *The Sky Above, The Mud Below.*

The Chairman of this Board is Thomas R. Mulroy, a well known attorney. Other members are Sydney R. Drebin, who is Corporation Counsel for the city, Dr. Matthew Schoenbaum,

Dean of the School of Social Work, Loyola University, Henry Rago, Doctor of Psychology, University of Chicago and Dr. Ner Littner of the University of Chicago. The Board, however, meets at irregular intervals. It's very tough to get the members together because they're all busy.

Q. 39. *Have any court cases resulted from disagreements with distributors? If so, can you recall the motion pictures involved and the final decision of the courts?*[474]

Patrolman O'Neill: We have had no involvements in court in the last three years. The last dispute was over *Anatomy of a Murder* when the distributor took issue with our ruling.

Q. 40. *Which "adults only" statute do you think is better, the first one that limited movies to persons over twenty-one or the one you are now using?*[475]

The new ordinance is better. It is fairer to the movie industry and for the public. Kids are more "hep" now, more mature. "But we all need censorship."

Q. 41. *Have you had any schooling other than high school?*

Yes.

Q. 42. *What other schooling have you had?*

Sergeant Murphy: I took a divinity course of study after high school.

Patrolman O'Neill: I had one year of college and two years in a police training course.

Q. 43. *Along with your work as a censor do you have another job? What is that?*

No.

Q. 44. *What did you do before you held your present position? How long ago was that?*

I came to work here in 1961. From 1947 until then I worked in the Youth Division. Jim worked in the same Division from 1950 through 1958 when he came over here. The censorship board falls under the jurisdiction of the Youth Division of the Police Department.

---

[474] Respondent's sweeping answer to the previous question made it unnecessary to ask Questions 46 and 47.

[475] This question was inserted for the purpose of obtaining an insight into how the censors viewed various kinds of age classification schemes.

Q. 45. *How long have the censors themselves been serving in their present capacities?*[476]

The newest of these women came five years ago. Another has been here for six years, another for eight and another for as long as fifteen years.

Q. 46. *Could you tell me in general terms what your yearly salary is? Would you say you earn: (1) less than $4000, (2) between $4000 and $6000, (3) between $6000 and $8000, (4) more than $8000?*

Between $6000 and $8000.

---

[476] This question was added so as to gain as much information as possible about these "line" officials.

# Appendix VI

*Interview with Mrs. Minter S. Hooker*

Q. 1. *How many people serve with you on the censorship board?*

There are seven of us, three of which are men. We used to have five but this was changed two years ago.

Q. 2. *Do you preview each full-length movie and each short subject before it is shown in Memphis?*

We preview each full-length film but we don't look at shorts or newsreels. There are usually about three members present at each screening. If we think the picture will be troublesome we try to have a quorum present.

Q. 3. *Aside from the censorship of movies the Memphis ordinance grants your board the power to regulate other public exhibitions such as plays and burlesques. How do you go about supervising these activities?*

The police take care of burlesques. As for other live performances, we have had no occasion to watch these. Plays show to selected audiences. There is no doubt that parents have better control over their children when it comes to attendance at plays.

Q. 4. *When the board finds that a film is objectionable does it make recommendations to the exhibitor or producer as to what changes ought to be made?*

Yes.

Q. 5. *Are the recommendations of the Board usually followed?*

We have had our ups and downs. I have been Chairman for about a year and we have had no trouble as yet but there have been difficulties previously.

Q. 6. *What does the Board do if the recommendations are not followed?*

If someone challenges a ruling we make we will go to the

city attorney to find out how solid our legal grounds are. If he gives us the "go-ahead" then we won't give permission for the film to be shown. Otherwise we relent. Lloyd Binford used to threaten to issue a warrant closing someone's place of business if he wouldn't go along, but we have never practiced this policy.

Q. 7. *Does the Board practice a policy of banning movies when it thinks such action is necessary?*

Yes.

Q. 8. *How many films have you banned in Memphis in the past five years and do you recall the names of these films?*

In the late 1950's we banned *Island in the Sun* but this has recently been shown as a re-release. In 1960 we suppressed *Hideout in the Sun,* a nudist film. Last year we banned *Paradisio* (another movie dwelling on nudism) and *I Spit on Your Grave.* The person who wanted to exhibit this last picture was arrested for showing it after we denied him a license. He is appealing. The other films we wouldn't allow a permit were *Mom and Dad* and *The Frigid Woman.*

Before I was appointed to the Board, there were attempts made to ban *Jack the Ripper* and *The Hypnotic Eye* but the bureau, meeting with resistance from distributors, was forced to relent when the city attorney advised that only a provable charge of obscenity could be levied against movies of that sort. Thus, permits were issued to them of necessity.

There were two other pictures which were not shown. These were *The Rebel Breed* and *Smiles of a Summer Night.* There were no legal reasons for not allowing these films to be exhibited but "for the best interests of the community" we thought they shouldn't be shown. We were able to convince exhibitors of this "on a mutual agreement basis." That means there were eight pictures that were not shown here for one reason or another but we don't think of the last two as being banned because they weren't disallowed for legal reasons.

I might point out that I am sometimes called down personally to look at movies in what you might call an advisory capacity. One movie chain manager, for example, who represents many movie house owners in Arkansas, Tennessee, and Mississippi won't buy films unless we think they are "proper." He is, of course, trying to avoid any trouble we might cause him after purchase.

Incidentally, there was a movie that came around called

*Poor White Trash* which was originally entitled *Bayou.* We thought this title might cause some trouble so we required that the exhibitors change it back to its original name.

Q. 9.  (a) *How many films shown in Memphis in the past three years have been altered or cut in some way before they were exhibited?*

I think there have been only three.

(b) *What are the names of these films and how many times were each of them cut?*

One was a Bardot movie. Then there was *Lady Chatterley's Lover.* Recently we ordered cuts in *Hud.* We are waiting for word on whether they will comply with our decision on this. We don't keep written records on the number of cuts made but as I recall we made two deletions in each of these pictures.

Q. 10. *Could you tell me what specific material was excluded with each particular cut?*

We do not think it serves anyone's best interests to reveal these. Besides, the content of some of the cuts slips my mind and we do not keep official records that I can refer to. However, we will eliminate nude scenes as well as any profanity we think goes too far. I am apologetic about the fact that we don't have records on these things but the Board has no offices of its own or secretarial help so it's just impossible to be as systematic as we would like to be.

You might be interested in knowing that many of these movies that stress nudism don't come to Memphis. People used to avoid our censorship policies by showing these items across the river in West Memphis, Arkansas, but there was so much protest over the fact that a great many people went over there to see these pictures that "they follow our decisions pretty much now."

Q. 11. *Have you placed other kinds of restrictions on movies during this time? For example, have you restricted some films to certain kinds of movie houses, or have you placed a minimum age requirement on those viewing some films?*

In the past we have done both of these things even though the ordinance does not authorize such practices. We have one art house in the city which for a while received preferential treatment. For instance, we allowed *Lady Chatterley's Lover* and that Bardot picture I mentioned to play there in expurgated form. This sort of priority was resented by other exhibitors and, furthermore, the owner used to let minors in to see films of that kind. Finally, he tried to show the movie *Paradisio* and at that point we decided to step in and regulate his fare on an equal footing with the other houses. However, we often will not allow people under eighteen to see certain movies.

Q. 12. (a) *How many films have required such action in the past three years?*

We keep no records on films we restrict through age limit procedures. I would guess there have been about twenty-five or thirty in the past three years. I remember one such film was entitled *The Vampire and the Ballerina*.

As far as art house restriction was concerned I am afraid we again kept no records. If I were to guess I would say that about fifty pictures were shown at the art house on an exclusive basis over the same period. *A Taste of Honey* was one of these and another was *The Green Mare*. No one on the Board previewed these. The way things worked as a general rule was that the art house was given carte blanche in its selection of movies with the exception of certain "hot" items. We just ignored what it did for the most part. This period lasted from 1957 to 1962 but then, as I say, the owner attempted to show *Paradisio* and we had to shut him off.[477]

Q. 13. *When there is a question of whether a movie is to be restricted or not, are formal votes taken to decide on what the Board ought to do?*

Yes.

Q. 14. *How many votes are needed to ban or to alter a movie?*

Four.

Q. 15. *Do you keep a record of such votes?*

The Chairman keeps a record. Usually the vote is unanimous.

Q. 16. *When you have voted to restrict films in the past three years could you tell me how many members of the Board voted for and how many voted against each restriction?*

---

[477] This answer precludes asking the second half of this question. Items 24 and 58 were also omitted for similarly apparent reasons.

I would say that ninety-five percent of the decisions to ban or to cut movies have been unanimous. The only picture I can think of where the disagreement was at all vehement was with *Hud*. We never disagree on a question of age classification.

Q. 17. *Which of the standards in the statute, if any, do you find difficult to interpret?*

We have stopped enforcing certain parts of the statute because of court decisions in this area. The city attorney has advised us that this was necessary. We don't apply the section of the law which checks movies that denounce or deride the present form of national government nor do we ever, except on the rarest occasion, put to use the provision about films that are inimical to the public interest.

The standards that we are using to evaluate movies are the terms "lewd, lascivious and immoral" which you will find specifically mentioned in our law. These, of course, are terribly difficult to interpret. In practice what we try to do is to construe these guidelines as if each was related to obscenity because we know that when we go into court we must be able to show that a film is obscene. The situation is unusual because this term is not used in the law, yet it is the basic factor we know we must try to demonstrate exists.

Q. 18. *Is there much disagreement among members of the Board as to how these standards should be interpreted?*

All three guidelines give everyone trouble "as much as they do me." The Supreme Court can't decide what obscenity is.

Q. 19. *What are the usual differences of opinion as to the meaning of these ambiguous standards?*

We apply them on a case-by-case basis. How else can you do it?

Q. 20. *Does the Board keep records of why it banned, altered or restricted certain films?*

We keep no records on this.

Q. 21. *Which of these standards do you feel films probably tend to violate most often?*

I would say that most of them are "indecent." "They defy all moral codes." Also, they are obscene. *I Spit on Your Grave* was "obscenity for obscenity's sake. It was merely an appeal to the prurient interest."

Q. 22.  (a) *Would you say that objectionable American films tend to violate the same standards as foreign films or do they seem to violate different standards?*

Different standards are involved.

(b) *Which standards do each seem to violate most often?*

American movies are more violent and vulgar. Foreign films deal more with "decadent sex."

Q. 23. *Do you feel the Board is too strict or not strict enough in judging the suitability of films? Why?*

For years we were too slack. We had a "what's the use" attitude. But we've made improvements so that now we have acquired a reputation for being strict and we are happy about this. All the Board hopes that we will be even stricter in the future if this is at all possible.

Q. 24. *Should the standards the Board is now using be amended and, if so, in what ways?*

We would like to see the law amended so that it will be consistent with Supreme Court rulings and the Tennessee criminal law against spreading obscenity. Our statute is basically obsolete even though it gives us plenty of leeway. We must include the word "obscene" in our ordinance.

Q. 25. *Some people wonder how important movie censorship is. Do you feel a community needs film censorship? Why?*

If a majority of the public wants it, then there is a need. We must have censorship because the movie industry has not taken steps to clean itself up. We must protect "immature minds" from certain films—children and adults as well.

Q. 26. *Do you feel a film censorship program that uses a system of prior restraint is better than one that would punish the exhibitor of an objectionable movie after he has once shown it to the public?*

Each scheme can complement one another. Prior restraint is more practical and less unpleasant for everyone.

Q. 27. *Can you think of any other changes in the way your film censorship program is devised that might be helpful? I am thinking now in terms of the way members of the Board are selected, their terms of office, the system of appeals, etc.*

The Board needs an office and a secretary, Also, we are not

salaried employees. We feel we are performing a public service so that salary is not a prerequisite, but I do think our expenses should come out of the tax dollar. This would help me be more efficient in my work.

Q. 28. *Does the Board keep in touch with the censorship policies and decisions of other cities and states? If so, which ones?*

This is very hard to do. We rely only on newspaper publicity and the word of "film people." From these sources we know a little about what is going on in Atlanta, Chicago, and New York. I don't know anything about any of the other boards and I don't know much about the makeup of even these three. We do not communicate with any of them. I tried to get in touch with Mrs. Gilliam in Atlanta but I don't know her address or her first name. I couldn't get through to her. I never got an answer.

Q. 29. *Are there any standards adopted by the courts that you feel are helpful to you in your work? Which ones are these?*

We have had no court action in recent years except for the exhibitor who was indicted for showing *I Spit on Your Grave.* So far as other courts are concerned, none of them have laid down any standards that are especially helpful.

Q. 30. *Are there any standards adopted by the courts which you feel make it more difficult for you to do your job? Which ones are these?*

The New York courts hurt us by making it impossible to censor *The Connection.* There is no point to having a censorship program if a picture like that can't be restricted. The producers didn't bother to send that film down here because they knew it wouldn't get by us.

Q. 31. *Do you think the courts as a whole are doing a good job in this area? Why?*

"They are bending over backwards to favor freedom of speech considerations."

Q. 32. *Do you base your decisions at all on whether or not a movie was given or denied a seal of approval by the film industry itself?*

Yes. We do not look with favor on films that don't carry the seal.

Q. 33. *Do you feel the film industry's P.C.A. is stricter or less strict than it ought to be?*

The Code is strict enough but its specifications are often not enforced. The Code is actually stricter than what any censor board would require.

Q. 34. *Do you base your decisions at all on ratings issued by any private groups? What groups are these?*

We get literature issued by the Legion of Decency and the Film Estimate Board and I keep a file on what they say of importance. However, as a rule we don't get the "Green Sheet's" reactions to a picture until after the film has come here and we have made a decision about it.

Q. 35. *Do you ever come in contact at any stage in your work with representatives of any private groups? What groups do they represent?*

Not on a personal basis.

Q. 36. *How would a person go about appealing the Board's decision to restrict a film?*

First of all, a person would make an appeal to the Board itself asking us to reconsider our ruling to ban or cut a picture. In this situation we will have a conference with such people during which they try to persuade us as to our course of action. If we vote against them they must go into court.

Q. 37. *Have any film executives or movie house owners challenged any of your decisions in the past five years? Which decisions and what films were involved?*

All appeals have stopped with reconsideration by the Board. I can remember that the exhibitor of *Lady Chatterley's Lover* appealed, for instance. The only time in recent years that things have gone further was the incident where a movie house owner tried to show *I Spit on Your Grave* illegally.

Q. 38. *Could you tell me if your board falls under the state civil service system.*

No.

Q. 39. *In order to obtain a position on the censorship board was it necessary for you to pass some kind of examination?*

There are no exams given. We are political appointees. When Mayor Loeb came into office he appointed all seven of us. In choosing each of us the Mayor looked at our records, elicited our views on censorship, and wanted to know if our religious convictions would affect our work in any way. He had an interview with each of us.

Let me say this. When Mayor Loeb leaves office he will take us with him and I'll be quite happy to leave. This job definitely has its drawbacks. The newspapers criticize you and take what you say out of context. There is no compensation given and no staff is provided.

Q. 40. *Have you had any schooling other than high school?*

Yes.

Q. 41. *What other schooling have you had?*

I had two years of college and a year at the Sorbonne.

Q. 42. *Along with your work as a censor do you have another job? What is that?*

I have no other job.

Q. 43. *What did you do before you held your present position? How long ago was that?*

I was in the real estate business for five years. I also have been an officer of the Memphis Little Theater Group (a nonpaying responsibility). I have been on the Board of Censors for five and a half years and was last reappointed two years ago.

# Appendix VII
*Interview with Mrs. Christine S. Gilliam*

Q. 1. *How many people serve with you on the censorship board?*

I am the only full-time paid employee who reviews movies. When I was sick for a time last year a member of the Library Board took my place.

Q. 2. *Do you preview each full-length movie and each short subject before it is shown in Atlanta?*

I see all feature films and an occasional short. However, newsreels are not previewed. These movies are pre-screened at regular trade showings where exhibitors come to bid for particular pictures being marketed by distributors. Atlanta assesses no fee for reviewing films.

Q. 3. *When the board finds that a film is objectionable does it make recommendations to the exhibitor or producer as to what changes ought to be made?*[478]

We used to do this regularly under the old system, but since the *Murray* decision we only resort to this practice on infrequent

---

[478] The phrasing of a question of this kind, while appropriate to the work of censorship agencies already discussed, may seem inappropriate given the fact that Atlanta, at least on the face of it, is now involved in *rating* films rather than *censoring* them. If there is any methodological problem raised by using certain questions devised to gain insight into censorship practices, it is a result of the fact that I did not know about the new Atlanta ordinance until just prior to the interview. The reason for this was simply that Atlanta makes no effort to keep the publication of its ordinances up to date. Mrs. Gilliam was kind enough to supply a copy of the law which was studied carefully "on the spot" so that her answers about her work under both the old and the new enactments could be readily understood. It was, of course, impossible to redraft questions with the greatest of care at that point but, hopefully, questions of this type elicit the necessary information. See also footnotes 480 and 481 for specific inquiries that were somewhat modified during the interview so as to take account of varying procedures under both ordinances.

occasions when certain alterations will change the category into which I might place the film. Our right to do this is very nebulous under the new law.

Q. 4. *Are the recommendations of the board usually followed?*

Yes. Up until we censored *Never on Sunday* and *Room at the Top* we rarely had a problem. These were the first real challenges.

Q. 5. *What does the board do if the recommendations are not followed?*

If the proper cuts were not made we would deny a permit for the movie. No exhibitor ever tried to show a picture contrary to our commands. The only route that was ever taken was an appeal to the Library Board and from there to the courts. From a practical standpoint, however, the appeal to the Board usually ended things until the *Never on Sunday* dispute came to a head. Prior to that we were involved in almost no courtroom activity.

Q. 6. *Does the board practice a policy of banning movies when it thinks such action is necessary?*

We used to do this but it is no longer allowable under the new law.

Q. 7. *How many films have been banned in Atlanta in the past five years and do you recall the names of these films?*

I can give you compete records on this. In 1958, for example, we saw 339 pictures and suppressed eleven. There was no appeal on eight of these and the Board concurred in my decision regarding the other three. We banned such movies as *Teen Age Doll*, *Cop Hater*, *The Case of Dr. Laurent*, and *Nana*.

In 1959 we looked at 291 and would not license sixteen. In ten of these instances no appeals were made and the Board upheld my ruling in the other six cases. Some of the pictures that we wouldn't show were *Lovers of Paris*, *Question of Adultery*, *Beat Generation*, *Call Girl*, *The Birth of a Nation*, and *Room at the Top*. *The Birth of a Nation* is "a race-baiter from way back." The paid publicist for the Ku Klux Klan told me that the Klan was behind the resurrection of this old chestnut. *Room at the Top* was the movie we banned that led to the *Murray* decision which threw out the old statute.

In 1960 I screened 267 pictures and refused to pass nine of them. Five of these were appealed and, once again, I was upheld in each case. We banned *The Pushers, Sapphire, This Rebel Breed,* and *Key Witness* among others. We have since classified all movies not approved in this year so as to see where they stand under the new law and my records show that each was given a "UY" rating.

In 1961 I saw 276 and failed to license ten of these. Surprisingly, only one was appealed. This was *From a Roman Balcony* which I have since held to be objectionable and this holding has again been appealed. I ruled that such pictures as *It Happened in Broad Daylight, Cold Wind in August, Never Take Candy From a Stranger,* and *Sin of Mona Kent* could not be exhibited.

The year 1962 was a year of confusion for us. First of all, I was sick for an extended period of time and an annual report for that year has yet to be made out. Then our censorship law was voided and we had to wait for two months until a new one was passed. Furthermore, there was a big drop-off in movies reviewed during the summer months because the "Johnston Office" and most distributors refused to invite me to previews in order to test the validity of the new ordinance. On advice from our attorney we did nothing about this for two months so as a result there were many pictures I didn't get to see.

Through April 8, 1963, I have graded 1226 movies under the new law. This includes ratings issued by my substitute during my illness, old pictures that I have catalogued by consulting my records and pictures coming to Atlanta for the first time. Of these, the following have been found objectionable: *The Balcony, From a Roman Balcony, Blaze Starr Goes Nudist, A Stranger Knocks, Jungle Street Girl, The Seventh Commandment, Too Young, Too Immoral, The Wild and the Wicked, Please Don't Touch Me, Not Tonite, Henry, The Connection, The Fast Set, West End Jungle, Girl Chasers,* and *Kipling's Women.* In spite of our ruling an exhibitor tried to show *The Fast Set.* He was tried in court and the picture was found not to be obscene under the relevant state law. He was then tried under the new city law and convicted. As punishment he was forced to pay a fine and he is now appealing. Someone else tried to show *Kipling's Women.* This film was also ruled obscene under the new Atlanta law and a fine was exacted. The exhibitor did not appeal this decision after a warning from the judge that he faced a prison term if there was a next time. The distributors for the remainder of these films have, as a rule, not appealed my ratings but there are two exceptions, *Too Young, Too Immoral* and *From a Roman Balcony*. The Library Board will have to decide about these.

Many of the pictures that were banned under the old law simply cannot be rated as objectionable under the new ordinance. *Never on Sunday* and *Room at the Top*, the two pictures that have given us so much trouble, have since been shown with a "UY" label. *Victim* and *A Taste of Honey*, two other well-known movies, are other examples of this. On occasion we will give a picture a "UY" if certain cuts are made. This has happened about three or four times. One I can remember was entitled *Case of Patty Smith*. Two more are now pending. I will give the Bardot film *Please, Not Now* a "UY" if "nudity scenes" are removed and another is *The Fruit is Ripe* where I am waiting to see if the distributor will make certain cuts. Still another one that I can recall of this type was *Sin of Mona Kent*.

This task of going over files on old movies and classifying them would not be possible without a complete set of records. We keep a catalogue on every film we have seen in which we include Legion of Decency rating, whether it was given a seal by the Hollywood code people, "Green Sheet" rating, Parents Magazine rating and any comments by the Better Films Council, a local volunteer group. This is not easy to do either because I have no secretary.

As yet we have no figures on pictures rated as being only for adults as opposed to those approved for all. I don't know how typical this would be but for the first two weeks of March, 1963, I saw fifty-six movies. Of these, thirty-three were approved, twenty were given a "UY" and three were found objectionable.[479]

Q. 8. (a) *How many films shown in Atlanta in the past three years have been altered or cut in some way before they were exhibited?*

Under present conditions it would be hard to give you

---

[479] An examination of monthly and annual reports filed by Mrs. Gilliam with the Library Board offer further data in this regard. Thus, she reported in May of 1962 that by the time the new law went into effect she had graded 397 movies but only eighteen of these were "first runs." Of this group, 272 were approved, 114 were given a "UY" rating and eleven were found to be objectionable. While the new law does not require Mrs. Gilliam to file reports with the appeals board she is continuing to do so.

accurate data because, of course we don't do this anymore. When this practice was a routine task for us, we had this information at our finger tips.

*Q. 9. Could you tell me what specific material was excluded with each particular cut?*

Again, we kept complete records of this as well.

*Q. 10. Have you placed other kinds of restrictions on movies during this time? For example, have you restricted some films to certain kinds of movie houses, or have you placed a minimum age requirement on those viewing some films?*

We did neither of these things.

*Q. 11. Which type of film would you say you have been forced to ban most often—foreign films or American films? Which type of film do you think you have had to alter or restrict most often prior to exhibition—American films or foreign films?[480]*

Many of these cheaply made nudist pictures have been coming in since the new law was passed. Most of these are American and they are the ones we usually are finding obscene. Some objectionable movies are foreign made, also. So far as the kinds of pictures that are rated only for adult consumption are concerned I can only guess but I doubt if there is much difference. The same was probably true under the old statute. We banned some well-known European pictures like *Never on Sunday* and *Sapphire* but if you examine the titles we discussed earlier you can see how much American junk there is.

Under the new law, incidentally, I take it upon myself to inform the police when a picture that I have held to be objectionable is being shown and, as I have mentioned, we have had two cases of this sort already. We have also had a few convictions obtained against exhibitors who have gone out of their way not to display our ratings on their billboards, but we do not require that they advertise the word "approved" because the movie-house owners have told us that this hurts business.

*Q. 12. Which of the standards in the new statute, if any, do you find difficult to interpret?[481]*

[480] This question was amended slightly so as also to determine the percentage of American movies that were rated "objectionable" or "unsuitable for children."

[481] This question was reworded in order to make it applicable only to the present law. Other inquiries that were modified so as to take ac-

The entire law is hard to interpret and that is why I try to find out what other people have said about particular movies by reading their ratings, etc. Basically I try to determine how each picture stands up when compared with community standards and I think these reviews I read are a good gauge of what community norms are.

Q. 13. *Does the board keep records of why it classifies films in the ways that it has? Did the board keep records of why it banned or altered certain movies when the old law was in force?*

We don't keep records of this under the new ordinance nor did we do this under the old one either.

Q. 14. *Which standards in the old ordinance do you feel films probably tended to violate most often?*

Under the old law we usually used either the terms "obscene" and/or "licentious." The others were too vague. The courts didn't like it when we said a picture would be detrimental to the morals and tranquility of Atlanta. However, we did ban *The Birth of a Nation* because of the good order of the city.

Q. 15. (a) *Would you say that American films and foreign films tended to violate the same standards in the old ordinance or did they seem to violate different standards?*

The same standards. This is also true under the new rule as well.

Q. 16. *Do you feel the board is now too strict or not strict enough in judging the suitability of films? Why?*

I thought the old system was strict enough. This one is not tough enough. I will be honest and say I preferred the old program. None of these "fly-by-night" operators could get

---

count of procedures under either one or both of the statutes were Questions 13, 14, 15, and 16 (the numbers used for these items refer to their order as listed here and *not* to their status in the master questionnaire). Question 14 was limited to procedures under the old enactment because it was felt that when a picture is classified as "UY" or "objectionable" there is little statutory discretion in deciding why these limitations are needed. This rationale is probably dubious because a question that asks, "What reason, more than any other, has led you to classify certain pictures as unsuitable for the young?" might well have been put to respondent. Of course, all questions dealing with differences of opinion among censorship board members were deleted.

away with anything when it was in effect. Most of them never even brought their merchandise down here. Under the old ordinance you had greater flexibility because you could just cut out the offensive material. Now what do you do when Bardot goes to take off her clothes? Before this we could just eliminate something of that sort or offensive dialogue like "bastard," "whore," and "by God." You can't do this anymore. The old law wasn't just a "yes or no law" like this one.

Q. 17. *Should the standards the board is now using be amended and, if so, in what ways?*

You have to operate under it longer than we have to make a proper evaluation, but I think this *Roth* definition we are using is not good enough as I have indicated already. What do you do about obscene words, segments, etc.?

Q. 18. *Some people wonder how important movie censorship is. Do you feel a community needs film censorship? Why?*

Yes. We must protect the immature regardless of age who comprise the vast bulk of the movie audience. Most patrons are children and we certainly want to protect them.

Q. 19. *Do you feel a film censorship program that uses a system of prior restraint is better than one that would punish the exhibitor of an objectionable movie after he has once shown it to the public?*

I prefer prior restraint of the kind we used before. We must stymie these cheap pictures before they hit the streets. It is important to remember that movies are made only for financial profit and not for educational or artistic reasons.

Q. 20. *Some people wonder how wise it is for just one person to censor films. What are your feelings on this?*

That's why we have an appeals board and why I try to keep a detailed record of what other people think. For example, I cut out a portion of a movie showing a man taking off his pants in front of several women because I thought this was "vulgar and coarse." The appeals board, comprised mostly of men, thought the scene was just funny and overruled me.

Q. 21. *Can you think of any other changes in the way your film censorship program is devised that might be helpful? I am thinking now in terms of the way members of the board are selected, their terms of office, the system of appeals, etc.*

Frankly, I think the appeals tribunal should be rejuvenated so as to better represent a cross-section of the community. We need leaders from various walks of life so that we can get the best possible insight into what community attitudes are. For instance, we might have someone from the P.T.A., a psychologist, someone from the juvenile board, and other professional people.

Q. 22.  *Does the board keep in touch with the censorship policies and decisions of other cities and states? If so, which ones?*

I am not in direct touch with anyone now but I used to have contact with the Ohio board when it was functioning. I read the trade papers carefully and I also subscribe to publications issued by the Legion of Decency and the "Green Sheet." When necessary I inform the Board of Appeals of information provided by any of these.

Q. 23.  *Are there any standards adopted by the courts that you feel are helpful to you in your work? Which ones are these?*

I can't think of any. The Chicago *Times Film* case which supported local censorship confused me more than anything else. The State Supreme Court's ruling on *Never on Sunday* was also confusing because it was decided on procedural grounds.

Q. 24.  *Are there any standards adopted by the courts which you feel make it more difficult for you to do your job? Which ones are these?*

The test set up in the *Roth* case makes it more difficult as I have mentioned earlier.

Q. 25.  *Do you think the courts as a whole are doing a good job in this area? Why?*

No. They are confusing the whole issue. They are too legalistic.

Q. 26.  *Do you base your decisions at all on whether or not a movie was given or denied a seal of approval by the film industry itself?*

We take this into consideration.

Q. 27.  *Do you feel the film industry's P.C.A. is stricter or less strict than it ought to be?*

Hollywood is not strict enough. If they lived up to their Code it would give me less trouble.

Q. 28.  *Do you base your decisions at all on ratings issued by any private groups? What groups are these?*

As I have said we take these into account and some of their ratings and criticisms are of value. The "Green Sheet" people are at long last reviewing pictures that have not been given the P.C.A.'s seal. This is a help to me. They are doing this to fight a proposed rating ordinance in New York State. However, this service, even though it is a good idea, cannot replace the work we are doing because we rate all pictures before they are distributed and, also, our conclusions are more accessible to the public because we insist that they be advertised.

Q. 29. *Do you ever come in contact at any stage in your work with representatives of any private groups? What groups do they represent?*

No.

Q. 30. *Could you tell me if your board falls under the state civil service system?*

My job falls under the civil service of the City of Atlanta which means that I can only be dismissed for cause. The classified service embraces everyone in civil service and provides for equitable pay, examinations that gauge merit, etc.

Q. 31. *In order to obtain a position on the censorship board was it necessary for you to pass some kind of examination?*

Yes.

Q. 32. *Could you briefly describe this examination? For instance, was it oral or written and, in general, what subject matter did it deal with?*

The test was both oral and written. The written part asked about movie censorship specifically but it was also a general knowledge examination. The oral test was much the same. They might ask you what you know about almost anything. They also were interested in your appearance and diction and, of course, censorship. The top three candidates were then given a special interview by the Library Board from which one person was finally picked. One of the things they asked was how I felt about Negroes on the screen. "I told them I wasn't going to be like Binford in Memphis and cut them all off the screen just on principle." After all, they're part of the community too.

Q. 33. *Have you had any schooling other than high school?*

I have a college degree as well as an M.A.

Q. 34. *Along with your work as a censor do you have another job? What is that?*

This is my only job.

Q. 35. *What did you do before you held your present position? How long ago was that?*

I have served as movie censor for eighteen years. Just prior to my appointment I held a paying job with the League of Women Voters. This was the first full-time paying job set up in the Atlanta area by the League. I was also writing articles on local government for the Atlanta *Journal* at the time. Before this I taught political science and history at Brenau College in Gainsville, Georgia.

Q. 36. *Could you tell me in general terms what your yearly salary is? Would you say you earn: (1) less than $4000, (2) between $4000 and $6000, (3) between $6000 and $8000, (4) more than $8000?*

Between $6000 and $8000.

# Table of Cases

# Bibliography

## Books and Pamphlets

Chafee Jr., Zechariah. *Free Speech in the United States*. Cambridge, Mass: Harvard University Press, 1941.

Crowther, Bosley. *Movies and Censorship*, Public Affairs Pamphlet No. 332, 1962.

*Forty-Sixth Annual Report of the Motion Picture Censor Board of Maryland*, 1962.

*Freedom Through Dissent*, 42nd Annual Report of the American Civil Liberties Union. New York: Oceana Publications, 1962.

Haney, Robert W. *Comstockery in America*. Boston: Beacon Press, 1960.

Inglis, Ruth. *Freedom of the Movies*. Chicago: The University of Chicago Press, 1947.

Kauper, Paul G. *Civil Liberties and the Constitution*. Ann Arbor: The University of Michigan Press, 1962.

Kilpatrick, James J. *The Smut Peddlers*. Garden City, N. Y.: Doubleday and Co., Inc., 1960.

Kronhausen, Eberhard and Phyllis. *Pornography and the Law*. New York: Ballantine Books, Inc., 1959.

*Memorandum on Motion Picture Classification*, issued by the Motion Picture Association of America, Jan. 19, 1960.

*Motion Pictures and Juvenile Delinquency*, Report of the Committee on the Judiciary Containing an Interim Report of the Subcommittee to Investigate Juvenile Delinquency, S. Rep. No. 2055, 84th Congress, 2d Session, 1956.

*The 1962 International Motion Picture Almanac*. New York: Quigley Publications.

Paul, James C. N. and Schwartz, Murray L. *Federal Censorship: Obscenity in the Mail*. New York: The Free Press of Glencoe, Inc., 1961.

329

Peltason, Jack W. *Federal Courts in the Political Process.* Garden City, N. Y.: Doubleday and Co., Inc., 1955.

Plato. *Dialogues of Plato.* New York: Pocket Books, 1950.

Pritchett, C. Herman. *The American Constitution.* New York: McGraw-Hill, 1959.

Pritchett, C. Herman. *Civil Liberties and the Vinson Court.* Chicago: The University of Chicago Press, 1954.

Schumach, Murray. *The Face on the Cutting Room Floor.* New York: William Morrow and Co., 1964.

Tappan, Paul W. *Juvenile Delinquency.* New York: McGraw-Hill, 1949.

*What Shocked the Censors,* a report prepared by The American Civil Liberties Union, 1933.

## Articles and Periodicals

Almond, Gabriel. "Comparative Analysis of Political Systems," Eldersveld, S. J. *et al* (eds.), *Political Behavior.* Glencoe, Ill.: The Free Press, 1956, pp. 34–42.

Alpert, Hollis. "Talk With a Movie Censor," *Saturday Review,* Nov. 22, 1952, pp. 21, 50–54.

Annotation, "Constitutionality, Construction, and Effect of Censorship Laws," *American Law Reports,* LXIV (1929), 505–13.

Annotation, "What Amounts to an Obscene Play or Book Within Prohibition Statute," *American Law Reports,* LXXXI (1932), 801–8.

"Arbitrary Movie-Censorship Invalidated by Supreme Court," *Weekly Bulletin* #2232, published by The American Civil Liberties Union, May 10, 1965, pp. 1–3.

Bartholomew, Paul C. "Movie Censorship and The Supreme Court," *Michigan State Bar Journal,* August 1961, pp. 10–16.

Carden, Philip M. "The Supreme Court and Obscenity," *Vanderbilt Law Review,* XI (1958), 585–98.

Crosby, John. "Movies Are Too Dirty," *Saturday Evening Post,* Nov. 10, 1962, pp. 8, 11.

"Detroit's Film Capitol," Roto Magazine Section, *Detroit Free Press,* March 27, 1955, p. 4.

*Detroit News.* August 3, 1962, p. 3.

Emerson, Thomas I. "The Doctrine of Prior Restraint," *Law and Contemporary Problems,* XX (1955), 648–71.

Freund, Paul A. "The Supreme Court and Civil Liberties," *Vanderbilt Law Review,* IV (1951), 533–54.

Goodman, Paul. "Pornography, Art, and Censorship," *Commentary Magazine,* March 1961, pp. 203–12.

Harris Jr., Albert. "Movie Censorship and the Supreme Court: What Next?" *California Law Review,* XIII (1954), 122–38.

Hyams, Joe. "What Should We Do About the Crisis in Movie Morals?" *This Week Magazine,* Feb. 26, 1961, pp. 8–10.

Kupferman, Theodore R. and O'Brien, Philip J. "Motion Picture Censorship—The Memphis Blues," *Cornell Law Quarterly,* XXXVI (1951), 273–300.

Lasker, Edward. "Censorship of Motion Pictures Pursuant to Recent Supreme Court Decisions," *U.C.L.A. Law Review,* I (1954), 582–92.

Lawrence, D. H. "Pornography and Obscenity," Beal, Anthony (ed.), *Selected Literary Criticism.* New York: The Viking Press, 1956, pp. 32–51.

Leary, Thomas B. and Noall, J. Roger. "Entertainment: Public Pressures and the Law," *Harvard Law Review,* LXXI (1957), 354–62.

Lockhart, William B. and McClure, Robert C. "Censorship of Obscenity: The Developing Constitutional Standards," *Minnesota Law Review,* XLV (1960), 5–121.

McAnany, P. D. "Motion Picture Censorship and Constitutional Freedom," *Kentucky Law Journal,* L (1962), 427–58.

Morse, Howard N. "A Critical Analysis and Appraisal of *Burstyn* v. *Wilson,*" *North Dakota Law Review,* XXIX (1953), 38–41.

Nimmer, Melville B. "The Constitutionality of Official Censorship of Motion Pictures," *University of Chicago Law Review,* XXV (1958), 625–57.

Note, " 'For Adults Only': The Constitutionality of Governmental Film Censorship by Age Classification," *Yale Law Journal,* LXIX (1959), 141–52.

Note, "Motion Pictures and the First Amendment," *Yale Law Journal,* LX (1951), 696–719.

Patric, Gordon. "The Impact of a Court Decision: Aftermath of the *McCollum* Case," *Journal of Public Law,* VI (1957), 455–64.

"Seek Changes in Censor Ordinance," *Chicago Tribune*, March 19, 1965, Sect. 2, p. 7.

Shaffer, Helen B. "Censorship of Movies and TV," *Editorial Research Reports*, April 12, 1961, pp. 265–82.

Sibley, John. "Film Censorship in State is Ended," *The New York Times*, June 11, 1965, pp. 33, 61.

Sorauf, Frank J. *"Zorach v. Clausen:* The Impact of a Supreme Court Decision," *American Political Science Review*, LIII (1959), 777–91.

Velie, Lester. "You Can't See That Movie: Censorship in Action," *Collier's*, May 6, 1950, pp. 11–13, 66.

Weiler, A. H. "Movie Censorship Seen in New Light," *The New York Times*, March 3, 1965, p. 35.

## Other Sources

Carmen, Ira H. "State and Local Motion Picture Censorship and Constitutional Liberties with Special Emphasis on the Communal Acceptance of Supreme Court Decision-Making." Doctoral Dissertation, University of Michigan, 1964.

Letter of May 24, 1963, received from Mr. Charles A. Brind, Counsel for the State Education Department, New York State.

Letter of October 12, 1965, received from Mr. Bosley Crowther, motion picture critic for *The New York Times*.

Letter of November 5, 1962, received from Mr. Reuben Goodman, Counsel for the Massachusetts Civil Liberties Union.

Letter of February 4, 1963, received from Mrs. Kitty McMahon, Chairman of the Kansas State Board of Review.

Letters of December 3, 1962, and April 30, 1963, received from Miss Barbara Scott, attorney for the Motion Picture Association of America.

Personal interview with Mr. Elwood L. Gebhart, Executive Assistant, Motion Picture Censor Board of Maryland, April 1963.

Personal interview with Mrs. Christine Smith Gilliam, Motion Picture Reviewer, Atlanta, Georgia, April 1963.

Personal interview with Mrs. Minter Somerville Hooker, Chairman, Board of Film Censors, Memphis, Tennessee, April 1963.

Personal interview with Mr. Sidney Lipston, Office of the General Counsel of the Post Office Department, April 1963.

Personal interview with Sergeant Robert E. Murphy and Patrolman James O'Neill, Film Review Section, Chicago, Illinois, January 1963.

Personal interview with Mr. Louis Pesce, Chairman, Motion Picture Division, New York State, April 1963.

Personal interview with Sergeant Phil Schoppe, Patrolman Edward Marks and Patrolman Roy Gutch, Detroit License and Censor Bureau, Detroit, Michigan, December 1962.

Personal interview with Miss Barbara Scott, attorney for the Motion Picture Association of America, April 1963.

Personal interview with Mrs. Lollie Whitehead and Mrs. Russell Wagers, Motion Picture Censorship Board of Virginia, April 1963.

*U. S. Congressional Record—House,* Feb. 14, 1963.

# Index

Motion Picture Association of America, 7, 125n, 128, 186, 249, 271-73, 279, 317.
Mulroy, Thomas R., 297, 303.
Murphy, Frank, 30, 43.
Murphy, Robert E., 195-99; interview with, 295-305.
Musmanno, Michael, 133-34, 138, 242-43.

National Board of Review, 127-28.
Neil, C. J., 208.
*Never on Sunday*, 215, 220-21n, 316, 318-19, 322.
New York Board of Regents, 48-49, 52, 56, 59, 96-97, 99, 122-23, 129, 142, 144, 148-49, 151, 266-68, 274.
New York, censorship policies in, 48-52, 56-59, 96-99, 122-24, 141-53, 181, 225-26, 233, 237-38, 266-75, 283.
New York Court of Appeals, 49, 56, 60, 62, 69, 97, 146-48.
New York, Supreme Court of, 48.
Nimmer, Melville B., 108n, 132n, 185n, 196, 233n, 251n.
Noall, J. Roger; *see* Leary, Thomas B.

O'Brien, Philip J., 209n, 215n.
Obscenity, criterion for censorship, 51, 63-64, 67-70, 90-96, 101, 107-8, 130, 133, 143, 147, 150, 154-55, 173-74, 180, 183, 190-93, 203, 205, 210-13, 215, 218-30, 236-38, 268, 270, 290, 310, 317, 319-21; definition of, 68-83, 85-89, 137, 152, 155, 217, 226-27, 235, 253, 281; criterion for age classification, 135, 194, 232, 239-40, 251-59.
Ohio, censorship policies in, 11-13, 59-61, 126, 129-31.
Ohio, Constitution of, 11-16.
Ohio Division of Film Censorship, 59, 93.

O'Neill, James, 195, 198; interview with, 295-305.
*The Outlaw*, 59, 144, 185.

Patric, Gordon, 2-3.
Paul, James C. N., 4n.
Peltason, Jack W., 2.
Pennsylvania, censorship policies in, 132-39.
Pennsylvania, Constitution of, 136-39.
Pennsylvania, Supreme Court of, 132-39.
Pesce, Louis, 150-53, 156, 162, 165, 283; interview with, 266-75.
*Pinky*, 54-55, 235.
Plato, 249-50.
*Please, Not Now*, 164, 276.
Pornography, 5n, 77-81, 88, 90n, 98-99, 108, 115, 148, 155-56, 172, 225, 227.
Post Office Department, 4-5n, 82-85, 190.
Pritchett, C. Herman, 6, 26n, 31n, 39n, 52-53.
Production Code Administration, 4n, 198, 237, 248n, 256, 264n, 273, 284, 292, 302, 312-13, 318, 322-23.

Reed, Stanley, 28, 37, 39, 41-44, 51, 66, 76, 86n.
*Revenge at Daybreak*, 117.
Robb, J., 63.
Roberts, Owen, 26-28, 30, 32, 245.
*Room at the Top*, 216, 220, 316, 318.
Rutledge, Wiley, 41-43.

Sacrilege, criterion for censorship, 49-53, 55, 58, 60, 62, 65n, 130, 133, 143, 146, 154, 168, 196, 225.
Sanford, Edward T., 18-19.
*Scarlet Street*, 214.
Schaefer, C. J., 190.
Schnackenberg, J., 92-94.
Schoenbaum, Matthew, 199n, 303.